Immigrants and the class struggle

Joseph Buckman

IMMIGRANTS AND THE CLASS STRUGGLE

THE JEWISH IMMIGRANT IN LEEDS 1880–1914

Manchester University Press

© J. Buckman 1983

Published by
Manchester University Press
Oxford Road, Manchester M13 9PL, UK
51 Washington Street, Dover, N.H. 03820, USA

British Library cataloguing in publication data
Buckman, Joseph
 Immigrants and the class struggle.
 1. Jews – England – Leeds (West Yorkshire)
 – Social conditions.
 2. Tailors – England – Leeds (West Yorkshire)
 – Social conditions.
 I. Title
 924.8'19004924   DS135.E55L/
 ISBN 0–7190–0908–1

Library of Congress cataloging in publication data
applied for

Library of Congress catalog card number
82-62264

Photoset in Times by
Northern Phototypesetting Co., Bolton
Printed in Great Britain by
Butler & Tanner Ltd, Frome and London

CONTENTS

		page	
	Acknowledgements		vi
	List of abbreviations		vii
	Introduction		viii
Chapter 1	The Jewish tailoring trade in Leeds: problems of interpretation		1
2	Condition of the Jewish tailoring workshop		36
3	Problems in the class struggle: the Jewish tailors and their organisation to 1888		59
4	Maturity and struggle: the Tailors' Union to 1914		90
5	The alien slipper industry: a study in heroism and decay		121
6	Conclusions		156
Appendix I	The sales and profits of four Leeds wholesale clothing manufacturers during the immigration period		168
II	Statistical analysis of spatial conditions in Leeds Jewish workshops in 1888		177
III	The address of John Lincoln Mahon to the Leeds Jewish tailors		178
	Index		180

ACKNOWLEDGEMENTS

The sources for alien economics and history are very widely scattered, and, in the main, fragmentary. Thus I have perforce imposed myself on many people over a number of years. Among these, I received generous assistance from the staffs of the Andersonian, the Mitchell, Stirling's and the University Library in Glasgow. In Leeds, the resources of the Brotherton Library of the University, the City Reference Library and the City Archives (whose curator, Mr J. M. Collinson, has ever demonstrated his interest) were made readily available to me. Visits to the National Newspaper Library at Colindale, the British Museum Reading Room, and the Public Record Office, have always been both enjoyable and fruitful. In London also, the staffs of the former Fawcett Library, the Research Department of the Garment Workers' Union, and the library of Jews' College, were ever ready to assist. I also enjoyed the hospitality of the Keeper of Records at the House of Lords. In Manchester, I owe a great debt to the willing staff of the Central Library, and especially to Mike Luft, the Head of Photography, for the technical facilities he made available, without which the translation of a large acreage of Yiddish microfilm would have been impossible. Many busy municipal officials in Leeds found time to assist, and I am especially grateful for access to Corporation Committee Minutes.

LIST OF ABBREVIATIONS

A.F.	*Der Arbeiter Freund* (*The Worker's Friend*)
D.P.Y.	*Der Poilisher Yidel* (*The Polish Jew*)
D.Y.E.	*Die Yiddisher Ekspres* (Jewish Express)
H.L.	House of Lords
J.C.	Jewish Chronicle
L.E.E.	Leeds Evening Express
L.W.E.	Leeds Weekly Express
NUBSO	National Union of Boot and Shoe Operatives
P.R.O.	Public Record Office
Y.E.N.	Yorkshire Evening News
Y.E.P.	Yorkshire Evening Post
Y.F.T.	Yorkshire Factory Times
Y.P.	Yorkshire Post

INTRODUCTION

This book arises from an increasing dissatisfaction with the content and methodology encountered in the mounting literature on Jewish immigration to Britain during the period 1880–1914; from the widening disparity between the 'unitary' models of immigrant society and the boyhood memories of a Leeds ghetto abounding in recent traditions of class conflict. To one born and raised in the Jewish Leylands and the immediate environs, and contemplating the spatial and ideological segregation of the economically successful from the Jewish working class, it appeared increasingly that current economic and social dispositions were the outcome of protracted intra-communal class struggle within the first generations of immigrants to Leeds. More recently the conviction was heightened and research along these lines was encouraged by the appearance, in 1964, of the sociological study *Leeds Jewry*, by Ernest Krausz, in which deeply stratified class differences in the later community were laid bare. These were clearly perceptible as the dialectical outcome of that older struggle.

Notwithstanding the outraged furore induced by Krausz's objectivity, it became apparent at an early stage of research into the historical background of his topic that the class struggle within Leeds immigrant society was marked by strife, largely industrial, of quite astonishing persistence, bitterness and frequency. So imposing, indeed, was the evidence of the incidence of worker/master combat, that the conclusion that the economic struggle had utterly overriden ethnic and religious bonds, and that it presented the key to the very articulation of the various parts of the community, became inescapable.

Against this, a strange quietus inhabited the literature of the subject. Cemented into eclectic postures and disabled by an institution-centred and establishment-oriented methodology, it seemed unable to conceive of a Jewish proletariat having an existence as a separate and distinct historical class. Hence a class-conflict model finds no place in the standard accounts of Jewish communal life, in which the Jewish bourgeoisie, occupying the entire foreground, exists in an antidialectical void with no socio-historic counterpart in the shape of an immigrant proletariat. Bourgeois communal institutions, especially those concerned with 'philanthropy', are never considered from the standpoint of their function as agencies of social control but are, instead, promulgated as the bases of spurious claims to pre-eminence as 'protectors' of the aliens against the hostility of British society. Of the Jewish worker, his voice, his institutions and their socio-economic meaning, little is heard. Thus serious economic analysis, which might illuminate and expose the sources of intra-communal conflict, appears to have been deemed equally superfluous. For the rich and varied experience of the alien worker dependent upon large-scale native industries, each having its own complex developmental courses, there appears merely the naive and omnipresent rubric that 'alien industries were in a state of transition'. Immigrant trade unions, so abundant in immigrant society, are a clear embarrassment to establishment pens. When treated at all (and there is no guarantee of this) worker organisations are never credited with the specificity of their functions as the organised battle units of a distinct class engaged in a special form of struggle. Rather, their role in the formation and development of a working-class consciousness is submerged by the method of their allotment to the socially undifferentiated ranks of Jewish communal institutions in general.

Prior to the 1870s Leeds had not attracted the degree of Jewish settlement which London and Manchester, in their due proportions, had already experienced. The foundations of the important and concentrated settlement of the post-1880 era, with its characteristic master/workman form, were laid in the 1870s as immigrant employment opportunity increased with the astronomical rate of growth of the local tailoring industry. Between the censuses of 1871 and 1881 the increase in tailoring employment in England and Wales was 7·19 per cent whilst, for Leeds, the figure amounted to 143·7 per cent. The occupational tables of the census also point to the rapid growth of the large Leeds clothing factory (the warehouse) with mass production based on the female machinist, the source of the living of a majority of alien settlers in Leeds, whose relationship with the native firms was that of an outworker and maker-up of garments after cutting within the factory. The proportion of females to total employees in the industry rose in Leeds by 46 per cent between 1871 and 1891. For the other two leading centres of the industry, London and Manchester, the comparative increments were 10 and 27 per cent respectively over the same interval.

Directories for the 1870s already reveal a marked correlation between identifiable Jewish names and the clothing trades of the district. In 1875 twenty-six such tailors are listed, the number rising to forty-three by 1878. These listings are generally the names of Jewish workshop masters. Similarly, the cap and slipper making trades are also shown as having attracted Jewish masters before 1880, though entries under these heads are necessarily sparser. For the remainder, the directories point to Jewish involvement during the 1870s in a wide variety of retailing, professional, merchanting, craft and dealership occupations. This group, prominent in the smaller community of the 1870s, formed no significant portion of the larger and more closed economy which centred on the Leylands district for residence and on the tailoring and footwear trades for sustenance after 1880. The slight but steady growth of Jewish masters employing alien workers in these trades, the system which was to form the substance of the later community, appears to have attracted no local attention during the formative decade of the 1870s.

Whilst the listed addresses of the Jewish businesses outside the clothing trades show no marked concentration into any single district, the alien clothing master was, by the same decade, commencing the transformation of the Leylands district of slum housing into what would become the 'Jewish quarter'. Already notorious by virtue of the health reports prepared in the 1840s by the distinguished inspector Dr Robert Baker, this low-lying area would entrap all but the few successful entrepreneurs before the Great War, and would provide the arena of an intra-communal class struggle aggravated by successive waves of newcomers.

By 1880 the small community had equipped itself with the institutional paraphernalia of synagogue, 'philanthropic', benefit, sick and mutual improvement societies. On the economic side the material symbols of class struggle were plainly evident by the same year. The decaying Jewish workshop premises, whether for suits or slippers, a differentiated social structure of masters and workmen, and a minuscule trade union of Jewish tailors which came into being as early as 1874, together signify the dawn of those social and economic tensions perceptible in so aggravated a form when mass immigration rapidly increased the Leeds Jewish population after 1880.

Population pressure, indeed, lay at the root of the long and complex two-way conflict endured by the immigrant worker of Leeds. The town carried the largest concentration of aliens, over 6 per cent of total local population, in the kingdom. This, as well as their concentration within a cramped township into so few occupations, produced a reaction from the native populace more dramatic than elsewhere, with a concomitant degree of hostility on the part of local labour interests. Simultaneously, intra-communal conflict waxed as alien numbers rose and the Jewish master, reinforced by the shopkeeper and landlord, battened on the Jewish working mass herded into the dark confines of the Leylands. Religious workers, encouraged by the local clergy, vied with the increasing segment of progressive, politically advanced workers produced both by the revolutionary ferment in Russia and by the bitter disappointments of free capitalist society. Together, these groups, in their turn, formed a heterogeneous and uncertain proletariat which struggled against the new master class which had called it into being.

In attempting, against such a class-segmented background, to pass beyond the historiographical and methodological attitudes by which the current literature of the subject is beset, novel treatment has here been deemed essential. The Jewish worker has been placed in the foreground and at the centre of events. Wherever possible he has been permitted to speak for himself through the Yiddish press so pointedly neglected by establishment writers. This is in accord with the Marxist stance taken in this book that, in communal as well as in social relations generally, the arrangements and alignments arising in the processes of earning a living are fundamental. From this it followed that immigrant history was equally work for the economist as for the historian, and every effort has been made to ask questions of the material and the evidence from that standpoint.

The dialectical processes observable in society as a whole are very pronounced and clear in a new, competitive industrial immigrant community such as that of Leeds in the period 1880–1914. Hence the resolution of that community into distinct and hostile classes has always appeared to provide its motive power as well as the basis of its ideological and political alignments. The motives imputed in this work are, therefore, *class* motives; whilst the struggles constantly to be observed in the foreground of the life of the community are here viewed as being undertaken by serious class battalions forming intra-communally rather than by the familial groups engaged in quaint, peculiarly Jewish squabbles common to so many pages of Jewish historical writing. The relatively modest application of Marxist method, however imperfect, in this book has, it is believed, paid some dividends. By a study of phenomena, in Schumpeter's phrase, *ex visu* of a point in time, and in their proneness to ceaseless change, much revision has been rendered possible on a number of important economic and social problems of the Leeds alien community. It has, above all, been possible to restore to the pages of history the appalling struggles of the immigrant Jewish worker and to reclaim for him a central role in the establishment of the Jewish community of Britain.

Chapter 1

THE JEWISH TAILORING TRADE IN LEEDS: PROBLEMS OF INTERPRETATION

The Jewish branch of the Leeds wholesale tailoring industry, the chief employer of alien labour, is of major importance in the study of the class struggle, and of the respective roles of organised Jewish labour and the masters as protagonist of that struggle. In the absence of a determined effort to understand the Jewish branch – its structure and development – no meaning can be ascribed to its characteristically bitter and incessant industrial strife. Nor, when the variable of virulent contemporary anti-alienism is considered, may a true assessment of the neglected role of the Jewish worker in the complex processes of host acceptance of the alien be made. For the many scholars who view capitalism as the ultimate stage in social evolution, and for whom there exist no dialectical historical movements, the high period of immigration has no other significance than a staging post along a road to universal alien bourgeoisification. V. D. Lipman, for example, equates 'acculturation' with 'keen ambition' to become self-employed masters, and to acquire the enhanced social status 'that went with an improved economic position'.[1] In such hands the industrial arena, with its own crucial social-dialectical processes, becomes a static backcloth on which are registered none of the dynamics which are essential both for historical accuracy and the fuller understanding of the alien social order and its conflicts.

The case of Leeds has been the special victim of inquiry in this spirit of stasis, commencing with so material a matter as the numbers of Jewish tailoring workshops. For J. A. Garrard, anxious to support his case that Leeds workshops were fewer in number but larger than those in London, the council inspector's figure of fifty-one in 1888 suffices for the whole period to 1914.[2] The expansionist tendencies of the 1870s were, however, strongly reinforced by the larger immigrant waves after 1880. By 1891 the Chief Constable's report put the alien population of Leeds at 11,000, whilst the Jewish statistician S. Rosenbaum estimated it at over 15,000 by 1905. Three years later the communal minister, Moses Abrahams, published the figure of 25,000[3] (representing a significant 6·25 per cent of the total Leeds population), so that it is difficult, in view of this rate of augmentation and of the preponderance of tailoring among alien occupations, to accept a single estimate of Jewish workshop numbers as satisfactory for the complete period. In any event, the official contemporary mind was itself rapidly altered, since, one year later, the same council inspector put the whole matter into perspective by his estimate of the workshops as 119 for the benefit of the Select Committee on the Sweating System, a figure with which the Factory Inspector, Mr May, agreed substantially.[4] From the standpoint of the Medical Officer of Health, moreover, there were 153 shops in 1889, 182 in 1892, and 180 in 1903.[5] These numbers (which represent only those shops falling beneath unsystematic official scrutiny) are more consistent with an increasing alien population, and must, therefore, be at odds with any view of the alien tailoring industry as a relatively small and static population of workshops.

The problem of alien workshops is strictly cognate with others relating to their scale — and, thus, to their true industrial function — as well as the nature and role of their founders, the workshop masters. These are more than mere academic matters. Taken together, these questions predominate for two main reasons. Firstly, much play has been made with them in scholarship and in 'standard' liberal defences of the alien both by contemporaries and by the more credulous among their latter-day adherents. Secondly, the standardised model of the alien economy of Leeds is radically unsatisfactory inasmuch as it substitutes socio-economic constants for variables leading to factual inaccuracy and obfuscation of the realities of Leeds alien industry beneath metaphysical pseudo-economic speculation, readily at the service of a special bourgeois historiography.

Metaphysical, indeed, is the expounded view of the origins and role of the alien tailoring master. Basing herself on a tradition established by the troublesome amateur, Beatrice Webb, and authenticated by a superstitious Administration,[6] even so radical a scholar as the late Shirley Lerner viewed the immigrant as a man 'normally trained in Talmudic logic, which gave him an eye for minute detail'. Switching smoothly from seminar to sweatshop, the application of this mentality to tailoring is held to have conduced to the subdivisional system which became 'the exclusive [sic] province of the Jewish subcontractor'.[7] This is both fanciful and far-reaching in face of the evidence for Jewish artisanship and proletarianisation in nineteenth-century Russia and Poland. On Jewish occupations in Russia and Poland, for example, S. W. Baron states that 46·7 per cent of Jews were occupied in industry by 1897.[8] In mid-century Lodz, the centre of Polish manufactures and of an imposing Jewish population, 56 per cent of Jews were either craftsmen or labourers.[9] In Galicia, with a Jewish population of 750,000, more than 25 per cent were industrial workers, chiefly in tailoring.[10] According to E. Mendelsohn, within the Pale of Jewish Settlement but excluding Poland, two-thirds to three-quarters of the entire artisan class was Jewish, and, for Russia in general, over 25 per cent of Jewish craftsmen were artisan-craftsmen tailors.[11] It must, therefore, be assumed, firstly, that workers rather than Talmudists constituted the source of immigrants, and, secondly, that the immigrant ranks contained more skilled workers than has usually been allowed. Anti-alienists often exploited the image of an army of unskilled aliens as a liability to Britain, and even sympathetic sources might agree. Lewis Lyons, the London-born machiner and union leader, observed in 1887 that the aliens 'having so far belied the famed shrewdness of their race as to land in England without being able to utter a single syllable of the English language find themselves unable to obtain employment'. They were, he stated, taken to the sweatshops and there taught only a small part of the trade. In a few days the 'embryo tailors' were proficient enough to enter into a period of 'close bondage'.[12] Mendelsohn, on the other hand, in his analysis of the industrial development of Russia to the end of the nineteenth century, pictures a diverse industrial society from which it may be inferred that finished skills were imported into Britain with the refugees. Further, although he finds that the industrial nexus of the Jewish worker was of no greater significance than that 'in the larger establishments, workers naturally found it more difficult to alter their status', he shows that, with increasing workshop scale, the social and economic functions of the old Jewish gilds were being replaced by hired-labour proletarian status,[13] a finding which illuminates the class conflicts in the immigrant communities of Britain.

Deeper penetration into the Russian background also produces the unnoticed probability that, so far from being technically ignorant seminarists, many immigrants were familiar not merely with the tailoring industry but also with its most modern variant: readymade clothing. Lenin, drawing on the 1897 Survey of Nizhni-Novgorod Fair in the journal *Vestnik Finansov* and the Petersburg publication *Successes of Russian Industry According to Surveys of Expert*

Commissions, 1897, notes the rapid growth of this branch as an example of capitalistic industrial development. 'The enormous development of this industry has taken place only since the eighties,' he writes. In response to increasing demand, the industry employed 20,000 workers in Moscow alone, where it had an annual output of clothing worth 16 million roubles. In St Petersburg in 1890 almost 40,000 were thus engaged, whilst in Russia as a whole the total employed was given as 2,780,376.[14]

Irrespective of origin, the gap between arrival as a poor immigrant and emergence as the proprietor of a tailoring workshop was bridged with some ease. The opportunities of Leeds were known in the east, and they had begun to attract in the 1870s. Russian and Polish Jews, as the *Yorkshire Post* put it with evident sarcasm, moved 'to the centre of the clothing industry' as soon as they landed. They 'trusted for safe dealings to their one word of English: "Leeds" '. Many had 'heard of Leeds as an earthly Paradise for outcasts and wanderers', and, on landing at Hull, they 'directed their steps towards the West Riding capital'.[15]

The classic route to entrepreneurship began with a rudimentary apprenticeship on the lines described by Lyons as applicable to London. Here the single, simple processes of the subdivisional system could be rapidly mastered. The newcomer paid his 'premium' by working without pay, but small sums were sometimes charged by the master. Despite the participation of at least some men of skill, this system, clearly born of desperate necessity, drew the scorn even of anxious friends such as James Sweeney, the Leeds president of the Boot and Shoe Operatives and unpaid secretary of the Jewish Tailors' Union until 1888, who observed, 'Few sweaters in Leeds are practical tailors. They have usually learned only a small part of the trade.'[16]

As well as for their style, Jewish masters drew attention for their numbers. The aliens were regarded as, to a man, apostles of Samuel Smiles – and not merely by those with hostile propagandist interest in the image. Hence the Factory Inspector could observe in 1887 that they 'live hard, do not drink, but save up every penny. The height of their desires is to set up for themselves as employers of labour.'[17] The 'Jewish preference to be a master rather than a wage earner' was officially reiterated in the *Immigration Report* of 1894.[18] In the meantime the distinguished economist J. A. Hobson, as archetype of many hostiles, was busily adding Shylockean colour and ascribing to the Jew motives which Marx, with surely greater precision, ascribed to all capitalists at the stage of primitive accumulation: 'The Jew craves the position of a sweating master, because that is the lowest step in a ladder which may lead to a life of magnificence supported out of usury.'[19]

The central role of this image in the anti-alien campaigns to 1914 has been well treated elsewhere in the specific context of anti-semitism.[20] Here the purpose is to examine it from the viewpoint of the economics of the industry penetrated by the alien 'entrepreneurial army', and for its profound implications for the class-conflict model of alien society. No progress appears possible by mere manipulation of the recorded observations, often paradoxical, made by interested contemporaries – friendly or otherwise. They did not possess the gift of foresight, but those able to employ hindsight cannot be thus excused.

The present situation of this important *economic* question is chaotic indeed. Hannah Neustatter, for example, overrides the class struggle in alien history, and, in promulgating a 'unitary' system of homogeneous bourgeois-aspiring Jewry, uncritically accepts the nugatory nineteenth-century image of the Jewish genius. To her it appears that there was a lack of working-class consciousness such that every [sic] Jewish labourer desired to become, or to see his offspring become, a master.[21] V. D. Lipman lends his authority to the view that 'spiritually, most of the immigrants did not wish to remain in the proletariat'. He acknowledges, however, that they could be regarded as 'economically proletarian'. Thus his immigrant is a socio-economic freak – an admixture of worker proletarian and bourgeois ideologue. Lipman's case rests on nothing more substantial than Beatrice Webb's classic but egregious comment: 'The chances of the trade are open to him; with indefatigable energy he may press forward into the ranks of the larger employers.'[22] The investigator does not always encounter such simple clarity. Garrard, for example, lets his reader know what the president of the Boot and Shoe Operatives thought about the willingness of the alien to make 'any sacrifice' to become a master, but, save a passing reference to the alien 'taste for entrepreneurship', what Garrard himself thinks is not certain.[23]

Economists working on themes cooler than anti-semitism and alien–host interaction have also retained the image in their models. In a much-quoted essay Lerner founded her version of alien Economic Man with his 'lack of working-class consciousness' – not on spiritual – but on hard economic values. In her version, the 'desire to emerge from the status of a wage earner to an employer' was due to the 'completely [sic] non-industrial, competitive middleman background of the immigrants'.[24] More surprisingly, E. H. Hunt's interesting work on regional wage-patterns also carries the view that most aliens thought of themselves as potential capitalists and rentiers [*sic*].[25] B. Gainer's contribution to the trivialisation of the complex panorama of alien proletarianism is to treat it as nothing more than a phase, but an undialectical one, during which, with evident masochistic relish, the immigrant was a willing party to privation and exploitation in order to further his desire to become a master. Professor L. P. Gartner, at once the leading exponent and victim of this static method, considers that the alien worker 'did not regard himself as one endowed with a fixed station in life', and thus accepted long hours and irregular seasons.[26]

Among critics of the image, W. J. Fishman, from a radical standpoint, has rejected out of hand the notion of a universal alien tropism to entrepreneurship, and, by an infusion of the economic reality that 'only a ruthless few made it', pointed to the conclusion that escape from the worker ranks was no routine matter.[27] C. Holmes, in work on anti-semitism, has unhesitatingly branded the imagery of both Webb and Hobson a hostile stereotype, so that it emerges as the antithesis of the encomiastic device wielded so paradoxically by contemporary anti-alienists and recent Jewish writers. He properly regards it as 'a categorical rather than an *ad hoc* treatment which discounts variety within that community'. How, he asks, are we to account for Jewish socialists and trade unions if every Jew were a capitalist?[28] From the standpoint of the intra-communal class problem this is a question and an interpretation of immense importance, forming the precise point of departure for an approach to the alien economy of a settlement such as Leeds as a system articulated by class hostility patently overriding religious and ethnic bonds. For scholars who, contemplating a sizeable alien industry, are able to conceive of its functioning classlessly, there will, of course, exist nothing like a proletarian consciousness, nor, indeed, anything other than an idealistic dream economy. Such scholars, to whom the contents of the Yiddish revolutionary press appear distasteful, may discover evidence of just such a consciousness in Leeds through the pen of a single alien worker, John Dyche, in more respectable places.[29]

From the socio-economic standpoint, the criticisms levelled by Holmes and Fishman need to be carried further. They have pointed clearly to the presence of differentiated economic groups within alien society, but such groupings are the reflection of the sum of the experience of their membership in the forms of economic organisation in which they have developed. More generally, therefore, the variety upon which Holmes rightly insists – the unions and the socialists – reflect a social basis of production resting on differentiated classes of masters and men, the outcome of a dialectical process involving capitalist and proletarian. Precisely why there was no indefinite aggregation of alien entrepreneurs is rather obvious and quite in accord with the situation in any competitive industry, alien or otherwise. Firstly, where is the industry with the capacity to absorb the infinitude of entrepreneurs naively envisioned by the Jewish and other proponents of the image? Secondly, since the idea of cut-throat competition has so often formed a part of the same image, it is strange that the consequences have hardly been considered. Yet conditions in the Leeds alien tailoring industry conformed well to the neo-classical competitive model. Here were the standard variables: many producers, apparent similarity of costs, undifferentiated product, freedom of entry, and, above all, the price-taker's situation.[30] The sole difference among 'firms' would, therefore, tend to be relative entrepreneurial efficiency – a differential pointing directly to the success of Fishman's 'ruthless few', and a rapid return to the status of wage-earner for many venturesome workers.

The most serious deflection from realism in the matter of the alien will-to-entrepreneurship, with its consequent distortion of the ideological structure of alien society, has resulted from the refusal to consider immigration as a 'thing in motion' with live individuals carrying with them the ideas reflecting Russian economic development, and, later, beneath the impact of the English ghetto, undergoing a reorientation of *Weltanschauung*. Although there are excellent accounts of the correlation between political events in the east and successive immigration waves, little attention has been accorded the effect on immigrant ideology of the economic changes described by Lenin, and their effect on Russian Jewry, as described by Mendelsohn.[31] Similarly, although Russian anti-Jewish legislation has been carefully studied, it has normally been treated merely as a causative factor in emigration. Yet one measure alone, the 1894 Law which forbade the Jews the liquor trade, was described by Dubnow as having created a Jewish proletariat of 'appalling proportions'.[32] The effect of Tsarist restrictionism was not simply to create a westward mass movement of Jews. As H. Sacher observed during the period of the movement, 'The Jew has become a conscious proletarian, has entered the revolutionary movement, has become a political portent.'[33]

Not surprisingly, the most unequivocal support of this thesis comes from the Yiddish revolutionary press, whose business it was to observe and analyse the development of the Jewish worker in Britain. In 1893, the anarchist-communist journal *Der Arbeiter Freund*, beneath the headline 'The New Jew', gave an account which, by its instinctive attention to the dialectics of class, goes far to remedy the perplexities occasioned by Jewish scholars in the approval they accord to grotesqueries fabricated by anti-semites. In the view of *Arbeiter Freund*, the ancient Shakespearean image of the Jew as a 'bloodthirsty money-percentnik' [*sic*] and the Dickensian image of the Jew as 'a thief who teaches children the light-fingered skills' had been replaced by the latest type: the 'little tailoring and footwear sweaters over whom the dunghill of the capitalist press pours its poisonous hatred'. The new Jew, however, was not prepared to suffer the opprobrium and bloodletting occasioned by the Jewish capitalist, whether banker *or* sweater:

With the beginning of the 1880s a new epoch began ... The persecutions in Russia were the cause of the immigration into England of intelligent young Jews and workers ... The Jewish workers who had believed that the streets of London were bestrewn with golden pounds only waiting to be gathered up were soon convinced that it was just a sweet dream, and that, here in England, the order of society rested on a hard and bitter bread question requiring solution just as in other parts of the world ... A new spirit enlivened the Jewish worker. They apprehended with a different eye the Shylocks, Fagins, and the little sweaters. They branded them as a class harmful to the welfare of humanity, and which would have to be eliminated along with all other parasites without distinction as to their nationality.[34]

There was more light on the matter in 1903:

A large section of the first immigrants ... were not workers in their homeland, and only in England, driven by economic circumstances, were they forced to work at a trade ... It is quite clear that these people had no trace in them of proletarian class-consciousness such as we find in the working classes of other peoples ... Later, when they lost their hopes of autonomy and began to understand that they would now remain in the workshop, they began to organise themselves ... Today, the position is far more favourable ... In Russia, there has been great industrial development which has thrown thousands of Jewish proletarians into social wretchedness in the workshops and factories. A large fraction of today's immigrants are already more or less acquainted with the idea of a labour movement from their homeland.[35]

The case of Leeds is, if anything, more difficult than the general. It is to be noted that the same image travelled northwards, where it broke ground in the Leeds press:

Problems of interpretation

As soon as the Jewish workman masters the rudiments of a trade, he looks round for greeners and sets up in business on his own hook. There are more employers amongst the Jews to the acre than amongst Gentiles to the mile.[36]

This is immediately irreconcilable with Garrard's fifty-one workshops, and even poses questions concerning the larger official estimates already noted. There are, however, further problems in the Leeds case, since, here, the 'fewness' of Jewish workshops accompanies 'largeness', 'regular work', and 'fair conditions' in a well rooted economic mythology wielded by apologists to exempt the town of the dread charge of sweating, and to construct a naive antithesis between its system and that of the East End.

This scheme is devoid of economic reason and misconceives the role of the alien in the Leeds trade. In some hands the mere category 'alien trades' suffices to account for the differential economics, structure and stage of development of industries of divergent history and experience. Thus, for Garrard, the alien trades of bootmaking, tailoring and cabinetmaking appear a homogeneous group, all 'undergoing the classic transition from domestic workshop to factory production'. The immigrant role in this fantasy-analogue of the Industrial Revolution was a 'compromise between the two systems of production'. Manufacture was divided between factory and workshop, between machine and hand production, 'with the immigrants taking the latter part of the process', and engaging in a 'machine style of production without the machine' (*sic*).[37] This romantic passage would have been improved by elucidation of the benefits obtained from this separation of production into concurrent mechanised and hand modes, of the technological basis of 'machineless' alien systems, and of the *special* stage of development of each separate trade concerned, from the viewpoint – not of ethnicity – but of its economic history and individuality. These requirements become acute when Garrard applies the obverse of his model to Leeds, where he finds that, although, here, the workshops were 'larger', there was no necessary connection between the immigrant and a minute subdivision of labour. Thus, in his view, the larger the scale of production, the less the extent of division of labour.[38]

Garrard is the most adventurous essayist in the 'economics' of Leeds Jewish tailoring. Gainer is content to propose the smaller number of shops, their larger size and high degree of mechanisation, and to conclude without further evidence that productivity was higher than in

London.³⁹ Similarly, for Hunt, Leeds production units were 'relatively large and heavily capitalised' so that they 'compared favourably with London'.⁴⁰ Gartner is the ultimate progenitor, however, of a Leeds system of homogeneously large workshops permanently transfixed in number and scale, blessed by 'regular work', 'fair conditions', an absence of sweating – the fair fruits of symbiosis with the giant Leeds wholesaler – and populated by a socially undifferentiated army of monomaniacal cretins all intent upon the single goal of tailoring masterdom. For Gartner, too, trades remain undifferentiated by the nature of their product or mode and stage of development. There exist for him only 'alien trades' and the rest; the former being always in the famous 'state of transition between factory and workshop' (*sic*).

In the 'special' case of Leeds, Gartner describes nothing but mechanised Jewish workshops of twenty to forty machines, in contrast to his general characterisation of alien trades as 'unmechanised'. At the heart of his model lies the assertion from which much else follows: that the London Jewish tailoring industry consisted of small workshops (with all their attendant evils) because the source of their work was the small merchant clothier; whilst the large Leeds workshops (with all their attendant benefits) received 'orders in quantity from the excess backlogs of clothing factories'. Gartner goes further, adding elsewhere to his model, alien clothing 'factories'.⁴¹

This thesis has spoiled many pages for many commentators. Gainer, for example, accepts it entirely, although, in his version, the Leeds masters only 'tended' to receive the 'backlogs of the large clothing factories', but, following Gartner faithfully, this suffices to dismiss from Leeds any charge of extreme sweating.⁴² Garrard also follows Gartner's 'backlogs' thesis, but without drawing from it such daring conclusions.⁴³

These apologist versions of the Leeds Jewish clothing industry remain obscure, and, in the light of both theory and evidence, deeply paradoxical. The very presence of the word 'backlogs' provides reason to ponder the situation of an industry dependent upon a supply of work of this secondary nature. The complex problems of the size-distribution of the industry – and the important social and economic conditions consequent upon such distribution – will not yield to the method of simple reference to the scale of the Leeds wholesale houses, and naive comparison between the latter and the London merchant clothiers as sources of work. The matter, so far from being qualitative, is really a question of scale economies, concentration ratios, and entry conditions.

Problems of interpretation 11

Professor Bain has written, in respect of concentration, that the degree necessary for 'reasonable efficiency' is the minimal scale required for lowest costs of production as a percentage of the total scale (capacity) of an industry. In order to attain a position of reasonable efficiency, a firm must supply a given (efficient) output-proportion of the total industry output. Where the single firm needs to supply only a negligible fraction of such output to be able to operate at an efficient level, there will be a disposition for new firms to enter the industry, since economies of scale are no barrier other than (small) absolute capital requirements.[44] In this light, the alleged absence of small shops in Leeds is mysterious, though the proliferation of small shops in London may be readily understood.

The latter, however, itself raises serious questions regarding the presentation by Gartner and his followers of the demand side of the London market. How large was the 'small merchant clothier' so beloved of this school? What was the size of his group, recalling that the sum of its demand was capable of sustaining over 2,000 Jewish workshops at an acceptable irreducibly minimal level of profit, leaving aside short-term phases of excess capacity? There is no provision, in the comparative statics of Gartner, for the postulate that even a London sweatshop might reap modest economies of growth and develop into a larger unit. Professor Bain's model is, after all, couched in terms of *minimal* scale necessary to the activation of a disposition for newcomers to enter the industry. The assumption embodied in the Gartner model (since all London alien producers are held to be small) is homogeneous entrepreneurship; but it is precisely in the differential ability of entrepreneurs that the source of most economies forming the basis of increased scale must be sought. Furthermore, since homogeneous entrepreneurship is unlikely in the real world, and in an industry of numerous entrepreneurs in particular, there must exist a serious theoretical doubt concerning the traditional views of the historian concerning London workshop scale. As for the growth-sustaining demand forces, it has only too often, and at great cost in the tedium of quasi-sociology, been pointed out that the Jews made for the East End because of the proximity of co-religionists, charities, and synagogues. Rarely has it been pointed out that London was also the world's richest and most concentrated centre of consumption. It is, therefore, difficult to comprehend Gartner's insistence on the universal smallness of the London merchant clothier,[45] and why he was unable to grow sufficiently to sustain larger Jewish shops. Nor is it clear why one alien master could not have done the outside making-up for more than a single merchant clothier – a manifestation of superior entrepreneurship. Hunt also restricts the scale of the London merchant by his suggestion that demand was entirely localised.[46] Some London clothiers, however, employed large staffs of travellers, pointing to a wider market.[47] Nor is it made clear why London manufacturers did not enter the export trade. In sum, the accepted model of the London tailoring industry on both the alien and native sides is devoid of any tendency to concentration whatsoever – an odd proposition which is difficult to sustain from a theoretical standpoint.

Evidence exists to support theory. Lewis Lyons considered, as early as 1885, that many East End workshops employed twenty people and that many employed up to 200. This accords with the view of the Inspectorate three years later that some London masters were 'well off' and worked regularly for single houses of substance.[48] Clara Collet, in her contribution to the 1894 *Report on Recent Immigration*, noted the presence in London of shops with 80–100, 100, and 287 workers respectively.[49] Large-scale London houses modelled on the Leeds style rose up, despite Webb and Gartner, before the Aliens Commission in the first years of the present century,[50] whilst evidence before the Select Committee on Home Work in 1908 strongly encourages the thesis that the London market supported many large alien workshops, including one East End shop of 160 workers. It suggests, further, that the average size of London shops had risen to between fifteen and twenty-five workers, and that variation in London shop size had become extreme.[51]

The question for Leeds poses itself in reverse. If all London workshops could not be small, could, *per contra*, all Leeds workshops be large? Moreover, although choice may be made between Garrard's fifty-five and Gartner's 101, could their number remain as unchanging as presented? Ultimately, the economic history of the Leeds Jewish branch is that of its general relationship to its sources of work, but that history cannot be encompassed in a vague reference to the great scale of the native houses, since, firstly, these did not constitute the sole source of work throughout the period, and, secondly, it will be argued that that very scale created special problems for the aliens, leading to anything but the Leeds conditions perceived by Gartner and his followers.

It is important to clarify the role of the immigrant in the Leeds trade. So far from entering an industry 'in transition',[52] or one experiencing 'a sort of long-delayed and long-continuing industrial revolution',[53] the alien master of Leeds was confronted by an intensely modern and technologically developed industry of immense expansive power. The number of large English firms grew from approximately fifty in the mid-1880s to almost 200 by 1914.[54] The scale of the individual firm was also enormously enlarged. By 1890 at least four firms of 2,000 were present,[55] whilst firms employing up to 1,500 were becoming commonplace.[56]

In order to put the role of the Jewish branch, and the odd innovatory claims made on its behalf, into perspective, it is emphasised that the distinguishing features of the native branch were the subdivisional system, the intensive application of new technologies, and the employment of uniquely high proportions of females. In Table 1 the proportions of females to males in tailoring generally are compared with those for Leeds. This preponderance of females immediately suggests a system of simple specialised processes – the subdivision so widely credited to the aliens themselves – without which scale expansion in the wholesale clothing industry is inconceivable. Typically, manufacture was divided into more than ten processes.[57]

Table 1 *Proportion of females to each thousand males employed in tailoring, 1881–1901*

Year	National	Leeds
1881	330	1276
1891	427	2287
1901	471	2420

Source: G. R. Porter, *Progress of the Nation*, London, 1912, p. 31; *Census Reports*, 1881–1901, Occupational Tables.

Treatments of this system as 'Talmudical', or having, in some other manner, an immigrant origin, are grossly superficial and thoroughly anachronistic. Stocks of ready-made clothing – the product of subdivision – were already present in the ledgers of one Leeds clothier by 1853, rising from a value of £1,859 in that year to £17,047 by 1869.[58] Marketing – a neglected topic – was well advanced by the 1860s, as the expenditure on advertising indicates.[59] Vast export markets had been created by 1860, with sales rising from £1,500,000 to £3,100,000 by the late 1870s. By 1895 the value of Leeds clothing exports alone reached £4,500,000.[60] These values represent manufacture on a scale unthinkable in the absence of a well organised system of mass production based on extreme division of labour.

The technological basis and its chronology have received little attention. In some accounts, indeed, notably those by Hunt, Gartner and Fishman, the very application of machinery and the concomitant increase in the scale of production are left entirely to await the arrival of the aliens.[61] By the latter event, however, the wholesale manufacturer had behind him a long tradition of innovation. In the period 1830–66 over 300 sewing-machine patents were taken out in England alone, and in the following decade at least a further 730. Cutting machinery was described by Scott as early as 1813, the circular cutter in 1853 (Dawson), and the endless steel knife which became the accepted principle in tailoring, in 1855 (Dusatory).[62] Each innovation marked an essential new stage in specialisation, in capitalisation, and in the division of labour. By 1884 up to thirty separate workers were required to complete a suit in many Leeds factories. Two decades later the minute subdivision of labour of the highly organised factory had 'necessitated the adaptation of the sewing machine to hundreds of distinct purposes'.[63]

In the first period of immigration the Leeds alien branch played a significant role in the industry, at least in terms of its contribution to total output. This may be misleading, however, unless it is realised that this role was always quite ancillary. The much-canvassed separateness of the alien, and his idealised 'preference' for the peripheral status of the workshop,[64] were, at least in Leeds, rather the objective outcome of the economics of the large firms in their particular stages of development. The situation was not specially Jewish, nor did the Jewish workshop represent an evolutionary end in itself. Its presence — and its own mutations — reflect the evolution of the parent English industry towards a scale at which demand and capacity approached an equilibrium. At such a point the alien worker would become supererogatory. Thus, whatever their scale, the Jewish workshops, so long as they remained in the outworker relationship, constituted a transitory and subordinate branch, exhibiting in the relationship many of the most pernicious aspects of domestic industry. So far from engaging in a struggle by hand against the machine, their rise was *facilitated* by the division of labour of the large factories. For this reason, a Russian system described by Lenin seemed to have been transplanted to Leeds:

> ... A typical feature of capitalist manufacture is precisely the small number of relatively large establishments ... the small establishments are merely outside departments of the manufactories ... in the overwhelming majority of cases

the connection between them is maintained by merchant's capital which belongs to the big masters and holds sway over the small ones.⁶⁵

Whether carried on in the largest workshops or under the bedroom system into which much Leeds work deteriorated, the master remained a middleman, collecting materials from the factory in the form of ready-cut garments and varying the classical homework system by organising and supervising the balance of processes personally. He therefore had the opportunity to bring workers together in a form imitative of the large factory with partial division of labour based on a petty-capital structure to which the sewing machine was central.

The 'grandness' of some alien workshops has obscured the economic realities of what was, in Lenin's terminology, a 'capitalist domestic industry'. The large manufacturer held the role of merchant clothier, handing out materials for processing. He dictated price, quality and quantity of work to be done on each garment. To the factory, the alien master was a device for the centralisation of outwork and reduction of the costs and problems of its distribution to countless individual hands. At the same time, by suffering through slack times, he allowed the factory to concentrate its work indoors and minimise its fixed costs. The trade journal *Men's Wear* frankly justified the alien in Leeds on the grounds that, without him, the large firms would require still greater capacity in busy seasons and be left with spare capacity in slack times. The Jews, it averred, also saved the reputation of the large firms by their readiness to break factory regulations in working excessive hours to complete specials – the orders for which there was little completion time. Above all, when work was given out to the Jews, its cost of production was absolutely predictable, whereas, thought the paper, this could not be said of indoor work because of the high associated fixed costs.⁶⁶

The scale of Leeds Jewish shops was often illusory. So far from generating uniformly large alien workshops, the factories, in blind pursuit of economic objectives, might induce the master to hoard surplus capacity. Tom Maguire, the Leeds socialist and friend of the Jewish worker, cast light on this matter by pointing out that, under factory pressure for completion of orders, masters employed twice as many machines as would be required for the normal conduct of business. This resulted in an average working week of three days and a large labour surplus.⁶⁷ Further, the large firms could affect the scale of the alien shop by retaining more work indoors, for example to avoid strike disturbances; or by taking on extra workers from the Leeds reserve army of the unemployed.⁶⁸ At times a rapid increase in small shops would be generated by the distribution of work to numerous masters in order to intensify competition and reduce prices.

Since, therefore, it does not appear to be an iron law that large workshops were the result of the Gartnerian 'large orders' of the large factories, other determinants require to be sought. At some stages the larger alien shops appear the survivors of rigorous competitive struggle rather than well nourished beneficiaries of a rich diet of regular orders. The master might compete by being all too acquiescent towards price reductions offered by his employing factory.⁶⁹ Alternatively, a species of perverse auction might occur as masters volunteered their own price reductions.⁷⁰ The most pernicious manifestation of the power of the factory, however, was the costly system of bribery set up by the competitive scramble for survival amongst the alien masters. Comment was widespread. The *Leeds Weekly Express* saw it as a part of the alien's ingenuity in 'getting round managers and the like', rather than as profit-maximising behaviour on the part of the large manufacturer.⁷¹ The *Yorkshire Factory Times* found the alien at the back door of the warehouse with 'magic gold' in sums ranging from £5 to £50. A horse and trap had been received by one foreman. The Jews were also 'great in the jewellery line', and many a passer's wife had 'a gold chain round her neck with a gold watch'. This, the paper perceived, was one of the major causes of low wages in the trade.⁷² The *Leeds Mercury*, the organ of Leeds manufacturing society, discovered that a set of gold-plated harness had been received by one manager, who, aware of the 'Hebraic origin of the gift', was unaware of the sender's identity.⁷³ Straying from its sanitary commission in 1888, *The Lancet* was also moved to comment upon 'unfair stratagems' in the 'Leeds sweating business'.⁷⁴ That these commentaries were other than anti-alien sour grapes is clear from the eye-opening testimony of the Leeds master, David Lubelski, to the Committee on Sweating. Had he not bribed, he asserted, he would not have received sufficient work. He had had to think of his wife and ten children, but, with so large a family, 'he could not afford to give bribery as much as the others do' (*sic*). Lubelski was a thoughtful man who did not go before the Lords to indulge in *braggadocio* about the mighty scale of Leeds Jewish workshops. He indicated, rather, that bribery was an evil which was inducing a 'tendency to monopoly' as large firms, their trade increasing the while, reduced their outlets to three or four, where they had once employed up to twenty.⁷⁵

More fundamental, however, was the sheer dispensability of the alien master — not merely beneath short-term seasonal influences — but also in the long term when, on the average, the factories had adjusted their fixed plant to scales at which the outside capacity provided by the aliens had become increasingly irrelevant and even burdensome. In this unstable environment of indefinite economic categories, and taking account of the growth of the Leeds alien population, it is no surprise that many gravitated towards the position of master, ready to exploit lower categories and to be servile towards the large capitalist clothier.

That some Leeds workshops were able to grow to impressive scale, at least as measured in numbers of workers, is clear. By 1889, according to Inspector Rickards, only two wholesale clothiers failed to employ alien outworkers.[76] The late 1880s, during which there was an outburst of factory building and extension by the large firms, also found the aliens producing an estimated 25 per cent of Leeds total output,[77] and it appears that demand was rising more rapidly than inside factory capacity. Individual alien shops of 150 workers were able to develop, as is clear from a fire report of 1894.[78] Davis Joseph, a Leeds master, informed the Sweating Committee that he employed eighty workers.[79] By 1898 it was possible to speak of 'large workshops ... containing as many as over a hundred workpeople'.[80]

Resort to official material for systematic data on scale presents difficulties. The single document produced locally was the 1888 survey carried out by the local authority. This was a hurried affair, ordered because both the Sweating Committee and *The Lancet* were beginning the investigation of provincial sweating. Here some fifty-seven Jewish shops are listed with addresses, male and female workers, and cubic space per head. The list is blatantly deficient in the light of the much larger estimates of workshop numbers made contemporaneously and soon after. Moreover, it is unlikely that a mere fifty-seven shops could have contributed up to 25 per cent of the output of an industry in which individual firms were capable of 500,000 suits per annum.[81] The size distribution of the listed shops is, however, given in Table 2. In this distribution, the median shop would employ twenty-one workers, whilst the ungrouped date of the survey yields a mean of twenty-five workers per shop. Grave suspicion as to its comprehensiveness leads to the consideration of the survey as a sample of a larger population. As the sample covers over 1,700 workers and has observations $n>30$, it may be employed to estimate population parameters. Point estimate for the population mean may be regarded as approximately equal to the sample mean of twenty-five workers per shop. For the interval estimate of the population mean, the standard error of the sampling distribution has been employed, and, at the 95 per cent confidence level, the true mean lies between 22·96 and 33·4 workers per shop. These conclusions hardly conjure up a picture of very grandiose scale, and the survey itself may well be biased towards the larger units catching the eye of the inspectors in a hurry.

Table 2 *The size-distribution of Leeds Jewish Workshops in 1888*

Employees	Shops
Less than 5	4
6–10	7
11–15	4
16–20	6
21–25	9
26–30	5
31–35	5
36–40	2
41–45	3
46–50	3
51–55	3
56–60	1
61–65	3
66–70	nil
71–75	nil
76–80	2
Over 80	nil

Source: Minutes of the Sanitary Committee of Leeds Town Council, 12–13 June 1888.

Much confidence has been placed by authors in two documents produced by central government. These are the 1888 *Report on the Sweating System in Leeds* and the *Report on the Effects of Recent Immigration* of 1894. The first was the outcome of a single day spent in the town by the Board of Trade Correspondent, Robert Burnett. His *modus operandi* was not a systematic survey but an interview with eight Jewish masters who each happened to employ an average of fifty workers. It is not surprising, therefore, that he concluded that the average Leeds workshop was large, and that a shop of twelve machines was considered small. He was also much impressed by the extent of division of labour in Leeds, feeling that it was carried to extremes unknown in London.⁸² Burnett, by his method, was clearly unlikely to arrive at an accurate picture of the average size of Leeds workshops. It should also be noted that, as he was writing his version of the 'largeness theory' and the 'superior' division of labour in Leeds, his colleagues in the Inspectorate were even then publishing the fact that the division of labour in London was equally extreme.⁸³ The second document, much more extensive, also contains conceptual flaws which render it useless as a general guide to scale, although it contains useful scattered information. Clara Collet, the investigator, did not intend a census of workshops but, rather, to explore the role of alien women in industry. Thus she expressly excluded shops of less than ten workers in Leeds, but included these in her data on London and Manchester, biasing her averages for all time. Despite this, and her Leeds figure of thirty-five workers per shop in one group of fifty-two shops visited, her information includes a further group of six shops employing an average of only fourteen workers.⁸⁴ The alien-watching *Factory Times* pounced on Miss Collet, grumbling that she had visited only seventy-five shops. 'She could find some sorry dog-kennels,' it complained, 'but, of course, on this, nothing is said.'⁸⁵

The small alien workshop is, in fact, essential to the solution of the problems posed by Gartner's model, in which penurious immigrants are able to set up large workshops without passing through so much as a transitional phase, however short, of growth. It is not difficult, moreover, to show that the Leeds trade numbered a considerable population of small workshops – and in the long as well as short term. This follows immediately from the idea of successive immigrant waves nourishing the alien sector with cheap labour – a stimulus to workshop proliferation – as well as a source of fresh masters. The small workshop could be started on as little as £25, and, as might be expected, some grew but many collapsed.⁸⁶ Early evidence of the small master's presence occurs in the Yiddish socialist journal *Der Poilisher Yidel*, in which, in 1884, the labour leader, Joseph Finn, described a totally undifferentiated crowd of workers and small masters making for the public house together to back horses as soon as they got 'their few shillings in their hands on Fridays for which they have worked so hard'.⁸⁷ A year later, as the first Jewish strike focused attention on the alien industry, the *Yorkshire Post* noticed that 'some employers had only two or three men in their service'.⁸⁸ In 1888 *The Lancet* sanitary commissioner reported that small Leeds workshops of six machines were increasing in scale, but, on penetrating the Jewish quarter of the

Leylands, he uncovered the small sweater with 'two machines plus four or five people' in the front rooms, and 'a number of homeworking tailors'. To the wife of one such, it was 'starvation for him and his workpeople'.[89] The *Yorkshire Post*, inspired by all this to investigate for itself, found 'thousands of Jews employed at their own homes without any factory inspector or local authority having power over them'.[90] In the same interesting (and convulsive) Leylands year the Sanitary Department began systematic inspection, producing a list of thirty-one dwelling houses used as workshops, each employing no more than four workers. Presented to the Sweating Committee in London, the list was greeted with a scepticism strongly reinforced by Inspector Rickards' assertion that 1,000 such shops existed in Leeds, each with two machines hired at 2s 6d per week. With renewal of the process of arrival, 'apprenticeship', and low-cost entry into 'business', the small master, little differentiated from his men, seemed an essential part of the industry. Many had little more than worker status. 'There is no great gulf between them,' reported the Inspector, inconsiderately breaching the East End monopoly of this hallmark of industrial wretchedness awarded by many authors.[91] Moreover, only very small masters could exhibit such breathtaking mobility of capital as to disappear when information was laid against them for breach of regulations.[92] Such a man penned a rare portrait of his species in *Arbeiter Freund* in 1903, wherein he wondered why that journal was so friendly to the workers of Leeds and so hateful to the masters. He, a master, was 'worse exploited' than any worker. He could not get a living unless he kept lodgers, and only his 'will to betterment' made him endure his situation.[93]

Trivialisation of the serious problems of the Leeds workshops in the standard apologetics has been compounded by disdain of the small matter of the tailoring revolution occurring before 1914. Secular trends in the wholesale sector, and their influence upon the vulnerable alien sector, have been entirely overlooked; whilst the dynamic realities of the industry have been translated into a comfortable stasis, typical of which is an uninterrupted flow of large orders between wholesaler and alien with an apparent immunity to the trade cycle. This somnolent vision (and the cosy conditions which are its implication) lies unclarified in many accounts, side by side with chatter about such dynamic matters as changes in fashion and fluctuations in demand. Nor has the rare recognition that an industry undergoes long as well as short-term experience served to cast great light. Garrard, for example, in considering Leeds to 1914, arbitrarily extends to that year Beatrice

Webb's observation of 1888 that Jewish and Gentile tailoring existed in 'watertight compartments'. In so doing, he effectively assigns to the former a single, unchanging role despite its intimate connection with the latter, and the uncertainties of trade that this implies.[94] Gainer, on the other hand, overturns all known laws of capitalist development – and, in particular, those relating to the interactions between domestic and manufacturing industry – by hinting at progressive stability in his assertion that, in Leeds, seasonal fluctuations were sharp 'at least in the earlier years of our period'.[95] Gartner, ever the victim of his own static method, also indulges in the idea that alien tailoring in Leeds underwent secular stabilisation – a luxury made possible by imperfect appraisal of the seasonal cycle, as well as an entire absence of attention to alternative sources of trade disturbance.[96]

In practice, the final years of the period were characterised by gross instability in the Leeds wholesale industry, with the profoundest consequences for the dependent alien sector. The central factor was a broad diversification into the market for made-to-measure clothing. The 'special-order trade' began rapid growth as early as 1895, when many large firms began to adjust their well tuned production systems to meet, on a wholesale basis, the rising demand for a better fit.[97] By 1902 it had become clear that the measure trade was 'the thing of the future' as this department appeared the busiest and even began to export.[98] The change to better quality was striking. Whereas the chief demand of the 1890s had been for serge suits retailing for as little as 6s 11d, the cheap houses found themselves lagging by 1902. The new market was welcomed avidly, not only as a source of diversification but as a relief from the competitive narrowing of margins in the cheaper trade. Changes in selling techniques influenced both factory and workshop. Stocks and stock production diminished. The retailer required no more than a few lengths of cloth for the window, a pattern book, and a supply of measurement forms. 'Why trouble keeping stock?' and, ominously, 'Why trouble keeping tailors?' asked the advertisers of the new product.[99] Although readymades continued to hold an important place in exports and in the cheaper domestic trade, an enormous growth of the measure trade occurred throughout the 1900s, and by 1911 it was described as 'at a peak'.[100]

In isolation these changes might have increased the long-term importance of the alien branch, since they depended to some extent on the advancing skills of the Jewish tailor. Associated by the Sweating Committee with the cheapest coat trade in 1889,[101] the Leeds aliens had caused Beatrice Webb's 'watertight compartments' between Jewish and Gentile tailoring — so cherished by her adherents — to spring a leak by 1894. 'The bespoke tailor is beginning to feel the pinch,' observed the *Leeds Weekly Express* in that year. 'Previously the Jews did the slop coatmaking but they have now become such adepts that high class work is being let out to them.'[102] Four years later, the *Jewish Chronicle* claimed that the Jewish masters now came 'from the most skilled and gifted ranks', whilst it regarded the smaller supply of work to the Jews in the highest quality trade in 1906 as the termination of a long-standing Jewish monopoly.[103] Well before the end of the period Jewish skills were frankly admired even by native craftsmen rivals. The presser, for example, was said by the Amalgamated Society of Tailors to be 'invariably a Jew'. No Englishman could 'rival him in the perfection of the presser's art'.[104]

Only beneath the cloak of spurious tranquillity in which this Leeds period has been clad, however, could these developments be regarded as benign. They were, in fact, accompanied by exogenous disturbances which acted catalytically upon the alien sector of the trade, and which were ultimately conducive to conditions quite opposed to those which have been so widely propounded. For their proper elucidation, the erratic course of development of the native industry requires examination.

With progressive concentration of capital elsewhere and consequent increase in the height of the cost barrier to entry to many manufacturing industries, Leeds tailoring — relatively labour-intensive and with new products of high potential — experienced a renewed outburst of expansion, apparently of greater magnitude even than that of the 1880s, and through the 1900s the reports of new entrants and of the enlargement of existing firms are abundant.[105] Nor was there any slowing of the technological progress essential to the increased concentration of tailoring capital which underlay the expansion. By the early 1900s, indeed, the contrast between the alien workshop and the turbine-powered native factory, with its batteries of mechanical cutters, novel finishing devices, and sewing machinery capable of 5,000 stitches per minute, was absolute.[106]

Increased mechanisation appeared to induce changes in the organic composition of capital of the type which form the basis of Marx's General Law of Capitalist Accumulation. Under this, an increase in productivity implies an increase in the means of production (constant capital) at the expense of the variable capital (wages). 'Since,' as Marx writes, 'the demand for labour is determined, not by the amount of capital as a whole, but by its variable constituent alone, that demand falls progressively with the increase of the total capital, instead of, as previously assumed, rising in proportion to it.' Thus, although accumulation reduces the *relative* magnitude of variable capital, and does not prevent an increase in its *absolute* magnitude, a relative-surplus or industrial reserve army is progressively produced. Marx's analysis of reserve-army behaviour is of profound importance for the tailoring industry during this period, with its special proneness to fluctuations. In cases of sudden expansion, he argues, there must be the possibility of throwing 'great masses of men' into work at decisive points without injuring the scale of production in other spheres. The cyclical course of industry depends on the formation, the absorption, and the re-formation of the reserve army.[107] Under the editorship of Sidney Webb the study *Seasonal Trades*, published in 1912, confirmed the views of Marx from the viewpoint of the clothing industry. It agreed that industrial concentration (the consequence of the increased organic composition of capital) eliminated 'leakage of employment'. The number of workers was diminished, though work was more regular for those remaining in their jobs. Where, however, as in the clothing trade, machinery was simple, large numbers of workers could be quickly taken on and seasonal concentration facilitated.[108]

A number of neglected aspects of Leeds wholesale tailoring – all bearing upon the role of the aliens – emerges. The periodic 'release' of portions of the labour force became a permanent affliction, as the anxious discussions in trade journals testify. The advance of the special order at the expense of readymades also produced the anomaly that, in large factories, a part of the labour force might be working overtime whilst the remainder were idle.[109] Productivity rose very rapidly. In 1903 it was said to have increased by 25 per cent in the previous three years, whilst the 'craze for cheapness', with measure suits selling at 10s 0d, 'insane competition', and reduced profits, called forth widespread trade condemnation. The leaders, noting the rapid consumption of the profit opportunities inherent in the new products, called for increased exports to fill the gap. In the 1900s, however, the Germans were 'fighting tooth and nail' for clothing markets, and colonial tariffs against clothing imports were rising steeply.[110] In place of the competitive equilibrium (with self-regulating entry) so beloved of bourgeois economics, the rapid inrush of new firms, and the ensuing productive anarchy, left the industry with what a Leeds clothier categorised as an 'overplus of labour' which came in 'useful only when things were humming'.[111] In other words, the Marxian reserve army was massing.

The cyclical nature of the wholesale clothing trade seeks more attention than it has yet received. Gainer has curiously equated the absence of any anti-alien pronouncement by the Leeds Trades Council after 1895 with 'permanent trade recovery'. This is very far-reaching indeed in view of the complexity and durability of the Leeds clothing cycle. To the end of the period the industry continued to be plagued by the basic seasonal cycle. So far from being confined to the early years of immigration, it was wearily admitted in 1904 that its hoped-for elimination seemed 'further away than ever'.[112] Matters were not one whit improved by 1912.[113] This failure of long-term efforts towards stabilisation followed from the expansion of the bespoke or measure trade in the 1900s which heightened sensitivity to seasonal influences. At the same time, the reduction in the relative output of readymades in uniform sizes and grades minimised the degree to which demand might be anticipated.[114] The seasonal fluctuations themselves, moreover, were irregular in incidence and intensity; and the trade would often be surprised by their timing and severity. This was the result of exogenous disturbances such as unseasonal weather, bad harvests, and random labour troubles in the basic industries of engineering, coal and cotton.[115]

More serious is the absence from commentaries of any hint of the industry's long-term demand experience. This neglect is surprising in view of the punctuation of these years by two major national slumps which cast odd light on Gainer's post-1895 'permanent trade recovery'. In Appendix I the graphs of the sales and profits of four major Leeds wholesale manufacturers are given. The group includes the largest Leeds firm and all are known to have employed alien outworkers.[116] Mathematical trend curves fitted to the undecomposed data generally assume markedly more positive gradients for the later years, confirming the expansion of activity and scale. More or less marked reaction to the trade crises of 1903–04 and 1908–10 is exhibited by all the firms. The graphs of the detrended series embody seasonal, cyclical and random variations expressed as deviations from trend, unsmoothed so as to reflect the precise extent of irregularity. It is immediately clear that these firms shared a similar experience in the form of significant and regular annual or biennial fluctuations in sales and/or profits. Furthermore, where the series extend back to the nineteenth century it is clear that the final years of the period did not see the relative stability which some scholars make contributory to the 'fair conditions' of the Leeds Jewish tailoring trade.

In relation to the modernisation, concentration and enlargement of the native wholesale branch, and the mixed economic experience implicit in these movements, the alien branch could hardly escape radical disturbance. Indeed, if the latter is viewed in its role as an external appendage of the larger system around it, rather than in the guise of perennial exception to the rules of alien industrial wretchedness in which it appears in the accounts of Gartner and his school, it becomes clear that the developments of the 1900s were bound to affect the balance between the two branches critically. Marx's account of the reaction of the factory system on domestic industry fits the situation well. The true, old-fashioned domestic industry, he writes, is 'converted into an outside department of the factory', which requires, in addition to the workers it commands directly, 'another army; that of the workers in the domestic industries'. In the apparel industry, Marx observes that the materials are supplied by the large manufacturer; the human material is that 'liberated' from the land or by machinery. The origin of the system, he considers, is the need for the capitalist to have at hand 'an army ready to meet any increase of demand'. The claims that there was a simple division between domestic handwork and factory machine work have already been considered. Marx observes, however, that there was 'a medley of transitional forms', which varied according to the extent to which the sewing machine had become prevalent in any branch of industry. 'Here the factory system proper. There middlemen receive the materials from the capitalist *en chef* and group around their sewing machines, in chambers and garrets, from ten to fifty or more workwomen.' As a model of the economics of Leeds alien tailoring, this requires amendment only inasmuch as the human material was liberated by the Tsar, and that most of the liberated workers in their chambers and garrets were men.

Marx does not fall into the naive error of Gartner and his followers in equating a large-scale work source with a beneficial situation of the outworker. On the contrary, such a source appears all the more dangerous since its capital structure is so highly developed. Marx perceives what they miss: that the variety of transitional forms 'does not conceal the tendency to conversion into the factory system proper'. This tendency is the consequence (in modern terminology) of the widening technological gap between the branches, and the resultant 'economy in the means of production' within the factory system – an economy which 'now shows its antagonistic and murderous side more and more in a given branch of industry the less the social productive power of labour and the technical basis for a combination of processes are developed in that branch'.[117]

This goes far to account for the vulnerability of the Leeds Jewish trade, despite the relative scale of some of its workshops and illusory similarity to the organisation of the large factory. In spite of a delayed transition – determined precisely by the rate of development of the native firms – it was clear by 1911 that the alien shops had moved towards the outermost circle of a trade in which they had, in the 1880s, occupied a central place. Overlooking the essentially domestic nature of the alien branch, a *Men's Wear* correspondent blamed the Jews of Leeds for failing to take advantage of new appliances. He perceived accurately, however, that reliance upon 'strenuous labour and long hours' was the basic cause of their being 'pushed out'.[118] Some months after these comments an English manufacturer confirmed that foreigners did not help them as much as they had once done.[119] As the *Yorkshire Evening Post* saw it in the same year:

> It will be cheerful news to some people that Leeds is no longer so inviting to the foreigner as it used to be ... Jews whom the tailoring trade in Leeds formerly attracted in their thousands now find their Jerusalem in New York. The Leeds tailoring trade, they say, is a dead letter.[120]

To another Leeds manufacturer it was 'a joke' to think that they 'nowadays relied on the Jews'.[121]

The widening technological gap, which improved the quality of machine work and permitted the factory, utilising more female labour, to do more for itself, presented the wholesalers with problems of maintaining the output of their own capital-rich systems, of keeping their own large forces employed, and of coping with the unstable demand curve mirrored in the graphs of Appendix I. The disharmony between English-factory and alien-workshop methods of production became increasingly clear, whilst the opportunity-cost of outside production was prohibitive for many large firms by the later 1900s. The consequences – falling demand upon alien services, downward pressure on making-up prices, and the alien role in general – came under broad discussion from the mid-1900s. Significantly, the slump of 1903–04 had called forth nothing more than complaints of temporary, if very severe, unemployment. In 1906, however, a year of revival in trade, the *Jewish Chronicle*, with the following, commenced an agonised commentary on Leeds Jewish prospects which was to continue to the end of the period:

Almost every few months witness the abolition of some Jewish master . . . the large establishments deciding to make the garments on their own premises.

The large firms, it was noted, were increasing their business whilst a simultaneous decrease occurred in the number of garments made in the alien branch. *Jewish World*, its contemporary, saw the growth of the older Leeds houses and the addition of new ones as 'a striking anomaly' at a time of declining demand on the aliens.[122]

Two years later, as the signs of a new slump appeared, withdrawals of work and Jewish shop closures increased. Connections of twenty years' duration were broken, and the largest firm, Messrs John Barran, withdrew all its work indoors.[123] Christian missionaries in the Jewish quarter reported in 1909 that employment was 'lower for Jewish men'.[124] A year later the *Chronicle* viewed the extinction of the Jewish middleman in Leeds as 'merely a matter of time',[125] a sentiment echoed by *Jewish World*.[126] The continuing debate on this theme in *Men's Wear* indicates also that these were not simply the complaints of Jewish interests.[127]

The effects upon the alien branch of the trade in the final years require consideration. In general, those masters losing their erstwhile warehouse contacts disappeared from the scene. The survivors found themselves in a transformed market, forming a labour reserve of greater servility than ever, and tolerated for no more than their readiness to bear the burden of slack periods.[128] Their area of manoeuvre also narrowed as the quality of factory work rose and they were forced to rely increasingly upon their differential skills for a place in the trade. Down to 1914 they were involved in a race against the increasingly competent factory girls armed with ever-improving implements. The input of greater alien skills was not, however, rewarded by higher prices, and, although price complaints abound in the period before 1900, it came to be regarded as a golden age by the later 1900s. These tendencies were persistently aggravated by the continuous invasion of the better-quality trade by the wholesalers in response to the demand of the Edwardian male for cheaper clothes in better styling. As early as 1902 some who rejoiced at the new market for measure goods were also able to see that the cost to the trade would be 'increased quality at low prices'.[129]

In 1907 the *Jewish Chronicle* took the measure of the alien situation in the Leeds trade. It concluded that the Jewish tailor had fallen to the position of mere maker-up of surplus garments after the factory had provided for its own workers. Unlike Professor Gartner, however, it did not draw optimistic inferences from this: rather, it saw that the prices paid to the Jewish branch were 'almost infinitesimal' compared with those of a dozen years earlier.[130] A year later, the position was that 'whilst the Gentile manufacturer periodically evolved new ideas involving additional labour, he indulged in the practice of cutting prices based on the cost of production by Christian females'.[131] *Jewish World*, at this time, also harked back to the previous years as a period of falling prices and rising material costs.[132]

In 1910, under the impact of heightened factory competition, considerable numbers of skilled Jewish tailors began to leave Leeds for Canada and the U.S.A., creating actual labour shortages in the busy seasons.[133] Despite the boast of the *Chronicle*, however, that '... when any new style of garments are to be produced ... they are given to Jewish masters to make up ... where special skill is required, that is where the Jewish workman is indispensable'[134] these movements did little to generate countervailing trends, and complaints of 'increased work on style – no advance on pay' continued to the eve of the Great War.[135]

On the structural side of the alien branch, there is evidence of great importance that, as a direct consequence of the disturbances of the 1900s, Leeds had acquired numberless replicas of the London sweater's den well before 1914 – the objective manifestations of adaptation to a much altered situation. Pre-1900 accounts, as has been seen, stressed the large scale of workshops in Leeds. With the turn of the century, however, little is heard in this vein, whilst there is a striking increase in the extent to which small shops figure in comment upon the town's tailoring affairs. The causes seem clear. With the withdrawal of work indoors, many large Jewish workshops were abolished and alien unemployment was created.[136] Warehouse policies towards the survivors tended to reduce their scale, since large external establishments became difficult to supply with regular orders in the erratic bespoke market. This was reinforced by the advance of the pernicious 'specials', invariably farmed out to the small alien ever willing to compete by finishing the work in record time.[137]

The distribution of outwork changed radically. Whereas the earlier years heard complaints of monopoly because of the restrictive distribution of outwork, 'an indiscriminate increase in the numbers of small middlemen' and a propitious environment for price reductions were created by 'the issue of work to excessive numbers of masters'.

Thus one firm, 'by no means the largest', farmed out its work to thirty-three masters when a handful would have sufficed.[138] It followed, therefore, that some Jewish employers of more than 100 workers were now able to sustain no more than a dozen.[139]

The chief impact on structure, however, was made by those thrown out of the wholesale sector by work withdrawal. The adaptable Jewish tailor did not stand still. Exploiting a limited tradition of cheap bespoke work extending back to 1889, he promptly invaded the better bespoke trade on his own account, there to exist in direct competition with the English craft tailor. By 1908 over 25 per cent of Jewish work in Leeds was said to be for the quality trade, despite the fact that Jews were often expressly barred from this area.[140] The market grew more complex, and, by the early 1900s, was further removed than ever from the simplified scheme of Gartner, involving merely the large warehouse and the large alien workshop. To a degree, the new system arose from the blurring of the distinction between hand craft work and machine work under which orders were directed to Jewish shops and away from the English back-room craftsman, though the customer often paid a premium for the latter's skills.[141] As High Street trading developed along with communications many small alien shops catered as makers-up for retail front shops in other towns.

The danger in rejecting the complaints of contemporaries in order to sustain a case is very clear. Gainer and Garrard, in whose models the alien tailor never moves out of the cheaper market, reject out of hand the complaints of native labour displacement uttered by the craftsmen of the Amalgamated Tailors. Owing to the shifts in Leeds, however, English craft tailoring shops declined from 450 in 1889 to 250 in 1903. By comparison, in Belfast, where there was no concentration of aliens, the number of craft tailors remained steady.[142] As the 1900s advanced, the role of the alien in Leeds was increasingly held by trade journals to be that of the skilled needleman.[143]

The new role was acted out in a new environment as a rash of bedroom workshops appeared which, overflowing the Leylands, spilled into the equally insalubrious Newtown to the north, Camp Road to the west, and Meanwood Road to the north-west, there to face an existence more casual and precarious than ever. By 1906 the *Jewish Chronicle* was struck – not by the scale of Jewish workshops – but by the fact that 'the majority of the Jewish men are tailors and they work very largely in their own homes'.[144] Hundreds of small masters, said the paper a year later, were competitively clamouring for work.[145] Although Mrs Lerner claimed that homework did not exist in Leeds, and although the phenomenon makes no appearance in more recent work such as that of Gartner and Gainer, the accounts of large workshops were rapidly replaced by distressed talk of the Leeds Jewish bedroom master with his chamber containing no more than six workers and 'not more than $3\frac{1}{4}$ yards by 4 yards' in area.[146] So rapid and widespread was the retreat from workshop to bedroom that, by 1908, the prevalence of the system was blamed for the complete ineffectiveness of the Truck Acts in Leeds.[147] Whilst nineteenth-century battles against homework appear to have been exclusively English affairs,[148] labour sources began in the 1900s to stigmatise Jewish homes for the first time as places in which there was 'much to be done' about homework.[149]

More revealing was the assumption of the Jewish Tailors' Union in 1911 that young Jews entering the trade would normally have to work in small shops and houses when they would have preferred the factory.[150] Union policies in these later years confirm the rise of the bedroom master as a major preoccupation. At the Trades Union Congress of 1908 Moses Sclare, the union secretary, moved that the Parliamentary Committee urge the government to render all dwelling houses used as workshops illegal.[151] Five years later so serious was the problem that Sclare himself led a deputation of the committee to the Home Secretary on this subject.[152]

Received assessments of the Leeds alien tailoring industry, in the light of an approach seeking to trace the course of its development, suffer from a variety of methodological faults. They are damaged by the centrality of the large alien workshop – a concept which takes little account of the dialectical variations experienced beneath the stresses of intra-communal competition, as well as those imposed from without through the anarchy of the parent wholesale industry. For these reasons, the role of the alien in Leeds tailoring has been quite misconceived, and conditions credited to him which, under objective material conditions, were chimerical. The basic thesis of those scholars whose work suffers from a misleading static approach to economic problems is that Leeds conditions were superior to those found in other alien centres. This question will be tested in the following chapter.

NOTES

1 V. D. Lipman, 'Jews in British urban society, 1880–1914: from ghetto to suburb', paper read at the Economic History Society Conference, Leeds, 1975, pp. 13–14.

2   J. A. Garrard, *The English and Immigration, 1880–1910*, Oxford, 1971, pp. 159–60.
3   *J.C.*, 17 March 1905; 29 May 1908.
4   H.L. *Select Committee on the Sweating System, 1889*, P.P. 1889, XIV, 331, appendix F; *Sweating System, 1889*, P.P. 1889, XIII, 165, appendix A.
5   Report of the Leeds Medical Officer of Health, 1889, 1892; *Royal Commission on Aliens, 1903*, P.P. 1903, IX, Cd 1742, qq. 14293–4.
6   *Reports on the Volume and Effects of Recent Immigration, 1894*, P.P. 1894, LXVII, C 7406, p. 42. The authors let their imaginations go, describing the Jew as a 'formidable competitor' because generations of study of the casuistry of the Talmud had sharpened his wits.
7   S. W. Lerner, *Breakaway Unions and the Small Trade Union*, London, 1961, pp. 86–7.
8   S. W. Baron, *The Russian Jew under Tsar and Soviets*, New York, 1964, p. 104.
9   J. Raba, 'On the occupational structure of the Jewish population in the kingdom of Poland in the middle of the nineteenth century', *Zion*, new series, 1960.
10 J. Bross, 'The beginning of the Jewish labour movement in Galicia', *Yivo*, IV, 1950, p. 56.
11 E. Mendelsohn, *Class Struggle in the Pale*, Cambridge, 1970, p. 6.
12 *The Anti-Sweater*, VIII, 1887, p. 2.
13 Mendelsohn, *Class Struggle*, p. 10.
14 V. I. Lenin, *The Development of Capitalism in Russia*, Collected Works, III, Moscow, 1964, pp. 450–1.
15 *Y.P.*, 15 September 1891.
16 *Sweating System*, qq. 29987–30100, 30107–39, 30250–51.
17 *Report of the Inspector of Factories, 1887*, P.P. 1887, XXVI, C 5328, p. 95.
18 *Recent Immigration*, p. 41.
19 J. A. Hobson, *The Problem of Poverty*, London, 1892, p. 98.
20 See B. Gainer, *The Alien Invasion*, London, 1972, pp. 84–90; C. Holmes, 'J. A. Hobson and the Jews', in C. Holmes (ed.), *Immigrants and Minorities in British Society*, London, 1978.
21 H. Neustatter, 'Demographic and other statistical aspects', in M. Freedman (ed.), *A Minority in Britain*, London, 1955, pp. 109–10.
22 Lipman, 'Jews in British urban society', pp. 13–14.
23 Garrard, *Immigration*, pp. 158–60.
24 S. W. Lerner, 'The impact of the Jewish immigration of 1880–1914 on the London clothing industry and trade unions', *Bulletin of the Society for the Study of Labour History*, XII, summer 1966, p. 13.
25 E. Hunt, *Regional Wage Variations in Britian, 1850–1914*, Oxford, 1973, p. 309.
26 Gainer, *Alien Invasion*, p. 28; L. P. Gartner, *The Jewish Immigrant in England, 1880–1914*, 2nd edn, London, 1973, p. 66.
27 W. J. Fishman, *East End Radicals, 1875–1914*, London, 1975, p. 50.

28 C. Holmes, *Anti-Semitism in British Society, 1876–1939*, London, 1979, p. 20.
29 J. A. Dyche, 'The Jewish workman', *Contemporary Review*, 385, January, 1898, pp. 37–9.
30 C. J. Hawkins, *Theory of the Firm*, London, 1973, pp. 17–21. Strict homogeneity of product is not essential to the model, given the nature of the market for the products of Leeds alien tailoring.
31 Lenin, *Development of Capitalism*; Mendelsohn, *Class Struggle*.
32 S. M. Dubnow, *History of the Jews of Russia and Poland*, III, Philadelphia, 1920, pp. 22–3.
33 H. Sacher, 'The pogroms', *Jewish Review*, April, 1910, p. 38.
34 *A.F.*, 6 January 1893.
35 *Ibid.*, 10 July 1903.
36 *L.W.E.*, 27 January 1894.
37 Garrard, *Immigration*, pp. 157–8.
38 *Ibid.*, pp. 159–60.
39 Gainer, *Alien Invasion*, p. 18.
40 Hunt, *Wage Variations*, p. 314.
41 Gartner, *Jewish Immigrant*, pp. 63, 66, 89, 138.
42 Gainer, *Alien Invasion*, p. 18.
43 Garrard, *Immigration*, pp. 159–60.
44 J. S. Bain, 'Economies of scale, concentration, and the conditions of entry in twenty manufacturing industries', *American Economic Review*, LXIV, 1954, pp. 15–39.
45 Gartner, *Jewish Immigrant*, p. 89.
46 Hunt, *Wage Variations*, pp. 312–13.
47 See *Men's Wear*, 9 January 1904, for a report indicating that one London firm employed fifty travellers.
48 L. Lyons, *The Horrible Sweating System*, London, 1885, p. 5.
49 *Recent Immigration*, pp. 112, 203.
50 *Aliens Commission*, qq. 19664–5.
51 *Select Committee on Homework, 1908*, P.P. 1908, VIII, 246, qq. 2698–9, 2604–12, 1196, 1435; *Aliens Commission*, qq. 17967–8.
52 Gartner, *Jewish Immigrant*, p. 63.
53 Garrard, *Immigration*, pp. 157–9.
54 According to the Leeds Clothiers' Operatives, 187 wholesalers were present in 1908. See *Committee on the Truck Acts, 1908*, P.P. 1908, LIX, Cd 4443, q. 5446.
55 *Y.P.*, 14 June 1888; *Leeds Mercury*, 11 January 1889, 8 May 1890.
56 *Y.F.T.*, 19 July 1889; *Leeds Mercury*, 24 July 1889.
57 *Dundee Advertiser*, 4 September 1896.
58 Leeds City Archives, John Barran Stock Books, 1845–69.
59 *Leeds Mercury*, 7 January 1860, for an early example.
60 *Sweating System*, appendix P; *Clothing and Outfitting World*, 19 September 1896.
61 See Hunt, *Wage Variations*, p. 321; Gartner, *Jewish Immigrant*, p. 63; Fishman, *East End Radicals*, pp. 84–5.
62 Commissioners of Patents, *Abridgements of Specifications relating to*

Sewing and Embroidering, A.D. 1755–1866, 1867–76.
63 'British industries', *Mercantile Age*, VII, 1884; *Men's Wear*, 27 May 1905.
64 See, for example, Garrard, *Immigration*, p. 159.
65 Lenin, *Development of Capitalism*, pp. 438–9.
66 *Men's Wear*, 23 November 1912.
67 *Labour Chronicle*, 6 May 1893.
68 *Clothing and Outfitting World*, 2 May, 5 September, 19 September 1896.
69 *Y.P.*, 12 May 1888; *L.W.E.*, 14 July 1888; *Report on Strikes, 1888*, P.P. 1889, LXX, C 5809, appendix i, p. 82.
70 *L.E.E.*, 24 February 1893; *J.C.*, 9 July 1897; *Report of the Inspector of Factories, 1887*, p. 94.
71 *L.W.E.*, 27 January 1894.
72 *Y.F.T.*, 12 January, 9 May 1890.
73 *Leeds Mercury*, 21 January 1898.
74 *The Lancet*, I, June, 1888, p. 1210.
75 *Sweating System*, qq. 31654, 31657, 31665.
76 *Ibid.*, qq. 30966.
77 *Y.P.*, 14 June 1888.
78 *L.E.E.*, 25 May 1894.
79 *Sweating System*, qq. 30655–6.
80 *J.C.*, 4 February 1898.
81 *Y.P.*, 14 June 1888.
82 *Report on the Sweating System in Leeds, 1888*, P.P. 1888, LXXXVI, C 5513, pp. 4–5.
83 *Report of the Inspector of Factories, 1887*, p. 95.
84 *Recent Immigration*, pp. 117, 120, 126.
85 *Y.F.T.*, 10 August 1894.
86 *Y.E.N.*, 14 March 1911.
87 *D.P.Y.*, 25 July 1884.
88 *Y.P.*, 9 May 1885.
89 *The Lancet*, I, June, 1888, p. 1209.
90 *Y.P.*, 25 August 1888.
91 *Sweating System*, qq. 30431, 30926, 30928, 30934–5, appendix F.
92 *Report of the Inspector of Factories, 1896*, P.P. 1897, XVII, C 8561, p. 71.
93 *A.F.*, 1 May 1903.
94 Garrard, *Immigration*, pp. 166–7.
95 Gainer, *Alien Invasion*, p. 18.
96 Gartner, *Jewish Immigrant*, pp. 89, 98.
97 *Clothing and Outfitting World*, 7 September, 21 September 1895.
98 *Men's Wear*, 26 April 1902.
99 *Ibid.*, 3 May 1902.
100 *Ibid.*, 16 September, 30 December 1905, 11 November 1911.
101 *Sweating System*, q. 28927.
102 *L.W.E.*, 27 January 1894.
103 *J.C.*, 22 April 1898, 17 August 1906.

104 *Journal of the A.S. of T.*, November, 1910, p. 9.
105 See, *inter alia, Men's Wear*, 1 March, 9 August 1902, 17 January, 27 June 1903, 9 January, 16 January 1905; *Y.E.P.*, 4 January 1911.
106 *Clothing and Outfitting World*, 18 April 1896; *Men's Wear*, 27 June 1903, 16 September 1905, 27 October 1906.
107 K. Marx, *Capital*, I, Chicago, 1919, p. 671 *et seq.* See also G. Kay, *The Economic Theory of the Working Class*, 1979, pp. 92–116.
108 S. Webb and A. Freeman (eds), *Seasonal Trades*, London, 1912, pp. 35, 57.
109 *Men's Wear*, 3 December 1904.
110 *Ibid.*, 11 April 1903, 6 January 1906, 5 October 1907.
111 *Ibid.*, 9 January, 28 May 1904.
112 *Ibid.*, 19 March 1904.
113 *Ibid.*, 6 July 1912.
114 Webb and Freeman, *Seasonal Trades*, pp. 35–40.
115 *Men's Wear*, 21 March 1903, 9 July 1904, 13 October 1906.
116 Leeds City Archives, Business Records Collection.
117 Marx, *Capital*, pp. 504–6, 514–9.
118 *Men's Wear*, 20 May 1911.
119 *Ibid.*, 7 October 1911.
120 *Y.E.P.*, 4 January 1911.
121 *Y.E.N.*, 8 March 1911.
122 *J.C.*, 17 August 1906; *Jewish World*, 11 September 1908.
123 *J.C.*, 12 June 1908; *Homework Committee*, q. 3075.
124 *Report of the Leeds Auxiliary of the British Society for the Propagation of the Gospel amongst the Jews*, 1909, p. 4.
125 *J.C.*, 5 August 1910.
126 *Jewish World*, 1 July 1910.
127 *Men's Wear*, 18 August 1906, 23 November 1912.
128 *Ibid.*, 23 November 1912.
129 *Ibid.*, 10 May 1902; *Die Yiddishe Presse*, 3 February 1903.
130 *J.C.*, 8 February 1907.
131 *Ibid.*, 15 May 1908.
132 *Jewish World*, 11 September 1908.
133 *J.C.*, 5 August 1910; *Y.E.N.*, 9 February 1911.
134 *J.C.*, 12 May 1911.
135 *Jewish World*, 5 May 1911; *Men's Wear*, 8 July 1911, 19 October 1912.
136 See, for example, *A.F.*, 29 May 1908.
137 *Men's Wear*, 19 October 1912.
138 *Jewish World*, 11 September 1908.
139 *Ibid.*, 1 July 1910.
140 *Sweating System*, qq. 28978–80; *Committee on the Truck Acts*, q. 5888.
141 *Daily News*, 25 July 1906.
142 *Sweating System*, q. 30533; *Aliens Commission*, qq. 14293–4, 14317–20, 15038.
143 *Men's Wear*, 20 May 1911.
144 *J.C.*, 29 June 1906.
145 *Ibid.*, 8 February 1907.

146 Lerner, 'Jewish immigration', p. 13; *Y.E.N.*, 23 June 1906.
147 *Committee on the Truck Acts*, q. 5888.
148 *Labour Chronicle*, 6 May 1893.
149 *Y.F.T.*, 29 June 1906, 16 March 1911.
150 *Men's Wear*, 20 May 1911.
151 *Jewish World*, 18 September 1908.
152 *J.C.*, 9 May 1913.

Chapter 2

CONDITION OF THE JEWISH TAILORING WORKSHOP IN LEEDS

Most of the mounting number of assessments of the Leeds alien tailoring industry, as has been seen, are thoroughly suffused by the concept of the large workshop and relatively favourable conditions – an electic image formed without reference to objective material interrelationships. Its advocates have, consequently, been in no position to satisfy the imperative requirement of justification of their postulates in terms of the suggested scale of operations and its supposed advantages. Garrard has been content to apply the general label 'bestial' to alien working conditions, and to hint at Leeds as an exception, since here, although the alien was blamed for sweating, his workshops were larger than those in London and Manchester.[1] On this view, workshop scale appears the single variable in the determination of working conditions. Hunt treads precisely the same path on the Leeds trade. He properly perceives that the accompaniments of sweating were the whims of fashion, a large supply of female labour, and 'irregular work patterns', but why these forces were neutralised in Leeds goes unexplained other than in terms of large workshops.[2]

Gartner goes further on this problem, permitting himself a quotation from the highly critical *Lancet* report of 1888 on Leeds alien workshops. That this was an unimpeachably professional and highly authoritative exercise which must constitute an embarrassment to his model does not give him pause, however. For Gartner, too, largeness is all; and with the invocation of some small poetic licence that steam power replaced manpower 'at many points', his reader is tempted to envision a Leylands economy of miniatures of the large factories with no sweating, thriving in isolation from external disturbances, and moving majestically and ineluctably the while towards secular stability.[3]

Considering his adherence to the school which treats Leeds as the exception to the generality of appalling alien working-class conditions,

Gainer also does little justificatory work. Impressionism, rather than economic science, is his preferred technique. Stitching together scattered comment from several State Papers, he begins, promisingly, with the view that, before 1888, conditions in Leeds were 'simply appalling'. After this date, however, they were 'sometimes bad' but 'generally fairly good'.[4] This 'disclosure' of a 'sanitary watershed' at the year 1888 is the precise fictional counterpart of Gartner's 'steam revolution' in the Leeds alien workshop.

Models of this type depend upon a naive progressivist notion of the industry neglectful of the economics of outwork, especially in their dynamic nature – a failure which an application of the laws of capitalist development would have obviated. As has been seen, a central role is found in previous models for the large factory as the source of creation of large alien workshops, but the economic dynamics of the relationship remain unsullied by analysis. Manufacturers of the model appear so satisfied with it that, once postulated, so little is it supported that the Leeds alien tailoring industry seems to have its own momentum and independent existence.

So soon as alien conditions are approached from the standpoint of their entire dependence upon complex externalities, rather than the single factor of the large English warehouse, however, it becomes clear that their definition is quite unamenable to any simple linear evolutionary theory. Further, since these conditions provide the test of the much-implied benefits of economic harness with the large firms, they merit far wider treatment than they have received.

The study of these conditions is complicated – not merely by the neglected matters of working hours, sanitation, and work organisation – but by the special factors adhering to the Leeds alien branch in its association with the warehouses. The evidence is scattered, unsystematic, and far from abundant. Largely generated within the miasma of anti-alienist propaganda, it is also frequently misleading. At times it is at variance with what might be anticipated from a given source. In June 1888, for example, as the Committee on Sweating turned its attention to the provinces, the hostile *Yorkshire Post*, keen to obviate any suggestion that local magnates were in economic relations with the sweater, gave an assurance that the alien workshops were 'a vast deal cleaner, lighter, better ventilated, and altogether healthier to work in than the mills at which the cloth here stitched is woven'.[5] A mere two months later, that journal, in a breathtaking oscillation, discovered that Leeds harboured 'thousands [sic] of Jews' employed at their own homes with no supervision.[6] Alien labour sources, too, are often eccentric in their views, and are to be found indulging in *ad hoc* praise of their conditions, fearing to confirm the propaganda aimed at the restriction of immigration. Leeds Jewish labour leaders, in addressing themselves to Englishmen, often introduce a note of pride in their achievements, leading to a degree of exaggeration and the painting of pictures 'in roseate hues'.[7]

Consideration of Leeds conditions requires that the central factor — the subservient position of the alien branch — be kept in mind at all times, since it is only in this light, rather than that of the independent strength suggested by large scale, that the alien shops may be adequately treated. Further, the fundamental changes throughout Leeds tailoring, treated elsewhere, and their disintegrating effects upon the alien sector, are overlooked at peril.

The Leeds wholesale warehouse must be regarded in its primary role as a unit of an expanding and dynamic industry, as well as a large-scale, if fitful, source of alien work and large, if far from universally large, workshops. Many English firms were housed in modern buildings representing an industrial architecture which attracted wide admiration.[8] Such firms were not in the business of creating an outside department in their own image, albeit on a miniature scale. Rather, by the operation of objective economic laws, they attracted within their ambit a dependent sub-group, whose relations with the parent firms make classification difficult. Some writers have spoken of Leeds Jewish masters 'contracting' for the work of given warehouses. This seems a grandiose description of a relationship which, in practice, appears to have normally been far more casual, and one in which the warehouse manager wielded the arbitrary power to choose his favourites. In this environment, with its clear implications of an endless alien scramble for work, economic categories were indefinite. The Jewish master cannot be regarded as the employee of the large factory in the master-and-servant relationship in which the latter stood with its direct employees. Consequently, and irrespective of the size or scale of his operations, the alien master did not aspire to the wage-nexus typical of the industrial system as a whole, and from which the lowliest direct employee derived such benefits as were available.

These considerations of lowly status derive immediately from the enunication of the master's role as maker-up of the excess backlogs of the factories, the work being organised on the subdivisional system of labour. In work such as that by Gartner facile and optimistic

conclusions are drawn from the model. The organisation of production
– central as it is to the problem of working conditions – demands closer
examination. It has, in the first place, been demonstrated that the 1900s
witnessed wholesale reductions in the scale of Leeds alien tailoring
operations, induced chiefly by market dynamics. Along with scale, the
extent of division of labour bears vitally upon the same question.

On Leeds the literature is confused. Garrard, for example, treats the
alien subdivisional system as synonymous with the worst working
conditions in general, and supports his case for the superiority of the
Leeds trade with the suggestion that, here, the alien was not necessarily
connected with that system. There exists, however, abundant testimony
to the minute subdivision of labour in Leeds, and, indeed, in some
hands, notably those of Lerner and Hunt, this has been treated as the
hallmark of the 'favourable' Leeds system. The testimony of the
Factory Inspectors of Leeds and London indicate, however, that there
was little to choose between the alien trades of the two places on the
score of their respective degrees of division of labour, and this
commonality places the conditions in the alien tailoring branch of the
former under immediate suspicion.

From a theoretical standpoint, too, the Leeds workshops can hardly
have been the centres of the fair conditions so unanimously claimed.
Marx writes that, under the capitalist drive for cheaper output, the firm
achieves cheaper production by raising the productive power of labour
as much as possible. This power is raised, above all, 'by a greater
division of labour, by a more universal introduction and continual
improvement of machinery'.[9] Here, with perfect and simple clarity, is
the *economic* law that division of labour and its extension is a function
of capitalisation rather than some quasi-metaphysical ethnic preference
of the Hebrew tailor. In its light, the typical Jewish shop with its strictly
circumscribed capital stock could have achieved little more than
pathetic imitation of the advanced native giants.

Those who have lauded the superior extent of division of labour in
Leeds have rarely paused to examine the logic of their position. The
consequences of extended division of labour are amply defined by
Marx. As it increases, he writes, labour is simplified and the market
value of skills reduced. The skilled man's labour 'becomes a labour that
anyone can perform. Hence, competitors crowd upon him on all sides.'
The greater the division of labour introduced by increasing capital, the
more readily may one worker do the work of five, ten or even twenty. 'It
therefore multiplies competition among the workers fivefold, tenfold or

twentyfold.'[10]

On this basis, the enormous scale of production of the large native warehouses, so far from constituting a source of benefits, was the cause of extreme competitive stress within its subordinate alien branch. Since the extended division of labour and increased productivity were facilitated and guided by the technology of the large factory, costs of production and therefore making prices and wages of both inside and outside labour were determined in that arena. As the skill factor declined progressively with the simplification of operations, monetary rewards fell. Hence the conjunction between the rapid technological progress of the native factories and the mounting complaints about prices emanating from the alien division in the 1900s. At its extreme, in the later years of the period, fewer areas of skill remained unaffected. As the quality of machine work rose, the way was open for the reduction of the traditional distinction between this and hand work, for the rise of the bedroom master, and for the worsening workshop conditions associated with an increasingly tenuous hold by the aliens on the trade. A general approach to the effects of division of labour requires, therefore, that the emanations of the economic ascendancy of the parent English firms over the trade as a whole be taken into account. Without this, the problems associated with Leeds alien working conditions, as presented hitherto, remain insolubly paradoxical.

Another misleading bias current in accepted versions of the Leeds trade is that of progressive improvement. There is some evidence, however, that the organisation of work was inferior in some respects towards the end of the period. In 1884, for example, the advantages of association with the large warehouse seemed apparent even to a radical labour leader such as Jacob Finn. Writing in *Der Poilisher Yidel*, he observed:

Here in Leeds the workers have a time when they begin their work and a time when they finish ... The London and Manchester workers do not know a time, and they begin work at six in the morning and work until the master says: 'Enough.' In a word, the Leeds workers stand far higher than the workers of London and Manchester because of the regularity of their hours.[11]

This, from an era dominated by ready-made stock tailoring, may be instructively compared with the picture presented to the Truck Committee in 1908, by which year the pernicious specials, rigidly seasonal bespoke work, and the bedroom system were widespread. Not only had the infinitely elaborate English factory structure of fines and deductions invaded the alien branch, but every article of faith of the

The Jewish tailoring workshop 41

East End sweater had gone into the conversion of his Leeds counterpart. Thus, as in London, sub-contracting by workers, mixed piece and day rates, pace-setting, unpredictable deductions and a general dependence 'on the temper of the master' rather than the ubiquitously absent notices required by law had become the norm equally in Leeds. Further, in such workplaces, 'no proper time' was observed.[12]

The deleterious influence of the large factory is detectable also in terms other than its objective economic sway. Three months after his account of the regularity of Leeds hours, Finn was moved to complaint of the problems of obtaining overtime pay from the Jewish master. In order to persuade his men to extend their lengthy working day in the first place, the master exploited the shadow of the warehouse by suggesting that, if current work were not completed in time, he would lose the work in the future. Observed Finn:

When it comes to Saturday and time to get paid and we ask for our overtime, the master pulls faces: 'Hey! When did you work overtime?' An argument begins, the result of which is that the master grabs a few pennies. Another, when asked for the overtime, says, 'God will pay.'[13]

The warehouse again looms large in some of the chief complaints on the score of work organisation and the manner of the master's manipulation of his relationship with it. Orders handed out to the master late in the week placed him under great pressure for their timely completion – a situation increasing in frequency with the advance of specials and measure work. The workers would then be driven hard throughout the whole of Thursday and Friday nights. As is evident from testimony to the Sweating Committee, some masters working for the very largest warehouses might avoid this.[14] Other authorities, including some Leeds masters, were, however, quite clear on its widespread incidence.[15] Again, the warehouse might supply work for three or four days only. Instead of collecting it on Friday to be worked on during Sunday to allow tailors and pressers to commence work without delay on Monday, the master would collect it on Monday and thus, until the first processes were complete, tailors, pressers and finishers would suffer two days' 'waiting time'. In this manner a week's work could be crowded into the final few days – a position aggravated if a further batch of work arrived from the warehouse in mid-week and the master attempted to complete it by the same weekend. Inordinate concentration of work was the cheapest method of operation, since intervals between the receipt of batches of work by the master would have involved shop closure for two or three days. By crowding the week's operations into the final few days the master achieved an unbroken, if short, working week at minimal monetary cost but at the alternative cost of an intensively driven labour force.[16]

The presence of day rates for some operations encouraged the master to extract the maximum of concentrated output by maneouvres of this type, which do much to account for the paradox of the short average week in a trade with a reputation for good organisation and large units of production. Economy of time did not end here, however. Another Yiddish account by Finn points to great ingenuity on the part of the master:

... most of the masters ... create an artificial slack period in order to get out of the workers as much as possible and to pay less. If they see that the current work can't be got back to the warehouse finished by Saturday, they cease working immediately. We have to begin again on Monday as they regard Sunday as a short day, and that is, you ought to be aware, because Sunday is just half an hour shorter than any other working day ... And if that is not enough, he often carries out this swindle: when Thursday evening arrives, he tells the hands to hurry, and that they should come early in the next morning, as there will be work for the whole day. On Friday they get up quite early and their souls are driven out the whole morning. The master shouts in one voice: 'The work must be got to the warehouse!' When mid-day comes, however, he sends a boy to the warehouse for more work and the boy returns with the reply that there is none. That, you understand, is a contrived thing ... as soon as the workers leave, the master goes to the same warehouse and picks up work which he fears another master might get. As you see, the swindle has been made only to squeeze out of the poor workers a few hours' work for nothing.[17]

It is from Finn's pen also that the following account of an organisational curiosity derives – and one with ironic implications for the dignified model of the Leeds trade which reigns in the pages of Gertner and others:

... And now a new fashion has begun. The masters lend or hire out their men one to the other. If the man doesn't want to go where the master sends him, then he is given the worst trouble. If he does go, however, the second master can do what he wants with him, as he will not be staying there anyway. The poor worker is like a donkey with three owners.[18]

The telescoping of the working week, the persistent stresses deriving from the atmosphere of urgency ultimately generated by the large firms, plus the volatile Jewish temperament, produced scenes grossly inimical to the image of the Leeds tailoring shop as a 'miniature factory'. For the formal supervision and disciplines of the English factory, the Jewish master substituted his often-irate presence, employing the riches of the Yiddish tongue to urge on his men. Though the *Yorkshire Post* found Davis Joseph, a Jewish master, 'as gentlemanly a Jew as you might find in a day's march',[19] many Englishmen were shocked at the conduct displayed by some masters. Sweeney, long involved in alien industrial matters, was amazed at the 'foul and filthy language' of 'nine out of ten' Leeds masters, and at the manner in which they ran 'up and down the workshop ... like wild beasts, raising up their hair with their hands as though they were not right in their heads'.[20] Robert Sherard, in the Leeds section of his *White Slaves of England*, confirms Sweeney by his image of the master stalking about, 'scolding, inspecting ... whilst a stream of vituperation pours from his lips'.[21] The *Leeds Weekly Express* considered the Jewish masters 'not nice in the language they use towards their hands', and that they exercised a 'galling supervision' over their workshops.[22] Such were the accompaniments of the Leeds driving system, regarded by such professionals as Clara Collet as harder than 'customary in English and Scotch factories'.[23]

Consideration of the war of attrition between the Leeds master and the Factory Inspectorate further illuminates working conditions, and aids in the removal of the Gartnerian accretions overlaying the industry. Under section 58 of the Factory Act of 1878, Jews were permitted to open their workshops on Sunday until 4 p.m. where they were closed on Saturday. Pressures in the busiest seasons brought the temptation to utilise both days, to work later than 4 p.m. on Sunday, or to employ Christian girls on Saturday and Jewish men on Sunday. The *Jewish Chronicle* saw this as 'an abuse of special privilege and the meanest and most wicked offence'.[24] The inspectors held that the contravention conferred competitive advantage on those who disregarded the law, and prosecuted the culprits mercilessly. Despite this, the practice remained endemic to the end of the period, having been badly aggravated by the increase in small shops.[25]

In the alien branch, enforcement of factory legislation was, in any event, difficult. The many shops, their obscure and shifting locations and the relative privacy enjoyed by the small man, all served to facilitate contravention. The Leeds area inspection staff was grossly inadequate. In 1895, for example, two inspectors were responsible for 5,391 factories and workshops in Leeds, the whole of the East Riding and some West Riding towns other than Leeds.[26] Until 1891 the inspector could not enter a domestically based workshop without a warrant.

Armed with his warrant, however, the inspector was little better off. He was often greeted by the master claiming total ignorance of English, or professing to be engaged – not in the commercial production of clothing – but in the making of clothes for his own family. When the workers were members of the master's own family the inspector was powerless. Thus, thought the *Yorkshire Post*, the alien sweater pursued 'the even tenour of his way undisturbed by all the enactments of the British Parliament'.[27]

A combination of economic pressure and ignorance of English ways ensured frequent differences of view between master and inspector. At least according to the leaders of the Leeds tailors' union, few masters kept books, could read or even sign their names so late as 1908; whilst the printed regulations required by the factory laws were rarely seen in their workshops.[28] A stream of inspectorial prosecutions thus punctuates the whole period of immigration. In addition to those for infringement of the Sunday provisions of the Act of 1878, the most frequent offence listed by the inspectors was the employment of Jewish women and young persons beyond legal limits. This is surprising, since the employment of young persons has never been regarded as a problem of alien tailoring in Leeds, and there is no reference to such employment in contemporary inquiry. Other prominent offences include attempted bribery,[29] failure to display Abstracts of the Factory Acts, and to maintain lists of outworkers and registers of young employed persons. For throwing Inspector Wilson out of his shop and threatening to break his neck, one Myer Silverstone was heavily fined in 1898.[30] Inevitably, inspectorial descents upon the Jewish quarter were intermittent, but they were highly productive of prosecutions throughout the period.[31]

The alarm manifested by the *Jewish Chronicle* at these alien entanglements with statutory authority clearly concerned the danger they represented to the repute of Anglo-Jewry. Materially it consisted of little more than vague calls for more inspectors and for legislation against the 'real culprit': the English firm. What is significant here, however, is the journal's recognition that the presence of the large manufacturer – so far from promoting the order and regularity alleged by so many scholars – tended to transform alien productive operations into a series of *ad hoc* struggles to meet his demands. Equally, the large warehouses cannot be said to have provided the compensatory regularity of work upon which Gartner and his school rely so heavily to distinguish the Leeds from the London tailoring trade.

The background demand fluctuations experienced by the large firms themselves have been reviewed above. In the direct examination of the alien branch on this score, account is also required of the effects of the descent to the bedroom system in the later years. There are clear indications that the average working week in Leeds was, in fact, no longer than that in the East End. In May 1893, for example, Board of Trade investigators visited seventy-five alien workshops in Leeds, concluding that

the weekly wages cannot be obtained by multiplying by six. Ocular demonstration was given of the slackness of trade in these workshops and employers and inspectors agreed that . . . with but few exceptions, the average number of days' work in any branch since Christmas seemed to have been from three to three and a half days a week.[32]

Miss Collet, in framing her contribution to the *Immigration Report* of 1894, considered the average Leeds working week was no more than three days. A year earlier the Board of Trade had gone so far as to estimate the working week of the East End trade as one more than this,[33] whilst miscellaneous references place it at no more than four days in both centres alike.[34] A decade later Jacob Finn testified to the Aliens Commission that the Leeds working week had not improved, being still at no more than three to four days.[35]

Equalisation of the working week in both centres was, to some extent, due to the variable incidence of demand fluctuations in Leeds and London, resulting from the basic differences in their respective markets. Cyclical disturbance in other industries affected the readymade trade of Leeds more profoundly than the bespoke-dominated trade of London,[36] whilst seasonal variations were common in both. Later, in the 1900s, the Leeds trade was to share in the greater uncertainty associated with bespoke work.

That the Leeds working week should be so depressingly short occasions little surprise when the evolution of the English firms, reviewed above, is taken into account. The meaning of the erratic course of demand on the native branch was that direct employees were hardly better off than the alien outworkers: having, according to the Board of Trade in 1893, a working week of no more than four days.[37] One year later the *Yorkshire Factory Times* put it at only three days.[38] Confirming the impression of secular instability emerging from the material of Appendix I, the Women's Industrial Council Conference of 1907 demonstrated that things were no better in the early years of the twentieth century: 'In the tailoring trade the swing of the pendulum is very marked indeed. As one woman said to me: "It is slavery one half of the year and starvation the other." [39]

In spite of a reasonable supply of evidence, there has also been small contribution to the analysis of alien physical conditions of work in Leeds in immigration studies. The subliminal application of the appellation 'large' to Leeds workshops (with small additional ceremony) has been a pretty technique for the implantation of optimistic, if distorted, images. The method – so well worked in contrasting the alien trades of Leeds and London – has already been criticised on the score of its effect upon the realities of workshop size-distribution. In the present context, two further criticisms may be levelled. Firstly, since the wholesale reduction in the average scale of Leeds workshops has been entirely missed in previous models of the Leeds trade, a concomitant neglect has inevitably been the consideration of working conditions in the smaller shops of the 1900s and, in particular, those in the bedroom system of that epoch. Secondly, it has never been suggested that even the larger Leeds workshops might do little more than replicate the London sweater's den, rather than reflect the Leeds model warehouse.

The attitude has, perhaps, been reinforced by the softness of the major State inquiries on the Leeds sanitary question, despite the production of material by local statutory authority. In the great House of Lords Sweating Committee inquiry of 1888–90, tailoring was regarded simplistically as factory work in Leeds and homework in London. The *Final Report* of the committee merely glanced at the general impact of the aliens on Leeds, without reference to sanitary matters, although the local Inspector, John Newhouse, had pointed to very dirty alien shops in his evidence.[40] The *Recent Immigration Report* of 1894 went into some fine detail on Leeds alien tailoring structures, but offered nothing on the sanitary side. The last major inquiry of the period, the Royal Commission on Aliens, also provides little by way of detailed material, despite the immense volume of evidence gathered.

To a high degree, official taciturnity was abetted by alien attitudes. Alien masters shunned the limelight with which they were constantly threatened as sweaters. Nor did they desire the drying-up of a supply of cheap labour by the closure of Britain to immigration; a consummation attained in 1905, and one to which anti-alien sweating propaganda contributed heavily. Jewish workers, adhering, for the most part, unwaveringly to the class view that Britain ought to be kept open to immigrant workers, found themselves in the same posture as their masters, if for rather different reasons. Thus the appearance of a Leeds master before any State inquiry was a very rare event. The Leeds proceedings of the Sweating Committee, for example, record the presence of just two, of whom one was already a small wholesale tailor in his own right, and therefore unrepresentative of the alien outworker master group. The Labour Correspondent of the Board of Trade, John Burnett, considered that many were afraid to come forward 'for fear of the consequences to themselves',[41] but the attitude of fear was not without elements of defiance. One master informed Commissioner Smith of the *Lancet* that people were always calling to inspect his shop just because he was a Jew. He had received 'one big letter from the House of Lords', inviting his evidence to the Sweating Committee, but he did not know the House of Lords and would not reply. The House of Lords, he insisted, 'won't give me anything if I am hungry'.[42] Leeds Jewish labour leaders, by contrast, lost no opportunity to appear in public, but, until the Truck Committee of 1908, they were silent on the physical conditions in their workshops. During the long period of agitation leading to the Restriction Act of 1905 the public appetite for anti-alien sensation was not to be fed from this source. Furthermore, the leaders of the only significant tailoring union among aliens in Britain were not likely to indulge in self-denigration.

The sanitary splendour of the Leeds alien workshop, then, was left to find its first chronicler in a freer-speaking English source. In 1885 the Bradford journal *The Yorkshireman* set up a tradition to which many English interests were to cling stubbornly: that the Jewish workshop, though it might house many machines, was yet a dirty place:

No one who has been permitted to enter one of these tailor establishments can fail to have been struck with the contrast that it offers to an English workshop. Like the Russians, the Hebrews give little attention to outward attractions. They make no attempt to adorn their business places. For the most part these places are dreary, unhealthy attics littered with the refuse of days, and reached by dark corridors and malodorous steps.[43]

By contrast with recent historiography, the Leeds Town Council was in no position to employ the pen as an instrument of whitewash, and, a year before the publicity afforded by the *Yorkshireman*, it had been compelled to employ the real thing. The Sanitary Committee – an offshoot of a local authority notorious for its philistinism in regard to public health[44] – was already in established battle with a novel municipal hazard: the 'fair conditions' of the Jewish tailoring shop. The Medical Officer of Health, Dr Goldie, began by instituting a group of control measures born of desperation and the lack of suitable administrative machinery. A system of 'voluntary inspection' of the workshops was set up with the hope that 'responsible Jews' would be 'coadjutors in the work' and report any particular cases of nuisance. Additionally, supplies of disinfectant, 'to be liberally handed out', were made available to the volunteer Jewish inspectors.[45]

It was not until 1888, however, that reality was truly confronted. Before that year it was quite possible to avoid the worst of publicity on sanitation provided that the location was other than the East End, and that circumspection was employed. In 1888 the general strike of the Jewish tailors produced a new situation for the Council. It was fought out amidst unusual publicity, and attracted visits by Beatrice Potter[46] and John Burnett, whose *Report on the Sweating System in Leeds* was directly provoked by the events.[47] Some local opinion was inspired to commence linking the alien sweating and sanitary questions hanging over the proliferating workshops, and to call successfully for the Lords to extend the jurisdiction of their sweating inquiry to the provinces. Despite the softness of Burnett's verdict on Leeds alien tailoring, liberal newspapers, from the strike onwards, were adamant that 'sweating had been proved to exist in all its hideousness'.[48] The Tory *Yorkshire Post* remained a solitary, uncharacteristic, but merely temporary defender of the workshops. That journal pointed to 'miniature factories' where, when more than forty people were employed, there was usually gas or steam power.[49]

The Council knew better, preferring the view that 'the sanitary aspect of the question is considered by many to be important if not serious'.[50] The 'many' happened to include Alderman Ward, the Sanitary Committee chairman and a familiar of the alien workshops well before 1888. His opinion was that the Jewish tailors were 'very filthy' as they came 'from beyond the pale of civilisation'.[51] At this moment also, the *Lancet* sent its investigating commissioner on a tour of the Leylands. His report was unequivocal in its condemnation of the crowding, the lack of proper closets, the open urinals, and the dilapidated condition of the workshop premises. It dealt, too, with the alleys and courts of the Leylands, which, at this early date, were already pullulating with homeworkers of the immigrant community; and concluded by equating the Jewish quarter of Leeds with that of London as a place which, from the sanitary viewpoint, equally required reform.[52]

This was a serious blow to the reputation of Leeds, spurious as it was, and to its alien 'miniature factories'. Nor were matters improved when the *Lancet* published the names of four of the largest masters and the locations of their workshops. The information was found of such abiding fascination that the Sweating Committee enshrined it in its *Fourth Report* of 1889. The Leeds factory inspector, E. T. Dawson of Headingley, affirmed that the *Lancet* articles 'were not one whit exaggerated in the description'. He found it impossible to describe many Jewish shops, instancing cases where four water closets were provided for 250 workers of both sexes. Old, dilapidated and broken properties, he confirmed, were being used as workshops, and there were many closets of the 'tub' type.[53]

The Council went into vigorous action. A separate inspector for Jewish workshops was appointed immediately, and Dr Goldie was instructed to make a special report on the problem. The Jews, he responded, were 'not notorious for cleanliness and order'. Their workshops were 'disused old mills and sheds', and many had no ceiling, being open to the roof. One such shop was in a disused old workhouse, and closet accommodation was 'defective in many instances'.[54] Despite this confirmation of the *Lancet* findings, the *Daily News* accused Dr Goldie of whitewashing the alien workshops, which, it thought, 'ought to be whitewashed oftener'.[55]

The sanitary authority viewed the report of the medical department seriously enough, however, and special Jewish inspection was rigorously maintained. Separate returns were made monthly and annually until 1891, when the Factory Act of that year extended local authority powers to all workshops and particular Jewish information was lost in the general returns of city-wide inspections and actions taken. In 1888, however, action was taken against alien masters in 197 cases arising from 252 inspections of 119 shops. Five shops were closed down, new closets ordered in seventy-two cases, and ninety notices served in respect of dirty conditions.[56] In the following year fourteen shops were closed as unfit from a total of 153, and 126 dirty premises notices were served.[57] In the same year Dr Goldie was sacked and his pathetic plea for three months' salary curtly rejected, apparently for the failure of his staff to control the Jewish branch.[58] The vigour with which his successor, Spottiswoode Cameron, concentrated on the alien shops suggests that the overburdened Goldie, who had grappled with the filth and disease of Leeds since 1867, had truly found the Jewish problem to be his final straw. In 1891 – the final year for which distinct Jewish figures may be identified – Cameron's inspectors carried out 660 alien workshop inspections, at which 301 cases of defective ventilation, 226 of dirty workrooms, and 180 of dirty closets were recorded. Of the 182 shops involved, fifty-nine were without any form of drainage and fifty-five had outside privies.[59]

That all this activity constituted a minor revolution in the sanitary administration of Leeds may hardly be doubted. Whether it conduced to such improvements in conditions as to permit acceptance of the optimism of Gainer on the Leeds workshops after 1888 is far more debatable. For later years, materials are less abundant, especially if blatant anti-alien propaganda is shunned. The absence of separate returns after 1891, and the loss of the diaries of the inspectors of Jewish workshops, make matters exceedingly difficult.

Some improvement in the course of time may be readily assumed as the largest masters became more habituated to regulation through the need to run their workshops in a more formal manner. There is, however, little evidence to indicate that the events of 1888 marked the opening of a permanent revolution in sanitary conditions in the alien sector. The energetic action of the Town Council certainly produced some short-term gains, recorded by the Home Office inspector in 1892 as an improvement in Leeds workshops, 'especially in those occupied by the Jews'.[60] Dr Cameron, in the same year, was surely going too far, however, in reporting that Jewish workshops were regularly examined and that there was 'nothing to complain of'.[61]

Appraisal of the objective relationships between the domestic alien industry and the wholesalers, from the viewpoint of their dynamics, suggests deterioration in the position of the former branch. The prolonged instability of the wholesale trade, falling prices, the phenomenon of burgeoning small shops, and an increase in the Jewish population, may all be adduced as components of the long-term experience of the alien branch tending to influence working conditions adversely.

The continuation of the sanitary problem beyond 1888 is, in the first place, hinted at strongly in the appointment in 1899 of H. M. Raskin as a Yiddish-speaking special inspector of nuisances with responsibility for the alien workshops. This post was still a part of the establishment in 1914.[62] The pseudonymous Yiddish writer 'Cohenovitz' confirms the pessimistic view in a scathing article in the *Yiddisher Ekspres* in 1897:

> The main element of Leeds Jewry is the working class. When all the so-called progressive elements in Jewry in Russia, who are always crying that the Russian Jews will improve their lot by working and that the only way out for the Russian Jews is honest toil, they should have a look at the working class of Leeds. They should visit their workshops, the places in which they spend

twelve or more hours a day, breathe the air which surrounds them in these places, see the surroundings in which they work ... they would long ago have given up agitating and banging the drum about work.[63]

With the turn of the century, official opinion, though expressed less frequently, tended to the adverse. So late as 1910 the 'old fashioned pail-closet system' was still only in decline. The general standard of sanitation remained 'deplorably low', though, 'by degrees, a sense of pride in brighter and more wholesome conditions' was being instilled. The worst air samples obtainable in Leeds were to be found in the Jewish workshops.[64] The problem may be identified at the very end of the period. In 1914, for example, the view of the Medical Officer was quite opposed to what it had been in 1892. There was, indeed, a degree of resignation in his view that cleanliness in the tailoring shops was at a minimum, and that it was impossible to enforce where tenement factories were shared by many occupants and tenants came and went with great frequency.[65] With the single amendment that cleanliness was merely *almost* impossible to enforce, the Home Office inspector's opinion in 1919 echoed that of his local authority colleague on the eve of war very precisely.[66]

The contribution of the bedroom workshops of the 1900s to the perpetuation of adverse conditions must be to a large extent assumed, since there is little sign of systematic penetration of this sector by the Inspectorate. The tailors' union secretary, in his admission to the Truck Committee in 1908 that the bedroom master was beyond control, gave a strong hint as to domestic workshop conditions. Direct complaints were rare, since the bedroom workshop was staffed by the head of the family with two or three children, and the occasional assistance of the wife. The sole outside labour was the presser, who came in after hours, and who regarded the work as overtime.[67] The wider public connection between alien homework in Leeds, the new factor of bespoke tailoring and unsatisfactory conditions, was forged as early as 1903 in testimony to the Aliens Commission. William Marston, who, as town councillor and official of the Amalgamated Tailors' Union, claimed expertise on alien conditions, acknowledged generously that the Jewish tailors' union had done much to improve the conditions in the larger workshops. It was, for him, in the bespoke business that increasing alien identification with homework and its unregulated conditions occurred.[68]

There is evidence to suggest that the Leeds alien workshop, despite frequent large scale, possessed few advantages over the worst of the

East End, with which bourgeois scholarship has so often favourably compared it. Failure to investigate the economic consequences of dependent association with a powerful wholesale sector, functioning in accordance with its own laws of capitalist development, has led commentators to equate many workers with favourable conditions. It has been suggested, however, that this measure is inadequate, and that the organisation, regulation and frequency of work require equal consideration. In these respects the Leeds trade appears to have represented little improvement over that of the East End, which exhibited to contemporaries the classic sweated conditions. Evidence for Leeds suggests, further, that, even where many machines are added to the model, it cannot be taken for granted that sanitary conditions were in advance of those of the East End. Comparison with the latter centre is, indeed, most misleading. Contemporaries inevitably compared Leeds alien shops with Leeds wholesale factories; and whether the alien shop, even on the largest scale attainable by the alien master, can ever be said to have raised itself out of the category 'sweatshop' into that of true factory, with the conditions associated with the latter, must remain doubtful.

Some quantitative analysis is made possible by data from the 1888 survey by the Leeds council and an analysis of ten wholesale clothing factories which appeared in the *Report* of the Factory Inspector for 1910. In Table 3 the Jewish shops in the 1888 survey are in frequency bands according to numbers employed, along with the mean space per worker within each group based on the recorded measurements for each workshop. Here it is apparent that, so far as the fifty-nine shops in the survey may be regarded as representative of the whole shop population, there is clearly no correlation between the larger shops and better spatial conditions. Shops of fewer than ten workers actually offered the best space per head, whilst the largest shops holding up to eighty return a very low average. The data of the same survey were employed in an attempt to establish a precise correlation by ranking of individual shops, between size and average space per worker. The method is given in Appendix II. This calculation produces the meagre coefficient of 0·01, a result which confirms the impression given by Table 3. A further effort was made to establish a distinction between large and small shops, but on a broader and less demanding spectrum. On this occasion shops were divided into 'large' and 'small' categories: those of more than twenty workers and the remainder. The differences between means and standard deviations of the two groups were examined as indicated in

Table 3 *The distribution of space per worker in fifty-five Leeds Jewish tailoring workshops in 1888*

Workshop size	Mean space in cubic feet per head
Fewer than 10 workers	515·75
11–20	478·43
21–30	360·75
31–40	484·57
41–50	414·38
51–60	497·50
61–70	514·50
71–80	372·50

Source: Minutes of the Sanitary Committee, 12–13 June 1888.

Appendix II, and no statistically significant difference was found.

The concern evinced by contemporaries with interest in the condition of alien workshops in Leeds becomes clearer when the excellent information presented by the Inspectorate on ten Leeds wholesale factories in 1910 is considered. Here the mean space per worker was 1,715 cubic feet, and, in certain specialist rooms such as pressing, it was over 3,000.[69]

The 1888 survey of Jewish shops additionally provides descriptive comment upon the sanitary conditions offered. These, with the locations, are presented in Table 4 for sixteen of the largest examples. Additionally, five shops employing between thirty and sixty workers were passed as clean. The survey also includes nineteen alien shops of twenty or fewer workers. Of this group, thirteen attracted adverse comment on dirt, inadequate closets, dirty privies, darkness, dangerous and dirty staircases, and unsuitability of premises.

The 1888 survey was admittedly deficient in its coverage of the true numbers of alien workshops. At the same time, there is no reason to suppose that the worst were deliberately singled out. It is, on the contrary, likely that, owing to the 'crisis' atmosphere in which the operation was undertaken, it is biased towards shops with prominent locations, at the expense of those in more obscure places. It is, therefore, likely that the survey provides a reasonable representation of the condition of the workshops.

The impression of insanitariness is heightened by the question of topography. Numbers of machines or workers were never employed by the Inspectors as criteria in their assessments, but much attention was given to topography, with special reference to the suitability of buildings – a problem neglected by optimistic modellers of the industry. The analytic method of treating large workshops as the automatic superiors of smaller workshops may be traced directly to alien defence propaganda, especially in the 1890s; and, typically, to Jewish bourgeois sources. The *Jewish Chronicle*, for example, was at times given to the presentation of the alien tailor as the joyous possessor of 'large workshops in buildings several storeys high, each workshop containing as many as over a hundred workpeople'.[70]

Table 4 *The sanitary condition of sixteen major Jewish tailoring workshops in Leeds in 1888*

Location	No. of workers	Inspector's comments
Rockingham St	52	Dirty
Rockingham St	80	Urinal bad
King Charles St	45	Dark, dirty
Guildford St	32	Closets dirty
Old Workhouse Yard	50	Unfit building
Old Workhouse Yard	31	Unfit building
Lady Bridge Mill Yard	44	Ashpit in yard
Dyer St	65	Privies objectionable
Dyer St	48	Privies objectionable
Dyer St	61	Privies objectionable
Dyer St	46	Privies objectionable
Dyer St	40	Privies objectionable
Hope St	80	Closets very dirty
Hope St	50	Closets deficient
Hope St	22	Closets dirty
North Court	40	Closets arranged badly

Source: Minutes of the Sanitary Committee, 12–13 June 1888.

In practice, although the occasional alien master might claim proprietorship of a purpose-built workshop,[71] addresses indicate that few colleagues functioned in such splendour. As might be expected of a troubled and insecure industry constituting an outside department of the large factories, most of its workplaces were little more than the disused textile mills, old workhouse premises, attics, dwelling houses and tenements – the decaying remnants of declining industries and the erstwhile homes of the wealthy of Leeds. In confirmation of the

Inspectorate, the *Yorkshire Factory Times* saw, in 1889, 'a sight not easily forgot'. This was a group of forty Jewish tailors packed into a single attic room.[72] In a back tenement a year later the heat was described by the same journal as 'intense' and the overcrowding so great that some aliens were at work on the floor.[73] Sherard also left a glimpse of the reality of a large Leeds Jewish tailoring shop. In the Leylands he visited a 'filthy room' where fifty people were 'all huddled together sewing as for dear life'. The stench and dirt, he affirmed, surpassed description.[74] In place of the illusion of the large Leeds workshop as a miniature version of the great factory, the evidence implies that such establishments were closer to the East End sweater's den on an enlarged scale.

The conditions of the alien branch were determined precisely by the policies of the large firms. Models of the alien branch which depend upon 'fair conditions' rest equally upon the implication that the large firms were something other than energetic profit-maximisers with a concern for the aliens transcendental to this fundamental capitalist emotion. Yet the clothing industry was not unique in the conditions created in the relationships between master and outworker. Rather, they were typical of the economics of such relationships. In such light, the eccentric hours and driving of workers were the direct consequences of the irregular output of work by the warehouses – in turn the victims of the anarchy of the competitive system. Price pressures omnipresent within that system ensured that little was left for workshop improvements and the fine premises suggested by optimistic models of the trade. Thus the sanitary condition of the Jewish workshop became an outrage which conjured up a minor revolution in the local authority and confirmed some aspects of anti-alien propaganda.

Despite the immense significance of their place in the trade, the public attitude of the large firms towards the aliens is exceedingly obscure. The Jews, competing, as many thought, insanely amongst themselves, were very cheap and pliable labour, utilised in a ruthless manner in the cynical pursuit of the last unit of profit. The large firms, further, made the chief contribution to the aggravation of bad alien conditions by their direct encouragement of the bedroom system in the 1900s – a fact upon which the tailors' secretary left the Truck Committee in no doubt in 1908:

> I might say that the warehouse men, the manufacturers, have created the bedroom masters. It is to their advantage. They always threaten a large sub-contractor who employs from fifteen to sixty hands that if he does not do the

work at a cheaper price they will get a bedroom master and they will do the work even cheaper ... The warehouse man always keeps a staff of those bedroom master tailors as a threat.[75]

In the course of this development, which removed much work from the outside workshop and placed it in the domestic hearth, alien tailoring in Leeds acquired the semblance of a true pre-industrial domestic system, and a significant area of alien industry was thus entirely removed from the possibility of statutory regulation.

Nevertheless, rarer alone than the appearance of an alien master before State inquiry was that of the Leeds wholesale clothier representing the large firms. This was most notable in the cases of the Sweating Committee and the Aliens Commission, considering the wide scope of both inquiries and the anti-alien furore surrounding them. The attitude of the group to their outworkers is best epitomised by the statement of Rowland Barran, head of the largest Leeds firm, to the Chamber of Commerce in 1910, that the wholesaler could not concern himself with the wages paid by outside contractors to their workers.[76]

The ultimate victim was the Leeds Jewish worker, and it is hardly surprising that the class struggle was particularly bitter in the Leylands, though it has yet to become manifest in the pages of bourgeois studies of immigration.

NOTES

1. Garrard, *Immigration*, pp. 159–60.
2. Hunt, *Wage Variations*, p. 314, n. 3.
3. Gartner, *Jewish Immigrant*, pp. 69, 89.
4. Gainer, *Alien Invasion*, p. 27.
5. *Y.P.*, 16 June 1888.
6. *Ibid.*, 25 August 1888.
7. *Sweating System*, qq. 30655–6; S. Freedman, 'Sketch of the Leeds Jewish Tailors' Union', *The Trade Unionist*, July, 1899, p. 449; S. Freedman, 'Condition of the Jewish workers of Leeds', *The Trade Unionist*, August, 1899, p. 523; R. H. Sherard, *The White Slaves of England*, London, 1897, p. 112.
8. *The Builder*, LXXXI, 1896, p. 513.
9. K. Marx, *Wage Labour and Capital*, Moscow, 1952, p. 38.
10. *Ibid.*, p. 41.
11. *D.P.Y.*, 25 July 1884.
12. *Committee on the Truck Acts*, qq. 5913–6000.
13. *D.P.Y.*, 31 October 1884.
14. *Sweating Committee*, qq. 30655–6.
15. *Ibid.*, qq. 30237, 31661.

16 *Ibid.*, qq. 30238, 30241.
17 *D.P.Y.*, 19 September 1884.
18 *Ibid.*, 17 October 1884.
19 *Y.P.*, 16 June 1888.
20 *Sweating System*, q. 30283.
21 Sherard, *White Slaves*, p. 114.
22 *L.W.E.*, 1 June 1889.
23 C. E. Collet, 'Women's work in Leeds', *Economic Journal*, I, March, 1891, p. 469.
24 *J.C.*, 20 March 1896.
25 *Report of the Inspector of Factories, 1885–1911.*
26 *Ibid.*, 1895.
27 *Y.P.*, 4 July 1907.
28 *Committee on the Truck Acts*, q. 5906.
29 *Y.F.T.*, 10 May 1895.
30 *Ibid.*, 10 April 1908.
31 *Ibid.*, 2 May 1890, 8 January 1892, 28 March 1902, 17 February 1910.
32 *Labour Gazette*, I, May, 1893, p. 9.
33 *Ibid.*, I, June, 1893, p. 41.
34 See, for example, *J.C.*, 18 March 1898.
35 *Aliens Commission*, q. 20280.
36 *J.C.*, 10 April 1903.
37 *Labour Gazette*, I, June, 1893, p. 41.
38 *Y.F.T.*, 10 August 1894.
39 Women's Industrial Council, *Report of a Conference on the Unemployment of Women*, October, 1907, p. 13.
40 *Sweating Committee*, q. 1509; *Final Report*, para. 183.
41 *Ibid.*, q. 31111.
42 *The Lancet*, I, June, 1888, p. 1147.
43 *The Yorkshireman*, May, 1885, p. 314.
44 B. J. Barber, 'Aspects of municipal government, 1835–1914', in D. Fraser (ed.), *A History of Modern Leeds*, Manchester, 1980, pp. 302–7.
45 Minutes of the Sanitary Committee, 11 August 1884.
46 *Y.P.*, 25 May 1888.
47 *Leeds Sweating System*, p. 3.
48 *L.E.E.*, 16 May 1888.
49 *Y.P.*, 16 June 1888.
50 *Leeds Times*, 12 May 1888.
51 *Leeds Daily News*, 11 June 1888.
52 *The Lancet*, I, June, 1888, p. 1147.
53 *Leeds Daily News*, 11 June 1888.
54 Minutes of the Sanitary Committee, 25 June 1888.
55 *Leeds Daily News*, 25 June 1888.
56 Minutes of the Sanitary Committee, 1 April 1889.
57 *Report of the Medical Officer of Health*, 31 August 1889.
58 Minutes of the Sanitary Committee, 22 July 1889.
59 *Report of the Medical Officer of Health*, 2 January 1892.

60 *Report of the Inspector of Factories, 1892*, P.P. 1893, XVII, C 6978, p. 64.
61 *Report of the Medical Officer of Health, 1892.*
62 Minutes of the Sanitary Committee, 8 May 1899; *Report of the Medical Officer of Health*, 1914.
63 *D.Y.E.*, 5 November 1897.
64 *Report of the Inspector of Factories, 1910*, P.P. 1911, XXII, Cd 5693, pp. 52, 116.
65 *Report of the Medical Officer of Health, 1914*, p. 48.
66 *Report of the Inspector of Factories, 1919*, P.P. 1919, XXV, Cmd, 941, p. 48.
67 *Committee on the Truck Acts*, qq. 5949–50.
68 *Aliens Commission*, qq. 14306–9, 14325, 14357.
69 *Report of the Inspector of Factories, 1910*, pp. 70–1.
70 *J.C.*, 4 February 1898.
71 *Y.P.*, 18 June 1888.
72 *Y.F.T.*, 29 November 1889.
73 *Ibid.*, 29 August 1890.
74 Sherard, *White Slaves*, p. 114.
75 *Committee on the Truck Acts*, qq. 5949–50.
76 *Journal of the A.S. of T.*, January, 1910, p. 104. The question arose in connection with the enforcement of minimum rates in the workshops of sub-contractors under the Trade Boards Act.

Chapter 3

PROBLEMS IN THE CLASS STRUGGLE: THE JEWISH TAILORS AND THEIR ORGANISATION TO 1888

The extensive history of union organisation by Jewish immigrants during the period 1880–1914 has received peremptory treatment in the literature of immigration. Largely in the grip of a communal theory of a mystical Jewish ethnic unity, and impervious, beneath the carapace of an eternal, all-consuming 'Jewish culture', to the solvent power of industrial experience and struggle to create new class structures, such literature exhibits varied and embarrassed methods of accounting for Jewish labour organisations in the British settlements. Dialectical progression towards a specifically Jewish working-class consciousness generated in the industrial arena is regarded as a thing impossible. A Jewish trade union must be, at best, a sympton of acculturational drift from the centripetal, perpetual, exclusive Jewish culture universal in time and space. The art of concealment has been well applied in the service of this historiography, with profoundly obliterative consequences. In the first place, the 'unitary' interpretation of alien settlement has socially located Jewish unions among the typically luxuriant charity organisations of Jewish communities, contracted their significance, distorted their meaning, and obscured their role as the representative institutions of Jewish proletarianism and chief agents of expression of the class struggle. As a second consequence, the crucial importance of successful alien unions in the van of the struggle for acceptance by the host community has been entirely lost.

At the extreme, there exist sociological studies in which Jewish trade unions are found to be unworthy even of mention. In *A Minority in Britain*, for example, J. Parkes fails to include them in his summary of the secular institutions of the Jewish community. 'Alien defence', he considers, began around 1901 – a view from which comfort may be drawn only in the event that the contribution to 'alien defence' of worker organisations such as the Leeds Jewish Tailors' Union from the 1880s is ignored. The obscurantist syndrome which best represents the unitary system of immigrant Jewry is well expressed in Parkes's assertion that no anti-semitic feeling and 'boisterous xenophobia' appeared during the period of immigration because 'Anglo-Jewry was at this time very well equipped to receive' the immigrants.[1] This impertinent claim on behalf of the Jewish bourgeoisie clearly indicates that the long struggle of the alien worker to come to terms with English labour – as well as the Jewish master – was historically unnecessary in view of the ever-present availability of the 'protection' of Anglo-Jewry.

In his 1975 paper 'Jews in British urban society' V. D. Lipman is less complacent concerning the role of Anglo-Jewry in the immigration movement, but he too finds no place for trade unions either in the host-acceptance process or as socio-cultural agents.[2] Hannah Neustatter, on the other hand, deals in a weird Jewish labour movement which not only failed to manifest any working-class consciousness but was entirely a failure from lack of it. Her 'proof' is based on a treatment of chronology more suited to science fiction than science, since she finds the survival of only one independent Jewish trade union into the 1950s sufficient for the conclusion that the Jewish labour movement was a perennial failure, despite the struggles of seventy previous years.[3]

The case of the Jewish unions has fared little better at the hands of scholars who have acknowledged their existence and related them to their actual industrial situation. Shirley Lerner's insistence upon the Talmudic background of the alien tailor, intended to bolster her case for mass alien tropism to entrepreneurship, immediately fails to postulate a dialectical proletarian counter-group; leaving her little choice but to conclude that the immigrant was simply unsound unionising material.[4] Such a model naturally raises the urgent question of Jewish strikes and their interpretation. Since, in her scheme, they could not reflect class antagonism, she is impelled to the view that they were really nothing more than intimate family quarrels, devoid of class tensions.[5]

Duncan Bythell, the authority on sweated trades, is even less sanguine on trade unions as the loci of industrial struggle. For him, alien union history has no existence at all, since attempts to form unions for tailors and shoemakers 'in both London and Leeds' appear to have failed.[6] Hunt differentiates between London and Leeds. Religion, bourgeois ambition and language, he considers, handicapped unionism among the Jews of London. A proper appraisal of the strength of alien unionism in Leeds, however, might have led him to query the remarkable absence of these debilitating factors in that city. Instead, Hunt offers the view that unionism was retarded in Leeds owing to the 'nature of the trade': this in the face of his adherence to the group which considers the Leeds tailoring workshop to have been unique in scale.[7]

The cosy vision of the Leeds Jewish tailoring industry created by Gartner and his followers has also done disservice by its tendency to obscure the internal economic and class conflicts of the community. Yet by 1912, when the *Yorkshire Factory Times* realised the supremacy of economic-class loyalties over the religious by its comment that 'the sweater knows no race or blood bond', such conflicts ranked among the veriest commonplaces of the Leylands.[8] The large workshop of the Gartner school is exploited in explanation of the strength of the Leeds Jewish Tailors' Union, tempting the reader to thoughts of benign industrial relations based on a sound industrial structure. In the work of none of this group are questions asked concerning the sources of the bitter and incessant industrial conflict from which the Leeds union was so arduously forged. The union, rather, appears in their pages developed at inception – an integral part of the local economy of large workshops, which, in their view, shares with the union a weird waxwork world without antecedents or historical progression.

The origins of the Leeds union lay in the Tailors' Trade Society, first registered in 1876 but originating as early as 1874.[9] This is of more than antiquarian interest. The early 1870s represent a 'prehistoric' stage of the community when, as directories indicate, there can hardly have been more than thirty Jewish workshops in Leeds – the forerunners of the larger mass accruing after 1880. At so early a stage in the growth of a foreign community in a strange land it might be expected that the religious bond would be the sole and, perhaps, universal communal tie. Yet, in these circumstances, and in the face of so many scholarly findings as to the social, psychological, ideological and religious unsuitability of the Jewish immigrant for trade union life, a union was not only founded, but one which, according to Leeds tradition, actually engaged in industrial action.

Gartner and Garrard are the most serious commentators on the problems of alien unionisation, and some of their views have validity. This is especially the case in their treatment of the mobility of the labour force and the master, as well as the variations in trade. It is when they construct their Leeds antithesis – that, here, unionism was stronger owing to the presence of 'larger and stabler producers' – that credulity is strained.[10] It has been demonstrated that Leeds was by no means a city of homogeneously large workshops throughout the period. Masters came and went as readily as elsewhere. Movements in the labour force were quite as volatile as in other places of settlement as new immigrants made for the centre of large-scale tailoring and settled immigrants moved on, sometimes in batches of 200 at a time.[11] Aliens moved freely from place to place as, for example, when a migration of large firms from Glasgow to Leeds in the 1880s compelled the Jewish tailors to follow for their livelihood.[12] In spite of its 'stable producers', the Anglo-Jewish writer E. E. Burgess observed in a reminiscence published in 1925 that Leeds men who became masters 'equally easily dropped back into the ranks of "sweatees" when they failed'. As a countervailing trend there was the phenomenon of 'battalions of new employers' converting bedrooms and 'best parlours' into workshops.[13] Immigration movements into Leeds were spasmodic. In 1891, for example, the Leeds police, acting for the Board of Trade, reported 440 new arrivals. For most of 1892 there was a lull owing to cholera on the Continent, but by the end of the year 1,550 more had appeared. 'A further influx of indigent Jews' was reported the following year.[14] Clearly, also, the effects of the Restriction Act of 1905 must have been felt in Leeds.

Nor was the appelation 'tailor' necessarily more specific to Leeds tailors than those of London or Manchester. Leeds tailors were given to movement into the footwear trade, and, at the worst, into the Jewish bakeries, whenever prompted by their economic situation. For those acquiring early competence in English there were opportunities also beyond the alien trades, for example, as labourers in the Leeds City Markets.

Thus the strength of organised Jewish labour in Leeds can hardly be ascribed to the stability of its tailoring trade. A further problem left unresolved in recent literature is precisely how the canvassed stability of Leeds tailoring served to overcome the religious and temperamental antipathy which proved fatal to alien unionism in London. Perplexity may be overcome only when the tailors are viewed through the developing class struggle and against their shifting economic background, rather than through a search for a chimerical industrial stability remote from the situation of an outwork trade. Additionally, the tailors, as the most important alien group, were the most deeply and intimately involved in the interaction between the immigration movement and the anti-alien controversy, which, with variable emphasis, is traceable throughout the period. Thus, as union performance began to influence the views of the host society, the Leeds tailors acquired a second role and organisational incentive which were to become important to the immigration as a whole.

Much concerning the immediate incentives to organisation may be instantly inferred from the corrections made to the standard models of the Leeds tailoring trade, and of working conditions, in the appropriate chapters. The wretched workshops, the irregularity of employment, the driving, and, as Sweeney put it, 'the blasphemery of the masters',[15] were sufficient reasons for the drive to organisational strength. Worker reaction to these conditions was well documented in the Yiddish press by the mid-1880s.[16]

To these perennial factors in alien trades were added local developments driving the tailors on into their first major actions in 1884 and 1885. The union faintly traced in the 1870s emerged into the 1880s in the form of three separate organisations of tailors, machiners and pressers.[17] Leaders – thoughtful and capable men like Jacob Finn – were available to unite the branches and allay factionalism. In a handful of years after the dawn of large-scale immigration in 1880, and with, still, only rudimentary labour organisation, the stresses appeared which were the chief factors in the formation of hostile class lines. Finn's invaluable articles in *Poilisher Yidel* in 1884–85 illuminate – not merely the dissolution of religious and ethnic loyalties into master – worker antagonism – but problems of labour organisation. The earliest concern was with the latter:

There are few Jewish workers capable of writing a little letter, or able to read. Those who speak of a Yiddish newspaper certainly do not know this. English they cannot either, and Yiddish they do not want to know. That is why they are so uncouth and know only that the world is large and contains many horses.[18]

Finn's work rapidly acquired a less idealistic and more material and economic tone. Within a few weeks of his article on illiteracy all his attention was on a problem which was to engage the tailors throughout their organised existence: the competition of the female machinist. This was related to the masters' habit of 'constantly declaring half days'. The men had struck but had been defeated because women had been brought in to take their place.[19] Conditions were deteriorating and the workers, stated Finn, stood in 'a very lowly situation'. The tyranny of the masters was such that workers were afraid to pen complaints to the press.[20]

Soon there appeared the system of tensions by which the industry was to be permanently pervaded. In the first place, Finn clearly identified the master as the class enemy:

My master didn't want to let me go early but I didn't listen to him, for I have no fear of him. He doesn't give me enough to live on and laughs at me. I work hard and he goes around idle.

But the worker had not yet recognised his enemy:

But unfortunately there are many to hand who think he is God and they will not even unite with the societies which were founded only to better their lot.

Next came the dawn of the idea of mutual destruction, originating on the side of the masters but soon mutual in Leeds tailoring:

The masters themselves do not remain hungry but amongst them are those who also get nothing out of the work and for that reason the masters try with all their strength to destroy our society.

Finally, Finn overtly recognised the significance of English labour opinion on the Jewish worker:

My purpose is to show how we bring dark clouds upon ourselves. And in what way? Firstly, through our work. See, brothers, how hard and bitter is our work! And what is the end? The end is that all we hear from the English tailor is that the Jews have spoiled the trade and we make thousands of enemies for it.[21]

By early 1885 polarisation was extreme, and Finn himself was advocating the establishment of co-operative tailoring shops and the entire abolition of the master system.[22] This long-held ambition of the Leeds tailors was to imbue their numberless battles with a deadly quality unknown in English labour circles. There was outside support for the idea. The *Jewish Chronicle*, for example, had proposed it in 1884 as the only way to terminate the Jewish tailor's 'life of slavery'.[23] The prerequisite – a strong union – was encouraged not only by Jewish progressives such as Finn but by English press opinion. No class of workers was more in need of protection than the Jews, thought the *Leeds Express*. Christian workers had, 'in a measure, thrown off long hours and poor wages', and the Jews could do the same if they had equal courage and determination, and if they were united.[24]

Consideration of the developing confrontation during 1884 indicates that the strike of 1885, to which the situation led directly, was far from the 'spontaneous' event described by Gartner.[25] The encouragement accorded the tailors alarmed the masters, who formed a Jewish Employers' Association 'to crush the societies and to prevent the leaders of the men from having any employment in the town'. The blacklist was employed, the masters binding themselves under penalty to refuse work to the listed men. Despite this, thought the *Express*, the

Jewish working men – 'a long-suffering race' – could 'stand up in defence of those great principles of liberty won by past generations of trades unionists as well as a Gentile'. The list also aroused the active interest of the Trades Council, which publicly affirmed the right of the Jews to organise themselves.[26] Public opinion was incensed by the fact that the tailors had made no demand other than the right to have a union. Further, they had offered to submit to arbitration – at first accepted, then quickly rejected by the Masters' Association. When walk-outs had occurred at some workshops, union men had been replaced by blacklegs from Liverpool. The *Express* lectured the masters: 'An employer in England cannot do exactly as he would like with his own. The men have rights which the law will protect them in.' The masters, it accused, had imposed a ban of twelve months on any worker discharged by any one of their number. This had been done 'with the avowed object of breaking down the men's societies'.[27]

Efforts were made to organise meetings 'to draw up rules for the guidance of the trade', since, as the *Express* pointed out, public opinion would 'certainly not support either association in simply trying to break down the other'.[28] By 1885, however, visions of industrial harmony were vainly conceived. The views and pronouncements of the tailors were already those of a separate class with, as a central theme, the abolition of the Jewish master class. Led by James Sweeney, the three unions passed a resolution in March 1885 'approving co-operative principles as applied to production'.[29] Public meetings followed. On 2 May, Isaac Myers, the tailors' president, denounced the 'system of slavery' to which they were subjected, from which the middlemen were reaping large profits weekly, as was 'shown by their mode of living, class of residence, etc.'.[30] This insistence upon the gulf between master and man was a clear-sighted recognition that its intra-communal basis did not relieve the bitterness of the struggle. Myers's attitude was contemporaneously mirrored in the East End, where Lewis Lyons published figures demonstrating that the profits of sweating, if often arduously earned, were yet high.[31] Finn expressed the new radicalism as follows:

> ... instead of having over us a master who brings no good, and who, nevertheless, makes £10 to £15 a week, we would most prefer to be our own masters and the benefit the master gets will go to those who work in the shop.

The movement had, as early as 1885, attracted the labour interests not only of Leeds but also of London. Metropolitan forces led by James

Rowlands, one of the fourteen workers who were to be elected to Parliament with Keir Hardie in 1892, travelled to a meeting of the Jewish unions where, on 7 March, they undertook to obtain work from the wholesale firms for the proposed co-operative.[32]

Despite the optimism of Myers and Finn, however, the two-week strike which broke out in May – an attempt to gain uniform hours for all grades – was equally an expression of frustration over the matter of the co-operative system. Aware that by union action English tailors had 'obtained a great reduction of hours and increase of wages', the tailors sent a circular to the masters on 26 April, containing a demand for a reduction in hours.[33] Before the strike provoked by this circular the basic working day of the Leeds alien tailor, with the exception of the record-breaking Jewish slipper worker, was of outstanding length in the industry of Leeds. Whilst the machiners worked from 8 a.m. to 8 p.m., the tailors and pressers worked two hours longer, and underpressers – the lowest form of tailoring life – three hours longer. The modest demand for a uniform day of 8 a.m. to 8 p.m. was rejected, at which over 600 men walked out. With the busy season upon them, the masters hastily called a meeting with the unions at the Belgrave Street Synagogue on 10 May, and, in negotiations led by Sweeney, a one-hour reduction was conceded without loss of pay on condition that there was a speedy return to work.[34]

Writing some fifty-eight years later, Finn asserted that this was the first Jewish strike by the first Jewish union in the modern world. It was, at any event, a profound first experience of working-class action by the Jewish tailor. Organisation was good. The timing of the strike to coincide with the busy season had placed the masters under pressure for an early settlement. The railway station had been picketed, London blacklegs met, 'given a brotherly talk', and returned home with their fares paid. As the strike had been intended merely to equalise the hours of the other groups with those of the machiners, the latter had magnanimously participated, with nothing to gain.[35] The action had also come under close public scrutiny – a matter in which Finn took pride, discerning that the industrial performance of the Leeds tailors would form a touchstone of alien industrial behaviour in general: 'All the papers became full of the strike; even a paper which calls itself the *Yorkshireman* described how the Jews strike.'[36] The Bradford journal had done more than this. It had published the most thorough and sensitive account of the Leeds trade to date, making no bones concerning the condition of alien tailors working for 'stable producers'.

It had pointed to the fact that, although the strike ostensibly concerned working hours, the extension of the tailors' working day had the effect of shortening the working week, reducing the earnings of 'a two-guinea man' to 15s 0d. From the alien-host viewpoint, the strike had done much good, the paper praising the intelligence and calmness of the union, and pronouncing it 'a great industrial force'.[37]

This early strike, the harbinger of much conflict, already reveals the simplistic basis of the Gartnerian equation between stable producers and strong Jewish union. The strike had not settled the question of the abolition of the middleman, and it was to remain in the Leylands air for many years, always in the background of the many industrial conflicts. Thus the masters were driven in self-defence to pursue the goal of destruction of the unions of their trade. Although, as Finn reported, the men had determined to resist the blacklist,[38] he himself became an early victim, being forced out of the country some months after the strike. Effective banishment of leaders was, by this deed, instituted in Leeds, and it was to remain a problem for the union until the appointment of paid officers in the 1890s. Another problem arising in the 1885 strike was the masters' fear of losing the work of the large firms.[39] This fear was perforce shared by the union, however, and expressed on a number of occasions, so that the masters' subordinate place in the trade was a factor calculated to inhibit union action.

In the handful of years following the strike a number of problems overlooked or misinterpreted in recent immigration studies came to the fore. In the first place, few writers have made proper concessions to the influence of trade disturbance on the relationships between the masters and the organised tailors. The depression of the mid-1880s, nevertheless, strengthened the masters in many ways. The terms of the 1885 settlement on hours were by no means applied universally, and it soon became clear that such settlements were largely illusory. Also omitted from accounts of Leeds (though, oddly, not of London) is the effect of new immigrant arrivals on trade settlements. It is clear, however, that the effect was deleterious, in Leeds as elsewhere. By 1886, in fact, the established Leeds tailors were complaining of the greeners who 'messed the trade up' and forced them to 'lie in the shop eighteen hours a day using the heavy iron'. The call had to be renewed for a twelve-hour day, and for the 5s 0d wage 'which a good worker deserved'.[40] A year later, beneath this combination of conditions, it was as though no strike had ever occurred as press complaints of wide wage variations, long hours and 'unpleasant conditions' in Jewish workshops were renewed.⁴¹

Neither the 1885 strike nor any of the numberless later ones support the thesis that the Leeds tailors were strongly organised because of the stability of the local industry. On the contrary, later events indicate that 1885 witnessed merely the first steps along an arduous road traversed by the workers in the face of appalling conditions, a merciless class struggle, and the important complication of English labour enmity. The strike of 1885 had given the Jewish tailor a first taste of victory – if only temporarily. From this year also, the leadership of the unions tended to be socialist, reflecting the clearest perception of the master as class enemy first and co-religionist afterwards.

Gartner admits that the early leadership of Jewish unions was socialist, but he considers that leaders and led had different goals. The leaders, he states, immediately reducing diversity to identity, 'aspired to make of the Jewish worker a disciplined, class-conscious member of a revolutionary vanguard', whilst all that the worker wanted was collective strength and a better standard of living.⁴² No dichotomy of this nature is discernible in the long history of the relationships between the Left and the alien worker. A careful study of the most important Jewish revolutionary organ, *Der Arbeiter Freund*, indicates quite clearly that education for revolution and the support of effective trade unionism were inseparable strands in Jewish left-wing thought and action. Gartner treats alien politics as if they existed in a vacuum, but an important influence upon them was the socialist revival in Britain which coincided almost precisely with the high period of immigration. Thus the politics of the alien communities did not consist merely of an intra-communal dialogue, but encompassed also a number of significant intellectual interventions from the British outer world.

A major determinant of the comparative strength of the Leeds tailors was their steadfastness in regard to the dual objectives of socialism and battle on the industrial front. Anarchists and revolutionary social democrats held high office in the unions throughout the period. Their two paid secretaries before 1914, Sam Freedman and Moses Sclare, whilst they might pursue 'businesslike' and 'responsible' courses, both held to a belief in the ultimate abolition of capitalism. That the socialists were anything but the lunatic fringe implied by Gartner is clear – not only from their practical role in the Leeds unions – but in the revolutionary outlook of many of the ordinary tailors.

This adamantine Leeds foundation may be contrasted with the state of affairs in London through a consideration of the grotesque contemporaneous events in the metropolis, where the proximity of the large Jewish capitalist exerted an influence which the Leeds tailors were providentially spared. In London, states Gartner, 'upper class individuals' organised the unions. One such was F. D. Mocatta, 'a scholarly bullion merchant and a ranking communal worthy'. Gartner omits to mention in which community this bullion merchant ranked as 'a worthy', but there is a clue in the leader's Malthusian advice to the London tailoresses that they ought not to have settled in England, and that they ought to resign themselves to 'small remuneration'.

In 1886, states Gartner further, Sir Samuel Montagu 'assumed the role of founder and Maecenas of the Jewish Tailors' and Machinists' Society'. Under this Maecenas, it appears, the daring resolve was made to 'ask' for a twelve-hour day, with 'time for lunch and tea', but to abstain from 'asking' for dinner time; the whole daring scheme to be accomplished without that inconvenience so upsetting to the capitalist known as a strike. Working-class attitudes so draconian were the predictable outcome of 'leadership' by 'upper class individuals', and Gartner's conclusion that nothing came of these 'philanthropic approaches' because they were 'too tepid and timid' must occupy a chief place in the ranks of the superfluous.[43]

The Leeds tailors travelled by more direct intellectual paths, and thus more rapidly, towards a conscious apprehension of their economic situation. No pronouncement in the history of the Jewish labour movement in Britain surpasses in purity of working-class expression that with which Jacob Finn greeted the appearance of *Arbeiter Freund* in 1885. It was a journal, he wrote, whose object was to awaken the workers from their sleep, to get them to look about and consider their position in the world. As for Leeds, hundreds were tormented from early morning till late at night with heavy labours – people who were not even regarded as humans, but as machines. In a passage of testamentary quality Finn treated the class struggle:

The worker is the fundament of the world; he creates everything... Therefore, how comes it about that his situation is so bad? It is true that everything belongs to the worker, but the misfortune is that this fact does not strike him. Rather... everything passes over to a few capitalists who do not put so much as a finger into cold water. Now we can clearly see that the source of the worker's troubles is the existence of a capitalist class which robs us of all that we create... To the capitalist class belongs the earth from which we come and to which we must all return, and whose fruits we all have an equal right to enjoy ... So soon as we recognise that the source of our troubles is the capitalist class, so we must specifically destroy this surplus class and organise our society so that all must work and participate in what we create and ensure that it belongs to everyone.[44]

This was excellent preparation for what the Leeds tailors were to hear from the English socialists within a few years. There were many reasons for a coalescence between these particular forces. The profound trade crisis of 1886 had triggered a severe outburst of anti-semitism. In a worried account of this manifestation the Yiddish socialist journal *Die Tsukunft* observed that there had been a spate of hostile pamphlets, of which the pioneer had been by one Frank Gardner, a Grimsby master tailor. In this document Gardner had blamed the aliens for the distress in his trade. By this, and at a stroke, he had set up a tradition and placed the alien tailor at the controversial centre of alien-host affairs.[45]

This emanation from the host society, added to the sufficiency of internal industrial problems, produced in the Leeds tailors a reaction in which they sought to maximise their identification with the English working class whilst overriding any tendency to enclusivity on the ground of religious difference. The environment of mounting hostility assisted the tailors' three unions to survive the slump. In 1887 the tailors, led by the socialist, Lewis Frank, boasted 545 members, whilst the machiners added a further 232. Taken together, such numbers represented the largest group of organised clothing workers in the British wholesale industry before the 1900s. As reported in *Arbeiter Freund*, the unions were acting 'as brothers' in order 'to break the power of the masters'. Large workshops did not appear to be the source of union strength: the small masters were more vulnerable:

Nowadays in Leeds it is known that as soon as a worker is in dispute with a master, the union goes in and arranges settlement. If the master does not agree, he finds himself without labour. Many members of the society now joining are small masters we have turned into ex-masters.

Such demonstrations that the Leeds Jewish tailor did not intend to conform to the image of the helpless sweater's victim encouraged the Trades Council to recognise the unions, four Jewish delegates being elected on 4 December 1887. The event was hailed by the tailors as a sign that the alien workers were 'not shut out of the general company of the working classes'.[46] The link with the Trades Council was strengthened by James Sweeney, still honorary secretary to the Jewish unions and representative of his own boot and shoe union on the council.

By this important year in their history, however, it was the Socialist League which had entered into the more intimate relationship with the

Jewish tailors. Tom Maguire and Tom Paylor, the leaders of the strong Leeds branch, were well enough acquainted with the conditions of the local tailoring trade, and were on close personal terms with the more advanced Jewish leaders such as John Dyche and Morris Kemelhor. Improving the lot of the settled Jewish tailor was an objective with a strong intuitive appeal to the internationalist emotions of a Maguire, whose warm humanity is apparent in all his dealings with the aliens. The English socialists were, at the same time, convinced that the labour situation could not be improved so long as the Leylands continued to be crowded with new immigrants. Thus they were opposed to further immigration, but, such was their influence with the established Jewish workers, that relations were never soured and Maguire continued to be regarded by them as a good comrade.[47]

Maguire, who had gone with William Morris, Edward Aveling, Eleanor Marx and John Lincoln Mahon in the Social Democratic Federation split in 1884, from which the Socialist League had been formed, was less dependent on London for policy by 1888. As the League itself split into anarchist and parliamentarian groups, Maguire and Paylor led an independent effort to convert the Leeds district trade unions to socialism. The major proponent of this policy was the League's first national secretary, John Lincoln Mahon. Socialists, he considered, had a choice between broadening the movement to include the practical aspirations of the working class, or forming factions preaching principles with no influence on the masses. In 1887, on the advice of his friend, Engels, he based his policy on a view similar to that of many Jewish revolutionaries: that socialist propaganda should be more than preaching what the workers were unable to comprehend, but that it should take hold of the labour movement and mould it into a socialist shape. The trade unions were a means to obtain a larger share in the fruits of labour, but socialism meant securing the full fruits of their labour by the working class.[48] As union militancy increased in 1887 and the Federation and the League stood aside, Mahon's aims were to become involved directly in workers' grievances and to enter the struggles of the unions. In 1887 Mahon left the League but continued to campaign, and Maguire, his friend since 1884, maintained close links with him.[49]

By the final days of 1887 the ferment surrounding the Leeds Jewish tailors was sufficient to persuade Mahon to the view that his campaign in the North-east for socialism might be interrupted with profit. The Jewish unions in Leeds were under militant socialists. The hardships of the workshop, and increasing anti-alien criticism, drove the tailors leftwards into easy association with the English comrades. The notion of co-operative tailoring and release from the master's bondage revived with trade.

The Jewish revolt of 1888 (for such, rather than a mere strike, it was) received a flying start from Mahon's address to the tailors at the end of 1887. That this historic speech was not lost is due to the Yiddish summary made by a listener who, appreciating the distinguished nature of the speaker and the language problem of most of the audience, sought to ensure that all Leeds workers should have access to it. The summary, as published in *Arbeiter Freund*, is reproduced in Appendix III. The dialectical strain, as well as Mahon's strategy of working through the trade unions towards socialism, are clearly expressed. In the Leylands, Mahon's exhortation to the aliens to 'throw off the master-yoke' must have sounded far less an abstraction than might have been the case before an English audience. The tide was running strongly in a socialist direction, and the Leeds tailors were already in the van of the 'far greater masses' noted by Engels in 1889 as being drawn into the struggle for the eight-hour day and electing only openly declared socialists as leaders.[50]

With the partial recovery of trade early in 1888, the fruits of agitation began to be reaped. The general strike with which it culminated in May that year has generally been regarded as purely a tailoring matter. Yiddish sources, however, indicate that very ambitious plans were afoot for something more akin to a complete transformation of the Leylands economy. The tailors were in high spirits, reminiscing about the easy victory of 1885 and boasting of their strength:

In the history of the Jewish labour movement in England, Leeds will, without doubt, occupy one of the nicest places, if not, indeed, the first place. And, in truth, whilst in other towns such as Manchester, Liverpool, Glasgow [sic], Nottingham, Birmingham and others, the Jewish workers are not even organised in societies, or are entirely beneath the heel of the masters, having entirely surrendered their free will to them, the Leeds workers have, in this regard, made enormous progress. They have not stopped at this ... they have decided to open a co-operative grocery shop, and, by this means, to free themselves from the shopkeepers, butchers, ritual slaughterers, milk-and-butter dealers, etc., who live and get fat on the sweat of the workers like rats on a living corpse.[51]

The announcement – by Morris Kemelhor, the tailors' leader – was received with enthusiasm, and, if a report to *Arbeiter Freund* by

'Comrade J. R.' is to be believed, it did much to accommodate the rank and file to Socialism:

> Anyone who has left Leeds and returns there will certainly wonder at the altered opinions of the workers. For how long was the cry heard in the unions: 'We don't want any Socialists here?' Today, however, wherever one goes one hears it said that the Socialists are right . . . Now the workers understand that we are not unjust when we cry so much against the robbers, bandits and man-eaters. We hope that the Leeds workers will shortly be free of their exploiters.[52]

The Trades Council – a stronghold of Liberalism – could also overcome its scruples against working with socialists when the matter under review was the alien tailor. John Judge, a Liberal stalwart of the council, who, as an official of the Boot and Shoe Operatives, had good reason for his interest in the Jewish worker, urged a general strike, though without the revolutionary tone adopted by Mahon. He had, at the same time, something of value to offer the alien exposed to the enmity of the English worker:

> The sympathy of the English working folk will be on your side when they see you behave like men who do not wish to be worked like horses and treated like dogs. The English workers will no longer say that you are the cause of the lowering of wages as they say at present, and they will no longer hate you.[53]

A report in *Arbeiter Freund*, despite its humour, firmly fixes the background of the strike, and exposes the fabulous nature of the many optimistic accounts of the industry in Leeds:

> As everyone knows, the situation of workers in general, and of tailors in particular, worsens from day to day. The cause of this is that many workers, when they have been in England a certain time . . . begin to realise that it was not given on Mount Sinai that only Rabbi Solomon Burlander or Rabbi Moses Kovner can be masters, but also that Simon Goldman can be a master as well as anyone . . . Simon makes his way to the warehouse and asks that work be given out to him also. There, he tells the foreman that his sainted grandfather taught him that, in such matters, it was always necessary to give a little present, which, in the vernacular, is called *lapke*, or, as the English call it, 'bribery'. The foreman, however, needs to keep his boss happy, so he demands of Simon that he do the work more cheaply. He agrees, and the following day he becomes 'Rabbi' Simon – a master! He needs to put no money into the 'business', so why should he labour so long and hard for others? From this, no good will come to the worker, for, when the warehouse sees that the new man is doing the work for less money, they begin to tear at the prices of their other masters. The masters, however, seeking to hold on to the work, tear the skin off the poverty-stricken workers.[54]

The agreed solution was to persuade the masters to sign a document accepting union shops. A 'respectful' letter of invitation was therefore sent to the masters; but, despite the booking of a conference room, which 'cost good money earned with blood and sweat', none of the masters appeared. An angry workers' meeting ensued. Jacob Korn, the pressers' leader, rammed home the advantages of society shops. It would, above all, he asserted, 'be the means of restraining the wild beasts from imposing their will any longer on the workers'. No reasonable person, he thought, would say that they were unjust in their demand for a fifty-eight-hour week when the Christian workers worked only fifty-six hours. Sweeney asserted that the tailors would be guilty of supporting a system of bribery if they failed to make an end of it by having society shops. Kemelhor described the 'situation of the workers and compared the way of life of the masters with his own'.[55]

The strike upon which this meeting resolved began well for the workers. It was remarkably widespread, involving eventually more than 3,500 Jewish clothing workers and leaving few workshops unaffected. The press opened its colums to further grievances. Korn complained of the 'great number of strangers who poured into Leeds in the busy season', with the consequence that the slack season arrived in Leeds earlier than elsewhere. These strangers took away money 'that should have been earned by Leeds workmen', and society shops alone could end this evil. Sweeney announced that the time had passed 'when it could be said Jews would work eighteen hours a day. The Jews wanted to work the same hours as the Christian workmen.'[56]

In action, the tailors were backed by an enthusiastic alliance of the Trades Council, the Socialist League and miscellaneous entrepreneurs including the phonetician John Greevz [sic] Fisher, and David Lubelski, master tailor and labour agitator. Countless meetings were held. Tom Paylor's account in *Commonweal* states that the Leeds branch of the League had taken up the strike vigorously from the beginning, and that he, Maguire and Kemelhor had addressed numerous meetings.[57] The enormous ferment and enthusiasm, however, had the effect of concealing two fatal circumstances.

Firstly, the strike of 1885 turned out to be a bad precedent. Three years later the masters were not prepared to concede demands so readily despite the onset of the busy season, especially when so many advocates of their industrial mortality were in the field. This attitude led, in turn, to an unforeseen extension of the strike, straining union funds to breaking point. Secondly, the strikers were thoroughly unprepared for the manifestations of brotherly love and co-religious feeling evinced by the masters. On 7 May a letter from the Masters' Society appeared in the *Leeds Evening Express*. Its contents, it claimed, were intended 'to prevent any erroneous impression getting abroad amongst the public'. The latter, doubtless to their astonishment, learned that the strike was not, after all, really concerned with hours and wages. Though the Jews worked longer hours than the English workers, the latter did 'not command the same salary, our workpeople not making less than an average of 6s 0d per day'. Did the public, the letter continued,

know the meaning of their society shops? It means ... any journeyman from any other town must, before he can gain a situation in Leeds, pay a certain sum to their society and then, having become a member, he will be taken to a Jewish master tailor and employment demanded for him. Should the employer state that he has a full complement of hands, he would be compelled to dismiss one of the many females (some of whom have been brought up in the trade) and it would also be the thin end of the wedge for the gradual extermination of female labour in the trade.[58]

This cynical appeal to anti-semitic sentiment by a Jewish organisation representing an industry surrounded by enemies created consternation in the workers' ranks, cost them much public sympathy, and shocked English observers. Korn announced that the strike was not aimed at the English girls. They wanted to make themselves beloved, not hated. The English had done them no harm, and they did not want to harm anybody. Sweeney denounced the charges as a lie.[59] Lubelski asserted that the strikers merely sought 'the same for the girls as for themselves'.[60] Maguire wrote that he had never once 'heard a word spoken against the employment of females' at the many strike meetings he had attended. The thought, he asserted, 'never entered the heads of those moving in the strike', and the decision of the girls to form a strike committee of their own was 'the best answer to the calumny'.[61] Maguire was correct. By 8 May a second meeting of the English girls was being held at the Leylands Board School in support of the tailors. As the lengthy account in *Arbeiter Freund*, partly by John Dyche, indicates, reporters were invited so that the origins of the strike could be clarified:

the sweating system which was the cause of the systematic reduction of prices which the workers seek to obviate in the future by the introduction of society shops. Also, the monstrously long working hours, especially of the tailors and pressers, which they want to reduce to fifty-eight per week.

Tom Paylor was leading the counter-attack in the propaganda war, and seeking to employ the occasion to organise the women:

Mr Paylor, the secretary of the Leeds Socialist League, in a magnificent and loudly applauded speech, explained how oppressed the women workers were by the masters, and the necessity for their organisation ... A few of the working women ... declared that they had had sufficient opportunity to convince themselves that the Jewish workers always took the side of the Christian women against the masters, and, because of this, the men had earned more trust than the masters.[62]

The masters' shaft had, however, struck home. Whilst the demand for a fifty-eight-hour week was 'reasonable', sniffed the *Leeds Daily News*, the strikers had made only vague declarations, 'destitute of practical significance', of their intention not to injure English labour. From suspicion it was but a short step to the discovery of additional disadvantages such as the 'serious disorganisation in the wholesale clothing trade of the town' caused by the sudden onset of the strike.[63] In similar vein the *Yorkshire Post*, putting profits first, bewailed the damage done by the strike to the large firms, and stressed, correctly, that Whitsun orders might not be completed.[64]

By forcing the workers to protest their innocence in public, the masters' accusation turned the strike into a vociferous debate. Demonstrations had to be held:

It was decided to hold a demonstration the next day to march with the banner of the society to the square opposite the Town Hall, and to hold a meeting there in order to give the English people a proper idea of the justness of our demands ... and to protest against the calumnies with which the masters seek to besmirch the poor Jewish workers through the press.[65]

The latter aligned themselves along clear lines. The *Evening Express* took the view that the men might be foreigners but there was 'no reason for them to work seventy hours per week'. They were subject to 'an amount of driving' in Jewish workshops which, though it was present in other Leeds trades under Christian masters, was 'not altogether pleasant'. Wages were good, 'and the sole grievance relating thereto' was that full time was 'not always obtainable'. Thus, thought the paper, the men had full public sympathy in their desire to get the hours shortened.[66] The *Daily News*, on the other hand, managed to give the impression that a strike was hardly taking place. Touring the Jewish quarter, its reporter found the English workwomen at work and the shops 'not deserted at all'.[67]

Maguire, Paylor, Sweeney, Lubelski and the various union leaders addressed numerous meetings, some of which were impressive affairs, illustrating the extent of the interest aroused by the strike. Maguire, for example, organised a demonstration of the Socialist League and the Irish National League at which 5,000 people were addressed by ten speakers on 12 May in Vicar's Croft, the popular venue for open-air political meetings. John Dyche's Yiddish report of the occasion preserves in summary form the thought of the pre-eminent northern socialist, and indicates the perplexity occasioned outsiders by the bitterness of Jewish intra-communal battle:

Maguire, who was the leader, in a most resplendent and impressive speech, described the tragic situation of the Jewish tailoring workers, and demonstrated how shamefully the Jewish masters had behaved towards their co-religionists. To end with, he appealed to the English workers to support all other workers irrespective of religion or nation because all capitalists were also international in their oppression and in robbing the workers as widely as possible.[68]

The same meeting also heard the Socialist League renew the proposition for the abolition of the Jewish masters by the establishment of a co-operative system. On the following day Sweeney was informed by Messrs Hepworth that they were prepared to open a Jewish workshop with 100 machines.[69] English workers were in support, one tailor writing to the *Evening Express* that, if the men could not agree with the 'gaffers', they should 'gaffer' themselves; and adding, correctly, that the Jewish system lent itself readily to co-operative organisation.[70] Deputations of strikers also appealed to many other major firms of Leeds wholesale manufacturers for action on lines similar to that proposed by Hepworth's.[71] It is, therefore, not surprising that, by the end of the first week of the strike, it became clear that the men faced a determined foe.

An attempt by the men to obtain settlement on 10 May was rejected 'within two hours without a meeting'.[72] Fear of total elimination from the industry overcame the temporary inconvenience occasioned the masters by the strike and the loss of the revenues of a single busy season. The method of warfare, thought the *Yorkshire Post*, and the increasing fervour with which both sides stated their case, were also likely to prolong the strike.[73] Mass meetings heard Sweeney, Paylor, Korn and Kemelhor describe the masters as 'robbers and swindlers', 'foul liars', and 'villains whose object was to squeeze as much life as possible out of the men'. Before a very large audience Lubelski castigated his fellow masters so severely that a solicitor handed him a summons on their behalf. He promptly tore it up, asserting that he could prove all his statements.[74] A final factor making for an embitterment of the contest was the call by the unions, at a meeting attended by 10,000 people, for an extension of the investigations of the Sweating Committee to the Leeds Jewish workshops.[75]

How little a Jewish strike, at least in Leeds, resembled the quaint family quarrel of Mrs Lerner's model becomes clearer from a consideration of the second and final week, plus the terrible aftermath. The loyal *Express* was sure that public sympathy was with the men. It indicted the 'middlemen and big houses' as the source of the terrible condition of the Jewish tailors of Leeds. No Englishman, it thought, could contemplate the condition of the Jewish worker with equanimity.[76] Public sympathy, however, was not enough. As early as 9 May the *Echo* had noted percipiently that the Leeds unions 'had little or nothing to fall back upon'.[77] By 12 May hunger had become the dominant theme of the strike. The editors of *Arbeiter Freund* reported that they were receiving many letters from their 'brothers striking in Leeds'. One letter exhorted:

Friends! We beg you in the name of our great purpose, and from the Leeds strikers and their hungry families, to help us as much as possible with money. The struggle sharpens and becomes more intense. If the workers lose now, it will be the end of our organisations in Leeds. Many strikers have already left Leeds and many others are preparing to leave.[78]

The struggle was indeed sharpening. The masters fought bitterly, and financial aid could not be expected in large measure from collections taken among sympathetic workers, English or Jewish, in the year 1888. Nor, apart from a few sympathisers such as the remarkable Lubelski, were many Jewish bourgeois very concerned. The latter, indeed, were often openly hostile. When, on 26 May, Kemelhor and Mahon, in company with the London leader, Lewis Lyons, addressed the East End tailors at Mile End in aid of the strike, the anglo-posturing *Jewish Standard*, organ of the Jewish 'aristocracy', dubbed the event 'this curious gathering of foreign Jews'.[79]

Englishmen stood aghast at the lengths to which the masters might go. Sensing victory through hunger, they exploited their financial power and communal position to force or induce the shopkeepers of the Leylands to cut off supplies to the strikers. This manifestation of the Jewish unitary system was recounted by Lubelski and Sweeney to the Sweating Committee a year later. The masters, reported the former, had gone the rounds of the grocers to demand the refusal of credit 'to any of those people' as they would not obtain work, and the masters would let them all starve.[80] Sweeney's evidence indicated that the masters threatened to withdraw their own custom if supplies to the strikers were not stopped.[81] Vindictiveness was carried to extremes by individual masters. Beneath the headline 'The Inhuman Savagery of the Leeds Sweaters' *Arbeiter Freund* reported that Herman Freund, a leading light of the tailoring trade and chairman of the Jewish Guardians, had intervened to prevent the sick wife of a striker from receiving treatment at the Public Dispensary, claiming that the family were not entitled to free treatment, as the man was earning $7s\ 0d$ per day.[82] That these methods aroused execration even within the upper class of the Leeds community is clear from the testimony of David Isaac, a jeweller, who informed the Sweating Committee that he had investigated the accusation and had found it correct.[83] Beyond the community, also, the scandal was spread widely – not least by Tom Paylor's caustic account in *Commonweal*, which left readers in no doubt concerning the severity of the Leylands struggle, and the fact that 'nothing more mean than the tactics of the employers can be imagined'.[84]

The chief cause of defeat, however, as Sam Freedman put it in a reminiscence in 1899, was their error in that 'they went out without any funds'.[85] The financial problem was aggravated by a rapid augmentation of *ad hoc* membership occasioned by the strike. Opening with 1,200 strikers, the action soon encompassed several thousands, many of whom had not been members of good standing. In the interests of unity, the unions attempted to include the new members in strike pay arrangements, placing an intolerable strain on funds.[86] Strike pay did not always suffice to ensure loyalty, however. As a Leeds master observed in a critique of the local unions published in *Arbeiter Freund* in 1903, 'They strike, and the worker goes scabbing after he has accepted strike pay. A fine lot, eh?'[87]

The final days of the strike were thus taken up with desperate attempts to gain financial support. Benefit concerts were organised by English workers.[88] The Trades Council rather belatedly announced its 'moral and material support', organising a benefit at the Varieties Music Hall, and addressing appeals to the wholesalers to provide workshops for the aliens and to supervise them directly.[89] The English firms, despite their recorded promises, adopted their habitually taciturn attitude to alien industrial affairs. Pressure upon their capacity diminished when it was discovered that spare capacity – and willing workers – existed in London to execute Leeds orders. This was a bitter blow to the Leeds men. What was the use of the Leeds Tailoring Trades Union, queried Lewis Lyons in London, if, when they struck, their work could be done in London? The season, which had appeared favourable to a strike, now became a disadvantage as the approach of a Holy Festival, supplemented by privation, encouraged a drift back to the workshop.[90] The masters also succeeded in importing blackleg labour from London, despite the fact that their emissary provoked an East End socialist plot to beat him up, and a further demonstration in aid of the Leeds strike.[91] By 23 May the strike had ended in total defeat.

Aaron Rollin, the sole authority on Jewish labour to treat the strike in any depth, interprets its consequences in the most curious manner. He argues that, if the reasons for the decision to end the strike 'in a short time' are overlooked, the long-term results were positive and the union became 'ever stronger'.[92] The reasons for the termination are, however, overlooked at peril, since the defeat was total, its immediate consequences appalling, and its long-term effects retarding. Rollin overlooks the five difficult years which were to elapse before a permanent combination could be established — an event to which the disaster of 1888 can have made no material contribution.

For the masters, the fruits of their stubborn resistance and 'enterprising' tactics had yet to be gathered. Paylor did not require great prescience to forecast the immediate effects of defeat:

As it is, the men will have a harder life than ever after this strike and many have expressed a determination to leave the town. Comrade Kemelhor, Chairman of the Associated Societies, the head and front of the strike, and others who took an active part in the strike, will surely be boycotted from the trade in Leeds.[93]

This was echoed in the official *Report on Strikes*, which stated that, bad as their position had been before, the men were now far worse off.[94] The tailors were now in the hands of a vindictive, arrogant and often stupid class enemy, utterly insensitive to the effects upon English opinion of his retributive acts. The masters, the enemy routed, engaged in a punitive reaction against fellow Jews of a brutality which again shocked English opinion. The boycott was widely employed, despite the warning of the *Leeds Express* that, in England, such a course was 'looked upon as odious in the extreme', and that it was 'not policy in a strife of this kind for the victors to extract vengeance on the defeated'.[95] The masters had paid dearly for their victory through loss of revenue,[96] and were determined to compensate themselves by the destruction of the workers' organisations. The lords of the Leylands imposed quasi-serfdom:

The sequel to the ill-starred strike is already being felt by the poor Leeds workers ... the Masters' Society had passed a rule that one should not take on the other's workers without a written release from the first master, on which there must also be written his wages in order that the new master should not give him more than this.[97]

Towards the end of June it was reported to *Arbeiter Freund* that

Many workers still go around idle because the sweaters are putting themselves out to employ the boycott as widely as possible ... The well-known sweater, 'The Angel of Death', has sacked a presser because he had whistled at scabs in the street, and other damned things have been done by the accursed sweaters. Now the sweaters have discovered a new device: they have paid the police to wander around Bridge Street, where the workers congregate and take names.[98]

Sweeney presented a harrowing account to the Sweating Committee. So great was the fury of the victorious masters, he asserted, that the unions were reduced to two members in 1889. They could not keep members when men 'were expected to be turned out of the shop at any time if found to be a member'. Many had been subjected to the humiliation of being compelled to tear up their card ceremonially before the master.[99] The situation at the end of the strike was well summed up by the rising young anarchist Jacob Caplan, writing in *Arbeiter Freund* three years later:

In the year '87 [sic], when these same tailors lost their strike, they were forced to return defeated to their sweated labours. Then, naturally, they had lost everything ... They considered it impossible to improve their lot and bowed the head to any beast that cared to tread on it.[100]

In July the *Express*, concerned by the prolongation of the bitter aftermath, was again moved to preach that, in England, when a fight is over, 'the antagonists shake hands and eschew malice'. They were sorry to hear that the Jewish strike had 'left disillusion and ill feeling behind'.[101] Whether the editor expected the realities of the class struggle to be diminished in a Jewish context is not clear. The tailors, however, were left in no doubt that the struggle was itself extra-ethnic in nature. Thus the methods of the masters served to preserve and encourage the spirit of organisation in the face of disaster. On 23 May it was reported to *Arbeiter Freund* that the 'discovery by the Leeds sweaters of how to enslave their workers' by the use of the leaving certificate had its good side, since the workers were already beginning to feel more strongly that their only help was strong organisation.[102] On the same day the *Express*, on a similar theme, prophesied that, although the strike was over, they would 'be greatly mistaken if the matter was definitely settled', as the masters seemed to think.¹⁰³

The punitive attitude of the masters, and the starvation it threatened to boycotted workers, produced its first material reaction in the form of what the former most feared: a co-operative workshop. Initially, one shop was opened as a refuge, since it was the only place in Leeds where the boycotted men could get a living.¹⁰⁴ The Trades Council supported the venture because, in the long term, 'it would allow doing away with the middleman in the Leeds trade'.¹⁰⁵ Maguire, Paylor and the League were once more at the centre of affairs. The editor of *Arbeiter Freund* wrote that

... We received a letter from Comrade Maguire in which he described the piteous condition of the boycotted Leeds workers and begged us to try to send some money to enable them to carry on their small co-operative workshop which has been provisionally founded for a few hungry families. The honesty, courage and deep interest of this English comrade in the Jewish workers' strike was, for us, a sufficient guarantee of the accuracy of his writings ... On Monday £10 was sent to Comrade Maguire with the condition that it be devoted to the support of the co-operative workshop.¹⁰⁶

Other than this meagre collection taken among the East End poor, there is little evidence to indicate that the Leeds men had any other support than the representatives of English labour. Paylor's contribution took the form of a lengthy, over-optimistic account of the co-operative in *Commonweal*:

The right nail has been struck on the head, I believe, in this co-operative idea, and if, as there is every reason to believe, we can make a success of this, there will be no resting until every sweater is driven back to his original avocation of tinkering, glazing, organ-grinding, etc. Work is being obtained plentifully ... The action of a dozen men, in finding out how to work without the middleman, has done more to terrify the employers than all that the whole body of workmen had previously accomplished.¹⁰⁷

The co-operative, set up in the Ship Inn Yard, Briggate, with a complement of twenty-two male and nine female workers,¹⁰⁸ began most promisingly; and although it did not prove the millennial event anticipated by the Jewish leaders and the Socialist League, Paylor did not exaggerate the fear immediately excited among the masters. In June large orders were once more promised by the wholesalers.¹⁰⁹ A report to *Arbeiter Freund*, written in Leeds on 23 June, provides the best surviving detail of progress:

Concerning the co-operative workshop, we are able to inform our brothers that, provisionally, there are six machines at work. Until last week, 125 orders had been completed, and the warehouses were so pleased with our work that they expressed the conviction that, if the co-operative workshop produced such work for a period of six months, it would get the work of all the Leeds warehouses. Many warehouses have promised to provide work ... At present the workshop is a great curse to the masters, for out of this small workshop a great co-operative can grow, and that will enable us to get rid of the sweaters.[110]

The *Express* was also pleased to publish sinister pronouncements such as that of a Jewish worker that their only hope of freeing themselves in time 'from the control and power of the masters' lay in the co-operative. Kemelhor kept in mind the dual purpose of alien labour organisation, giving it as his opinion that it would be 'the source of plenty of bread and an end to English press talk of unsanitary Jewish workshops'.[111]

Noting that something dangerous was developing (in the form of a workshop without their presence and which they themselves named 'The Angel of Death'),[112] and that, in spite of defeat, a considerable body of tailors remained loyal to Kemelhor, the masters adopted grotesque tactics. As soon as the shop had been got ready for operations, wrote Paylor, it was suddenly discovered that the 'employing middlemen were violently in love with the workpeople'. With the aid of 'a party of four', a meeting was arranged at the Leylands Board School, where the masters were willing to concede all points at issue on condition that the co-operative be abandoned. What was more, continued Paylor,

the employers were desirous of joining the men's trade society, 'working hand in hand with them', and helping it by money and personal help. Somehow, this glorious and, by the way, startling idea, was not snapped up by the men as readily as was expected, and precautions were taken to go to the masters' meeting in a body.

As the tailors approached the Board School, the police pounced on Kemelhor and prevented his going further, when the men turned and

followed the banner to a piece of waste land called by the euphonious name of 'The Midden', where speeches were delivered by Maguire, Kemelhor, Paylor, Hill and Cohen ... The middlemen masters, deprived of the presence of the 'hands' they wanted to love so well, held a meeting composed of a sprinkling of slippermakers and the aforementioned four. No resolutions were passed as there wasn't audience to pass a good-sized resolution, and then some of the middlemen who had walked down to the meeting to benefit – be it borne in mind – the men, actually went home in cabs, fearful lest any of the workmen – who couldn't see things as masters see them – should punch their benefactors' heads. Such is the perversion of the sweater's intellect.[113]

The parallel report in *Arbeiter Freund* dubs Paylor's 'party of four' the 'scab committee'. It consisted of Abraham Korn, an old leader, Harris Balsam, Lewis Rosenberg and, surprisingly, James Sweeney, of whom Paylor remarked that, previous to this, he had always been credited with more sense. *Arbeiter Freund* provides more detail in its version. The body which marched to the Board School was 800 strong, and, upon assembly, its first act was to thank *Arbeiter Freund* for its warm interest 'in their bitter struggle against their bloodsuckers'. At the Board School

> one of the chief bloodsuckers was sent out to act as delegate, and he told them that, if they were to make peace with the masters and go hand in hand with them, they must first divorce themselves from Morris Kemelhor.

This had been the signal for the march to The Midden, where Maguire declared

> that it was impossible that a wolf should suddenly become a good friend of a sheep, and, for this reason, the workers should not trust their oppressors – the masters. And that is how nothing came of the meeting of masters and scabs at the Board School.[114]

If the attempt by the masters to penetrate the unions had ended in ludicrous failure, it remained open to them to act against individual unionists. Moreover, the 'party of four' symbolised the deep division in the movement into two hostile factions – the direct and, perhaps, inevitable consequence of defeat. As early as 23 May, Balsam had begun to form an anti-Kemelhor group hostile to socialism, and to blame defeat on lack of unity rather than of funds.[115] He was joined by Korn of the pressers and James Sweeney. Strong as was the support for what was essentially a socialist policy of co-operative working, a faction favoured a *modus vivendi* with the masters rather than their outright abolition.[116] Riotous meetings were held, which were to prove destructive of the leadership fabric. Although the actions of the masters appeared to confirm the contention of a Leeds socialist that

> The co-operative workshop is also a bone in their throats. They continue to read items about the workshop in the local press and that scares the souls out of their bodies ...

the three unions were busily encompassing their own disintegration. At a typical meeting on 18 June:

> The scab, Abraham Korn, was president. He climbed on to a table and,

opening his eyes like Balaam's Ass when he laid eyes on the angel, said: 'Brothers! Consider what you are doing! Why should you not go hand in hand with us? Do not believe in Kemelhor, Taylor and the other Socialists who seek, through power, to snatch the bread from your mouths and hand the work over into Christian hands!' One worker, who did not want to hear any more, cried: 'Down with the scabs!' This produced a terrible outcry and battle, and, were it not for the escort provided by the police, the little scabs would have been fortunate to escape with broken sides.

The same evening Kemelhor was elected president of the three unions, and, shortly after, a new amalgamated union of the three branches was formed, with a leadership which included Kemelhor and Isaac Taylor.[117] By the time of this event, however, the curtain was falling on the first phase of the tailors' union history.

No trace of the co-operative may be found after mid-July 1888, when an exasperated *Express* took the tailors to task for accepting a price reduction imposed by the English firms. This, it accused, was 'the very thing which the leaders of the strike so firmly denounced when done by the employers'.[118] Reviewing the tailors' history two years later, the *Yorkshire Factory Times* asserted that the co-operative, much to the regret of the Trades Council, 'was killed owing to their internal jealousies, bickerings and selfishness'.[119]

With the termination of the co-operative, the militant wing disintegrated. Kemelhor, the focus of residual loyalty, disappeared from Leeds under the influence of the boycott. On the other hand, socialists such as Isaac Taylor survived to play important roles in later developments. Elimination of the middleman was to reappear in the repertoire of the Leeds Jewish tailors on several occasions, but the attempt of 1888 was probably the most determined of those made throughout the period. Together with defeat in the strike, the failure of the co-operative cast a shadow over immediate socialist ambitions, though socialism would become important in subsequent Jewish tailoring unionism. The socialist leaders – in 1888 if not in retrospect – were firmly identified by many with the defeat and its baleful aftermath. Korn's accusation that they desired to hand over the work to other hands was a monstrous slander. It expressed, nonetheless, a genuine Jewish fear felt throughout the period and common to masters and men, irrespective of politics. The year of the general strike was one in which indoor manufacturing capacity was being much enlarged, and, indeed, the English movement to withdraw work indoors, if more rapid in the 1900s, may be traced to its origins in the general strike of 1888.[120]

Elimination of the Jewish master must have seemed a utopian vision to many in the circumstances of an outwork industry with a doubtful supply of work. Thus there emerged, from the recriminations inherent in defeat, broad agreement on refusal to countenance 'hand-in-hand' arrangements with the masters, but something less than unanimity on the practical possibilities of their abolition.

The experiences of 1888 were to influence the Leeds Jewish unions for many years. Adequate financial preparation for strikes and the avoidance of *general* actions, with all their financial and organisational problems, became hallmarks of the future organisations. The tailors had also been provided with a measure of the united power of the Leeds masters, their capacity for battle, and readiness to transcend – impervious to native opinion – the requirements of co-religious behavioural norms. After 1888 the most profound sceptic could not fail to be aware that the bond of ethnicity was incidental to the class struggle in the Leylands.

There were also external effects of importance directly traceable to the strike. Whilst, as the *Yorkshire Post* asserted, the tailors were mistaken in thinking that they would gain 'material assistance from the public attention' being drawn to their industry by the Sweating Committee,[121] the strike yet exerted considerable influence. The supporting demonstrations in the East End, the interest of metropolitan newspapers such as the *Echo*, and the Leeds visit by Beatrice Potter and John Burnett, induced the Lords to widen the scope of their inquiry to embrace provincial sweating. Locally, the strike may be said to have affected attitudes permanently. Although the sanitary question had not figured among the issues in the dispute, Leeds newspapers had carried out their own investigations. The *Lancet*, simultaneously attracted to Leeds, supported their unflattering findings, producing the cry: 'What are the inspectors doing?'[122] Within the local authority, as has been shown, a minor administrative revolution was provoked which, if unsuccessful in the long term, yet produced vigorous efforts based on permanent and special arrangements to supervise the Jewish workshops.

In the event, perhaps the most positive result of the strike in material terms was that delineated in an *Arbeiter Freund* report appearing at its end:

One thing annoys the masters more than any other: that they must now whitewash their hovels, and that costs money. They would not wish to do this but for the frequent visits of the uninvited guests – the inspectors.[123]

NOTES

1. J. Parkes, 'The history of the Anglo-Jewish community', in Freedman, *A Minority*, pp. 31, 38, 45–6.
2. Lipman, 'Jews in British urban society', p. 8.
3. Neustatter, 'Demographic and other statistical aspects', pp. 109–10.
4. Lerner, *Breakaway Unions*, pp. 66–7.
5. Lerner, 'Impact of Jewish immigration', p. 18.
6. D. Bythell, *Sweated Trades*, London, 1978, p. 205.
7. Hunt, *Wage Variations*, pp. 311–12.
8. *Y.F.T.*, 4 January 1912.
9. *Ibid.*, 16 December 1904.
10. Gartner, *Jewish Immigrant*, p. 119.
11. See, for example, *Y.F.T.*, 15 January 1904.
12. *Sweating Committee*, q. 26128.
13. *Y.E.N.*, 21 January 1925.
14. *Recent Immigration*, p. 12.
15. *Sweating Committee*, q. 30204.
16. *Die Tsukunft*, 1 January, 29 January 1886.
17. Leeds Trades Council Minutes, 6 February, 3 September, 1 October, 5 November 1884.
18. *D.P.Y.*, 1 August 1884.
19. *Ibid.*, 19 September 1884.
20. *Ibid.*, 17 October 1884.
21. *Ibid.*, 31 October 1884.
22. *Die Tsukunft*, 27 March 1885.
23. *J.C.*, 11 April 1884.
24. *L.E.E.*, 5 July, 23 August 1884.
25. Gartner, *Jewish Immigrant*, p. 118.
26. *L.W.E.*, 8 November 1884.
27. *Ibid.*, 15 November 1884.
28. *Ibid.*, 22 November 1884.
29. *Leeds Daily News*, 9 March 1885.
30. *Y.P.*, 4 May 1885.
31. Lyons, *Horrible Sweating System*, p. 6.
32. *Die Tsukunft*, 27 March 1885.
33. *Y.P.*, 4 May 1885.
34. *Ibid.*, 14 May 1885.
35. J. Finn, letter to A. R. Rollin, 27 October 1943.
36. *Die Tsukunft*, 29 May 1885.
37. *The Yorkshireman*, May 1885, p. 314.
38. *Die Tsukunft*, 29 May 1885.
39. *The Yorkshireman*, May 1885, p. 314.
40. *Die Tsukunft*, 5 March 1886.
41. *L.E.E.*, 1 February 1887.
42. Gartner, *Jewish Immigrant*, pp. 118–19.
43. *Ibid.*, pp. 117–18.
44. *A.F.*, 15 October 1885.

45 *Die Tsukunft*, 8 October 1886.
46 *A.F.*, 9 December 1887.
47 For Maguire on immigration, see *Labour Chronicle*, 6 May 1893.
48 S. Pierson, *Marxism and the Origins of British Socialism*, Ithaca, N.Y., 1973, pp. 185–6.
49 This section is based on E. P. Thompson, *William Morris, Romantic to Revolutionary*, London, 1977.
50 F. Engels to F. A. Sorge, 7 December 1889, *Karl Marx and Frederick Engels, Selected Correspondence*, Moscow, 1965, p. 407.
51 *A.F.*, 30 April 1888.
52 *Ibid.*, 30 April 1888.
53 *Ibid.*, 11 May 1888.
54 *Ibid.*
55 *Ibid.*
56 *L.E.E.*, 7 May 1888.
57 *Commonweal*, 26 June 1888.
58 *L.E.E.*, 7 May 1888.
59 *Ibid.*
60 *A.F.*, 11 May 1888.
61 *L.E.E.*, 9 May 1888.
62 *A.F.*, 18 May 1888.
63 *Leeds Daily News*, 8 May 1888.
64 *Y.P.*, 8 May 1888.
65 *A.F.*, 18 May 1888.
66 *L.E.E.*, 9 May 1888.
67 *Leeds Daily News*, 9 May 1888.
68 *A.F.*, 18 May 1888.
69 *Ibid.*
70 *L.E.E.*, 11 May 1888.
71 *Y.P.*, 12 May 1888.
72 *L.E.E.*, 10 May 1888.
73 *Y.P.*, 9 May 1888.
74 *L.E.E.*, 9 May 1888.
75 *A.F.*, 18 May 1888.
76 *L.E.E.*, 10–12 May 1888.
77 *The Echo*, 9 May 1888.
78 *A.F.*, 18 May 1888.
79 *Jewish Standard*, 1 June 1888.
80 *Sweating Committee*, q. 31785.
81 *Ibid.*, q. 30366.
82 *A.F.*, 18 May 1888.
83 *Sweating Committee*, q. 31744.
84 *Commonweal*, 26 June 1888.
85 Freedman, 'Leeds Jewish Tailors' Union', p. 449.
86 *A.F.*, 11 May 1888; *Commonweal*, 26 June 1888.
87 *A.F.*, 1 May 1903.
88 *L.E.E.*, 15–16 May 1888.
89 *Ibid.*, 19–22 May 1888.

90 *Leeds Daily News*, 16 May 1888.
91 *L.W.E.*, 26 May 1888; *A.F.*, 25 May 1888.
92 A. R. Rollin, 'Bletlach zu der geschichte fun der yiddisher arbeterbewegung in England', *Yivo Bleter*, XLIII, 1966, p. 276.
93 *Commonweal*, 26 June 1888.
94 *Report on Strikes*, 1888, p. 82.
95 *L.E.E.*, 23 May 1888.
96 *Commonweal*, 20 June 1888.
97 *A.F.*, 25 May 1888.
98 *Ibid.*, 29 June 1888.
99 *Sweating Committee*, qq. 30189–91, 30194–5, 30201, 30378.
100 *A.F.*, 11 December 1891.
101 *L.W.E.*, 7 July 1888.
102 *A.F.*, 25 May 1888.
103 *L.E.E.*, 23 May 1888.
104 *Ibid.*, 11 June 1888; *Commonweal*, 26 June 1888.
105 *L.E.E.*, 22 May 1888.
106 *A.F.*, 15 June 1888.
107 *Commonweal*, 30 June 1888.
108 Minutes of the Sanitary Committee, 12 June 1888.
109 *Leeds Times*, 16 June 1888.
110 *A.F.*, 29 June 1888.
111 *L.E.E.*, 12 June 1888.
112 *Ibid.*, 18 June 1888.
113 *Commonweal*, 30 June 1888.
114 *A.F.*, 15 June 1888.
115 *Ibid.*, 25 May 1888.
116 *L.E.E.*, 12 June 1888.
117 *A.F.*, 29 June 1888.
118 *L.W.E.*, 14 July 1888.
119 *Y.F.T.*, 18 April 1890.
120 *Report on Strikes, 1888*, p. 82; *L.E.E.*, 23 May 1888.
121 *Y.P.*, 10 May 1888.
122 *L.W.E.*, 9 June 1888.
123 *A.F.*, 29 June 1888.

Chapter 4

MATURITY AND STRUGGLE: THE TAILORS' UNION TO 1914

The phase of the Jewish tailors' union history extending from the disaster of 1888 to the Great War reveals no smooth progression towards mastery but, rather, the tortuous struggle punctuated by spasmodic – often temporary – gains which an unromantic view of their industry renders entirely plausible. So late as 1911 no more than 1,000 members of good standing could be counted after several decades of propaganda, education and, above all, the grim oppression of the workshop.[1] Of the London Jewish unions, Yiddish journalistic wits were fond of writing that they consisted of just three members: the chairman, the secretary and the rubber stamp. In this light, therefore, the Leeds union was a giant, but its potential membership was of the order of 5,000 – a figure attained only by 1913. The union battled on fronts unknown to English labour. Whilst the foundations of the immediate struggle with the masters remained firm, having been truly laid before 1888, the dynamic stresses within the parent wholesale industry imposed additional burdens upon the union by their influence upon prices and wages in the alien sector. The *Jewish Chronicle* saw clearly that 'the masters subcontract for the world's largest clothiers, but are slaves'.[2] Thus the struggle of the final phase of the union retained and, perhaps, intensified its sharp Leylands quality. Unique to the Jewish worker was his position as alien and soldier on the anti-alien front. By 1888 the scale of the actions involving the Leeds tailors, and the degree of their association with English labour interests, conservative and revolutionary, had placed them ineluctably in the centre of the cauldron of the anti-alien controversy. Whilst some writers have seen the termination of anti-semitic and xenophobic manifestations as coeval with 'permanent trade recovery' after 1895,[3] and others deny their occurrence at any time,[4] the problems and policies of the Leeds tailors derive significantly from the darkening anti-alienism extending across the whole period, as well as from internal industrial conditions.

The problems of the trade in the later Leeds period were far greater than can be deduced from the models which treat only the larger workshops. For the Leeds union, the small workshop proper constituted a ready target, but, with the spread of the bedroom master, a fundamental development of the 1900s, it had to be admitted that

as a union, I may acknowledge that we are powerless to deal with them at all because they can do a great deal of the work themselves, and if we strike against them, the result is that they do less.[5]

The route whereby the Leeds tailoring situation became more difficult in the later years, growing increasingly to resemble that of London, was clearly mapped in a *Jewish Chronicle* commentary of 1907, which, incidentally, provides a picture of pure competitive anarchy. The large Leeds warehouses had, 'in the old days', encouraged single firms of Jewish middlemen on efficiency grounds, with the result that the trade had been 'in the hands of a few fortunate individuals'. In the absence of keen competition, 'liberal' prices had been paid for the making-up of garments. By the 1900s, however, this structure had dissolved:

Owing to the prevailing competitive system, the adoption of modern scientific machinery, with the inevitable introduction of female labour, the clothing industry has, during the past decade, become almost revolutionised with disastrous results for the Jewish employer ... The doors of the large establishments were thrown open and, though the price paid for the making-up of the garment was by no means large, yet hundreds were found applying at the same firms.

The consequences, as the *Chronicle* saw them, were 'infinitesimal' prices for the Jewish masters, with the large English firms changing their outside sub-contractors weekly.[6] Here are important clues to the exacerbation of the Leeds tailors' struggles in the later period. How closely Leeds was following the footsteps of London by these developments is clear from Lewis Lyons's evidence on the latter to the Aliens Commission four years before the *Chronicle* article. In this, a mirror-image of the Leeds situation in 1907 emerges, with the conclusion that the alien state of affairs was 'comparable to the system that existed amongst the dockers before their great strike'.[7]

There were other evolving similarities with the East End to provide occasions for long-term conflict in Leeds. If the tailoring industry in the latter place were truly 'grander' than elsewhere, it remained, nevertheless, sufficiently undifferentiated to have its own large measure of such evils as internal sub-contracting – a system rightly regarded by Jewish organisers as a major source of disunity in the workers' ranks. The practice was a direct consequence of the subdivision of labour in alien workshops. Modern writers, including economists,[8] have lauded the system as the agent of rationalisation in tailoring without perceiving either its capacity for mischief or its great contribution to sweating. Beneath subdivision, as *Arbeiter Freund* analysed it in 1908, since it required little time for the immigrant to become a tolerable machiner or presser, there evolved a sub-group of workers for whom it did not pay the master to accept responsibility. Such workers, the plain machiners and underpressers, became the objects of direct exploitation by the skilled machiners and pressers:

For the plain machiner and underpresser, the master himself did not exist. His direct exploiter was, and is, the machiner or presser, who seeks to extract from him ever more profit. In this manner, there has developed a complete system of exploitation of worker by worker ... It is superfluous to demonstrate that this accursed system remains a hindrance to the development of a mutual trade union organisation.[9]

With the duplication of this London system in Leeds, it is evident that the northern city offered the Jewish labour organiser little comparative advantage as he observed the local growth of evils classically associated with London. How far the larger Leeds workshops eased the way for unionisation must also be doubtful. Their employees were vulnerable in larger masses to their master's dismissal by the employing warehouse. Their 'superior' organisation and capitalisation facilitated – not only sub-contracting – but the piecework experiments which formed a chief cause of bloodletting between 1891 and the general lockout of 1911. Furthermore, the disused workhouses and dilapidated mills of the Leeds trade were of sufficient size to accommodate elements arguably capable of making organisation more difficult in the larger workshop. Jewish females, hitherto an unconsidered factor, illustrate the point well. By 1896 they had created such problems that the men's union was compelled to set up a special committee under the anarchist, Louis Ellstein, in an effort to organise them. Ellstein's appeal to the women in that year through *Arbeiter Freund* is an eloquent document redolent of civil warfare:

Until now you have been the right hand of the masters. Whenever the men have gone on strike, you have completed the partly finished work, and, because of this, many strikes have been lost. Do you now understand against whom you are strike-breaking; who it is that you caused to wander the streets without bread for self and children? Without any feeling you went to work for the master's price. These men are your fathers, brothers, friends and future husbands. Yet, despite all, your situation has not improved — it has worsened ... Earlier, weekly paid workers got 15s 0d a week and now you work for 8s 0d, and the highest wages for a fellerhand are 12s 0d a week. And, to our greatest regret, we have never heard a word of protest from you and you have never tried to organise in order to better your lot.[10]

Socialism remained, in the later period, an integral aspect of the essential drive of the Jewish tailors. The dismissive and sub-elementary treatment received by this question at the hands of writers such as Gainer and Gartner betrays a patronising bourgeois historical method which treats the working class as an insentient mass. Gainer fails to credit the Jewish worker with the capacity to learn by his own experience or that of the English labour by which he was surrounded. Thus he fails to perceive that Jewish socialists and anarchists — groups which he brackets without differentiation — were, apart from a relatively few professional political penmen and orators, equally pressers, machiners and tailors schooled in precisely the same workshops as their fellows, and sharing in the delightful amenities of the alien slums. Never do they reveal themselves to careful research in the guise of Gainer's 'few' whose single activity was 'their persistent anti-religious propaganda' for which their punishment was to be ignored or despised.[11] Gainer does not trouble himself with journals such as *Arbeiter Freund* which would have provided a clear impression of the enormous range of Jewish socialist concerns, and, perhaps, induced him to consider how a journal devoted to a few communal pariahs could have commenced life with a weekly publication run of thirty-one years. Nor does he require class-conscious workers for union formation, leadership and battle. This is because he has access to Gartner's magic formula. Whereas aliens made poor trade unionists, he asserts, it was otherwise in Leeds, because the 'trade was organised along quite different lines from that of London'.[12] Gartner is prepared to allow socialism a role — at least in the early unions — and he perceives that the movement had a serious political programme. He also credits the Jewish worker with sufficient consciousness to desire to better his lot, but, for him, this represents the parting of the ways, since the socialists, in his grossly superficial view, pursued abstract and divisive revolutionary ideals alone, which separated them by a gulf from the ordinary worker. Turning to the case of Leeds, Gartner, like Gainer, asks no questions of the human, intellectual sources of the drive to unionisation, preferring reliance upon the 'large workshops' which were 'more fertile soil [sic] for trade unionism than London's chaotic congeries of small workshops'.[13]

No headway is possible in the comprehension of the role of Jewish socialism in the trade union movement unless its sheer heterogeneity is appreciated. Jewish socialism was unoriginal, following the passing parade of European movements: communism, anarchism, social democracy and syndicalism. Among these groups it is possible to discern Jewish revolutionaries in every centre of settlement conforming to the description applied by Gartner and Gainer to Jewish socialism in general. Yet no blanket description suffices, since alternative brands of Jewish socialism were fully committed to the Mahonesque theory that socialism was merely a higher stage of trade unionism. Thus their adherents worked consistently within and through the unions, pursuing the battle for short-term gains with a view to a socialist world in the problematical future. Marxists and Kautskyite social democrats were unambiguously in this category, but it is a curiosity of alien politics that elements of the anarchist movement were equally committed to trade union organisation. The presence of this special Jewish gloss can be explained only by the commonality of the experience of aliens of all persuasions as co-victims of the sweater, as well as the equal objects of anti-alien hatred. The most urgent task of the Jewish workers was seen simultaneously by multifarious revolutionary groups to be unionisation, both to improve their industrial situation and to hasten acceptance into the general world of English labour. These were objectives likely to shorten the distance between the socialist and the worker.

The whole question was well epitomised in an *Arbeiter Freund* editorial of 1908 – a convenient year from which to survey most of the period. This observed that the anarchists had always taken an active role in the unions, preaching and agitating among the masses. There were, however, differences in the 'tactical and theoretical perception' of the unions. Some groups were for amalgamation with English unions, some for independent Jewish unions, and some sought only revolutionary syndicates. The editor called these diverse groups to heel:

> It is of less importance for us to establish revolutionary unions than to develop the ideas and outlook of the unions already in existence ... Not by external criticism, but by working from within and by criticising from within we can obtain an influence over the strivings of these bodies. A union is not an Anarchist group ... A union views the worker as a producer and wage-slave to

the society of today: as tailor, shoemaker, carpenter, etc., and seeks to convince him that the sole means to the betterment of his economic conditions is the organisation – the union ... We have to reckon with the workers as they are and not as we would wish them to be. We have to work, work and work again to develop the present element.[14]

The unreality of the bourgeois position on Jewish socialism and the trade unions is heightened when the alien worker is viewed – not as an inert mass providing a passive target for left-wing evangelism – but as a group within which objective material conditions might generate specific proletarian reaction. Two dialectical dimensions are discernible. Firstly, as Mendelsohn has amply demonstrated, the strike movement among Jewish workers in the final quarter of the nineteenth century in Eastern Europe was very widespread.[15] Industrial development and experience of labour agitation was clearly acquired by many Jewish workers and imported to Britain by immigrants. This movement was perceived by *Arbeiter Freund* in 1903. Whereas the capitalist was able to exploit the imperfect class-consciousness of the first Jewish workers, many later comers were of a different stamp:

In Russia there has been great industrial development which has thrown thousands of Jewish proletarians into social wretchedness in the workshops and factories. A large fraction of today's immigrants are already more or less acquainted with the idea of a labour movement from their homeland, and, though their intellectual development is not very great, they nonetheless comprehend proletarian demands better and the necessity for organisation in the struggle.[16]

The second dimension of alien radicalisation was the outcome of English conditions experienced by immigrants owing no special political allegiances. The transition to a class-conscious worker was slow and difficult, especially outside London, where a great many former tailors turned into 'travellers'.[17] The necessary solvents were, nonetheless, at work. There could be no doubt, wrote *Arbeiter Freund* in 1908, that the conditions of the Jewish worker had altered greatly since the first immigrations:

The hard struggle for existence, the bitter disappointments of life, have gradually led him to the thought that his former hopes were, perhaps, after all, founded on false suppositions, and that it is impossible for him to throw up his work and create for himself new living conditions.[18]

There were no special conditions which would exempt the Leeds Jewish workers from those common to all Jewish workers. As 'Cohenovitz' put it in 1897:

If you stood on the street when the workers are at midday break, you would think that a graveyard had overturned and the dead were all going to their houses. You would see living skeletons, white faces, like a bag of skin and bones wrapped together in a couple of yards of cloth dragging itself slowly over the street. And that is the working class, the chief element of the Jews of Leeds.[19]

Under such conditions the intellectual level was low and the task awaiting the advanced workers clear. 'Cohenovitz' saw that the Leeds workshop – so far from being the well-spring of strong unionism – was actually a major disability:

I cannot say if it is an irony or accident that all Russian or other Jews who stand on a low moral plane have come together in Leeds, or if the hard battle of life, the blows of the iron, the noise of the machines and the driving of the masters deafen the brains in the heads of the workers; if it destroys their marrow and robs them of the power of thought.[20]

In the 1900s matters were no more propitious for unionisation. Bitter experience had simply been prolonged. As Arthur Hillman, the Leeds anarchist and union supporter, observed in 1905:

The dreadfully long working hours in the 'busy time' and the hunger in the 'slack time' do not merely occur in the East End of London ... You have it a thousand times worse in the provinces such as, for example, Leeds, Manchester, Liverpool or Glasgow.[21]

The Leeds tailors could claim some of the best men in the Jewish labour movement. Some, such as John Dyche and Jacob Caplan, were personages too large to be contained permanently in a provincial setting. For a Jewish union, however, there was a remarkable degree of continuity of leadership. Isaac Taylor, the lieutenant of Kemelhor in 1888, and the long-serving anarchist Louis Ellstein held high office in the various unions until the end of the period. The innovation of paid officials from 1895 also encouraged continuity. All these men were of the left, usually graduating from the anarchist ranks before moving into the camp of social democracy. In spite of diverse political tendencies, none would have accepted the view that, under contemporary economic arrangements, either accommodation with the masters or even social equilibrium was possible. Isaac Taylor's remarks in the debate of 1910 on the Trade Board illustrate how seasoned leaders might welcome legal methods without losing their radical outlook:

The next question is whether the present law is a good one. Will it destroy sweating? I will, firstly, state that, from a Liberal capitalist government, laws which are good for the workers are not to be expected ... As long as one person works for another, he will be sweated in order to make more profit. But, in the meantime, until the present system is overthrown, can we do nothing to help ourselves?[22]

That is not say that the political strife which enervated London Jewish unionism was lacking in Leeds. Anarchism against Zionism and practical trade unionism is exemplified in the following report in *Arbeiter Freund*:

It is high time I again wrote you something of our lovely city of Leeds. Let me first say a few words about our tailors. They established a fund within the union and did not know what to do with the money. They therefore called in Messrs 'R' and 'P'[23] to advise them. Both men are prominent Zionists and are certainly good advisers to the workers. That kind of progress will certainly make you smile, but don't be hasty – they are truly trade unionists and never forget practical work.[24]

Social democrats were, if anything, even harder on the Zionists, whose lecturers provided good sport. Of one Leeds lecture, the social democratic organ *Neue Tsait* reported:

He went out of his way to demonstrate that the Jews were already Socialists in ancient times. An example of this was that the Jewish prophets preached Socialism and love of humanity ... When asked why Elijah the Prophet had slaughtered 400 [sic] prophets who had differed from him on religion, he ignored the question.[25]

Mutual political regard between the major parties of the left was also no higher in Leeds. The 1904 programme for more union benefits and fewer strikes proposed by Louis Ellstein's social democratic brother, Saul, was anathema to anarchists, who could go so far as to demand that a union change its chairman weekly.[26] The report on the occasion of a speech by Saul Ellstein to the Leeds tailors shows how the parties were given to writing each other off:

Of the anticipated revolution in Leeds through the presence of the most important Jewish Anarchists a few years ago, nothing has resulted. The most important Anarchists have now gone away and the Anarchist Group is virtually non-existent for practical purposes.

The speech itself, however, points to the commonality between all Jewish workers – their condition and role in the alien–host interaction processes – and to the ultimate unity of outlook of Jewish worker-progressives of every shade. The tone is indistinguishable from that of the anarchists:

The speech by Comrade Ellstein on 'The Task of the Trade Unions', in which he showed us how the England of today has brought us fresh problems, also showed how these must be solved directly by the working class if the Jewish workers wanted to cease being the most degraded and insulted in society ... Stressing the need for the unions to take a broader interest in life, and to make the trade union – not merely a union of a certain trade in a struggle with a certain exploiter – but a labour organisation in battle for the liberation of the working class, his speech was greeted with great enthusiasm.[27]

It has often been assumed that, following the defeat of 1888, the tailors' union disappeared until 1893 – the year in which a continuous, independent union was founded. In her history of Leeds clothing, for example, Joan Thomas claimed that organisation among the Jewish workers did not reappear for several years.[28] Stewart and Hunter, the official historians of the tailoring unions, considered that no activity was pursued until 1893.[29] Before this year, however, the tailors had joined in broader labour movements in an experiment of profound importance.

After 1888 regrouping was difficult. One union was rapidly formed, and, as rapidly, it disappeared. In January 1889 an *Arbeiter Freund* commissioner found the tailors suffering terribly in the aftermath of the strike, but he was astonished, at the same time, at the great number of members, including English, of the Socialist Club.[30] The socialists, led by John Dyche and Lewis Frank, were taking the initiative, and on 6 January, the first amalgamated union was formed, Frank hoping that the new leaders 'would not be badly treated by the Society as they had been at the time of the strike'.[31] The determination of the masters to exploit their victory made recruitment difficult, whilst the factious situation at the end of the strike remained in evidence. A tailor complained that the quarrels among the socialists of Leeds were 'worse than the capitalist system itself', and that, if matters did not improve, all their efforts would be in vain.[32] Small as it must inevitably have been, the new union survived into late 1889, when the *Yorkshire Factory Times* named it as the only union in the wholesale industry.[33]

In November the socialists broke away, castigating the union as a scab organisation run for the sole benefit of the machiners. From a nucleus of 'forty-five honest tailors', led by Frank, there was a rapid enrolment of several hundred – not without anti-socialist disturbances.[34] Socialists were, nevertheless, pushing matters forward, and, by the end of 1889, high spirits were returning. Many 'fine speeches' were made to large gatherings, and education in elementary union principles was proceeding.[35] A Leeds speech by Prince

Kropotkin (who had many Leylands followers) delighted the tailors' future secretary, Sam Freedman, who informed *Arbeiter Freund* that, though he possessed only twopence, it had been worth far more to him.[36] To the individual worker, however, the survival efforts of the year 1889 brought no material benefit.

The union success of the year had been the June strike of the labourers, led by Maguire, Paylor and Sweeney, followed by the rapid establishment of a strong Leeds branch. In October, following the huge success of the London gasworkers in March, a Leeds branch had been formed, incorporating 'a bewildering variety of trades', including the labourers.[37] From June 1889 Maguire and Paylor played a leading role in the unionisation of the unskilled in the West Riding, and, by January 1890, the Jewish tailors had also been incorporated as a branch of the Gasworkers' and General Labourers' Union. Mrs Lerner considered that Jewish workers found it difficult to think of amalgamation with English unions which were opposed to immigration.[38] Such amalgamations did occur, however, where immediate stresses and the internationalist feeling immanent in socialism overrode disquiet on the immigration score. Further, though such amalgamations were frequently abortive, there is little to suggest that failure was due to simple anti-alien discord. The Leeds case is highly instructive. As has been noted, the local socialist leaders concerned with labour organisation were opponents of further immigration. Many Jewish tailors were on close personal terms with them despite this; largely through the joint socialist activity which was so hectic during 1888–90, with mixed-membership clubs and Jewish tailors joining the Socialist League in numbers in reaction to their defeat in 1888.[39]

Jacob Caplan's account, written in 1891, of this important but hitherto unregarded alliance was the first of many Yiddish documents – chiefly recriminatory – generated by its premature and controversial termination. It expresses clearly the Jewish motives in the early days:

The Leeds workers, who have had very strong unions since 1875 . . . have well and truly won for themselves the privilege of being enslaved from 8 a.m. to 8 p.m. . . . Enough blood and money have these regular hours cost these tailors! Enough people, who were inspired to open their bitter hearts, have fallen in these wars; and yet the end result of it all is that, until now, they have gained hardly anything . . . All this persisted until 1889, when there began to be found in Leeds people who cried with a loud voice that better times would and must come; and, if the Jewish worker could not help himself, then he must unite internationally and join with the Christian workers . . . The origins of this suggestion lay in the newly founded union of gasworkers, who, at that time, demonstrated such heroism in the battle for the eight-hour day ... Every sincere worker was inspired by the revolutionary spirit and held it as his duty to join with this union.

The alliance seemed not only a source of much-needed rejuvenation but also a method of neutralising anti-alien feeling among Leeds workers disinclined to stop and reason, in the way of modern scholars, that sweating antedated Jewish immigration by many decades:

> It was remarkable to consider the international feeling of Christians and Jews ... Instead of being met by sticks and stones and things of that kind as formerly, and being considered an enemy by the Christian workers, the Jews soon became quite another thing. They were soon regarded as friends because they were slaves to capitalism just like the Englishmen.[40]

The new situation produced a great wave of enthusiasm in the ranks of the tailors. Maguire, Paylor and Cockayne, the gasworkers' secretary, agitated ceaselessly, sharing their platforms with the great Jewish orator, Benjamin Fagenbaum, who exerted much influence over the movement.[41] To the Jewish masters, confrontation with Jewish workers backed by English forces was also novel, and there were grotesque reactions. One master, for example, proposed to his fellows that a petition be drawn up by 'men of substance' to the 'almighty Queen that all those who work to organise the workers in trade unions be driven out of England'.[42]

By May union membership had risen dramatically to over 900, and the tailors, by the scale of their part in the May Day Demonstration, had indicated their seriousness of purpose.[43] In the following month the gasworkers were tested as the Leeds Council sought to impose a four-month contract upon them. During the ensuing strike and the battles with police and troops a small group of machiners attempted to set up a rival union on religious lines. The stunning victory of the gasworkers, aided by Maguire, won over the majority of aliens, however. The long poles wielded so effectively in their battles by the gasworkers made a strong impression on the tailors. The anarchists preached unity:

> Workers of Leeds! Be united! Remember that your blooksuckers rejoice when they see you fighting amongst yourselves ... The labour question is a bread question, a stomach question, but never a religious question or a national question.[44]

Thus hardly had the gasworkers settled their own affairs with the Council when the Jewish tailoring trade, in which the masters had dictated terms since the general strike, was suddenly rocked by a 'revolt of the Israelites' hardly smaller in scale than that of 1888. The movement, according to the *Yorkshire Factory Times*, was against long hours, overcrowding, working on floors and being cooped up 'in attics and back tenements disgraceful for anyone either to work or live in'.[45] The central issue, however, was the masters' refusal to meet the old demand that those working from 7 a.m. to 8 p.m. should come into line with the machiners working one hour less. On 15 August, on the initiative of Jacob Caplan, a circular was sent to the masters, and, two days later, forty workshops were idle. Thirty masters capitulated immediately, but there remained problems with religious non-unionists. As it was reported to *Arbeiter Freund*:

> Nevertheless, there were still to be a number of sweaterish philosophers who reckoned to carry on the work through scabs, being quite aware that there are such sheep here who consider that their situation will only be bettered by the arrival of Moses riding on a donkey to drive them to the land of Israel.

The strike, in any event, ended in a rapid victory for the tailors, because

> the gas stokers with their long poles (who had been sent by the Gasworkers' Union to act as pickets) inspired such fear in the sweaters and their scabs that they found it to be more important to look after their bones.[46]

The gasworkers were soon again in action on the Jewish account, enforcing the new hours and acting against attempted victimisation of the leaders. Caplan relates that groups of gas stokers, sixty strong and armed with their poles, went the rounds of the Jewish shops which were under police protection:

> The police, who still remembered the flavour of the blows they had received in the last strike of the gasworkers, suddenly lost their desire to get beaten up in the protection of the capitalist beast, and they remained standing near the shops no longer than a flash ... And that's how the poles served the strike. Long live the poles – in the hands of the workers![47]

The contrast with 1888 was profound. On the masters' side, there was disunity and fear. Men working in shops where the new hours remained in dispute were offered jobs by masters honouring the agreement, and who were now in an uncompetitive position.[48] The boycott was not attempted, since it was known that this would encourage a visit from a band of 'armed' stokers. On the union side, the first result of the international alliance was a renewal of the almost forgotten taste of victory. Confidence returned and, from this year to 1912, there were few significant periods of tranquillity in the trade. A number of issues to become permanently contentious emerged during the episode with the gasworkers, and, with English union strength in their camp, the tailors initiated vigorous corrective action.

On the enforcement of agreements, the *Yorkshire Factory Times* warned the tailors to be watchful, as 'craft and cunning' would be used to impose the old hours.[49] For this, the sole remedy was the union shop, which the tailors began to enforce soon after the 1890 strike.[50] Action against driving was also initiated, and the incorrigible, their shops blocked, were driven out of business.[51] With the example of the swift achievement by the gasworkers of the eight-hour day before them, the union also launched into the general campaign, though they were not to obtain a significant reduction in hours until 1911. The campaign was given life by the extreme political wing of the union, despite the curious account of Jewish socialism standing in so many pages. Caplan's speech during the preparations for the Eight Hour Day Demonstration in October 1890 clarifies the anarchist approach to a practical union problem. Though the eight-hour day was 'a minor matter', the Jewish workers, stated Caplan, should participate 'in order to indicate their solidarity with their English brothers'. Apart from this:

the eight-hour day had a certain importance in itself, for it was better to be a poor man and work eight hours a day than to be the same poor man and work twelve to fifteen hours.[52]

Of enormous significance also was the opening in 1891 of the arduous campaign against piecework – a detested system which, equally, had to wait until 1911 for satisfactory settlement. In this connection, also, the anarchists can be seen at work on material problems, and even educating the still naive tailors. Caplan's warning to these tailors against piecework is highly illuminating:

The main topic of discussion in the Leeds tailors' union these days is the question of piecework. Until now we have all, with few exceptions, worked on a weekly basis, but it is clear that we have not become Rothschilds ... A slight difference has arisen between our workers and those of all the world. Whilst the latter, after much experiment, have concluded that, without the social revolution, nothing can help them, the Leeds Jewish workers still think that they can improve their position by the substitution of piecework for daywork. Do not forget that it will not be you who determine the piecework rates but your masters ... The prices will be very low and each man will seek to earn a living. What will he do? He will work his guts out labouring until fifteen o'clock. In short, he will do the work of two, and many will remain workless. These, however, wanting and having nothing to eat will destroy the prices, and your situation will be notably inferior to what it is now.[53]

Continuous action, backed by the gasworkers, occurred on one or other of these problems until late 1891. In October 1890, for example, non-union shops were attacked by crowds of workers who 'hooted and howled and broke windows'.[54] In June 1891 Paylor led negotiations in a number of disputes,[55] whilst the masters were 'showing more fight' and the piecework struggle was officially inaugurated.[56] The tailors appeared to have established themselves rapidly as a permanent branch of the English union – a triumph for Maguire in the control of alien industry. To the English socialists, indeed, such a conclusion appeared self-evident. *Commonweal* noted in June 1890 the remarkable enthusiasm and activity of 'our Jewish comrades in Leeds'.[57] Jewish tailors such as John Dyche were popular speakers at the meetings of the Socialist League.[58] At the gasworkers' Eight Hour Demonstration on Hunslet Moor in 1890 Cunninghame Graham, author of the abortive Eight Hours Bill of 1889, welcomed the tailors:

They were engaged in a class war and he rejoiced to hear that the foreign workers of Leeds had unanimously come forward and joined their union. That showed that they did not intend to be mere sojourners but were prepared to take their part in a struggle which was a bond of union between workers in almost all parts of the world.[59]

The impression of solidity was heightened by the action of Mahon, who, returning to Leeds in 1890 at the invitation of Maguire, was elected assistant secretary of the Yorkshire District of the Gasworkers in July 1891. Almost immediately he attempted to widen the movement to comprehend the Jewish workers of Manchester, London and Liverpool by organising a conference on 2 August to consider ways to abolish sweating. Cockayne, who, with Mahon, represented Leeds, pressed the predictable view that Jewish workers won more victories when combined with English unions, and a second conference was arranged.[60] In the same month an attempt by the masters to increase hours and reduce wages was successfully resisted.[61] In September two further disputes were won,[62], whilst September saw the tailors 'often in and out in the Leylands'.[63]

The conference and the industrial action of late 1891 were dying spasms, however; by the year's end the association with the gasworkers was virtually at an end. In a discussion of 1903 the *Jewish Chronicle* considered the cause of the rupture to have been that 'the quick-witted Jewish character could not brook the cumbrous and dilatory process of consulting the executive before the branch could take action'.[64] The reality was more complex. With their numerous branches of heterogeneous trades and occupations, the gasworkers could hardly have avoided a degree of centralisation, even at local level. The Jewish tailoring trade, with its peculiar arrangements, informal workshop arrangements, volatile demand for labour and the growing habit of ready striking, required speedier action than the English officials could supply. Thus the tailors grew increasingly impatient of delay, and the feeling grew that branch power was being lost to the executive.[65] Problems were reciprocal. To the English union the tailors appeared wild and unpractical, rather than racially different, in their approach. On one occasion the gasworkers were asked to provide 200 pickets for a period of three weeks at the Jewish workshops. The Jewish masters also had to be considered. In negotiation with the gasworkers' officials they 'bowed before them', yielded every point, then carried on as before. It was, observed the *Yorkshire Factory Times*, 'very hard to deal with such people'.[66]

These problems alone would hardly have sufficed to terminate a relationship so promising had they remained unmixed with political ingredients. At the May Day Demonstration of 1891 the anarchists had still been enthusastic:

The Jewish workers, for long sunk in the depths of dark fanaticism, are at last alive to their class consciousness. 'Workers of all countries, unite!' has also struck a chord in the hearts of the Jewish workers. Hand in hand with their English brothers, they marched out this Sunday to protest against the shameful exploitation which is being perpetrated against them.

But there was already a dark side: the demonstration was not as revolutionary as it had been before: 'not because the workers are more gentle, but because the leaders, the agitators, have become peaceful parliamentarians ... It makes one sick hearing them speak.'[67]

Caplan, the leader of a considerable body, began to discover confirmation of anarchist theory in the behaviour of the gasworkers' officials. The officers' wages had been 'raised to their hearts' content'. The right of the branch to protect its own members had been removed and replaced by the 'despotic rule' of the executive. The officers, fearing a reaction, had hastily amended the constitution so that a two-thirds majority of all the branches was required for their removal. A Jewish member had been expelled for accusing a gasworkers' secretary of drunkenness, and there were awkward questions concerning the disposal of monies raised through collections.[68] In a proper union, concluded Caplan, there ought to be weekly elections for office, for 'without leaders, there would be no misleaders'.[69]

As the anarchists and their followers tumbled out, after an appalling public scene between Caplan and Mahon,[70] John Dyche and his socialist group remained with the gasworkers. Enormous industry on the part of Maguire, Paylor and Mahon even produced a revival. In the heated atmosphere they were often in danger. The *Factory Times* describes a meeting they addressed at the Leylands Board School late in 1891, at which 'Jew after Jew spoke and chairs flew over their heads. Fists and boots were brought into play and forms were used.' Nevertheless, 'many prodigals' returned to the union, only to fall away by early 1892.[71]

It is evident from the recriminations still proceeding in the Yiddish press as late as 1896 that the final blow to the amalgamation came from a consensus arrived at beyond the anarchists alone, that there had indeed been some neglect of duties by the gasworkers' officials, and that the difficulty of removing them was widely felt to be irksome. According to his own account written some years later, Sam Freedman and many other socialists fought the leadership whilst attempting, vainly, to adhere to the principles of the union.[72]

The rupture produced profound gloom on both sides. So great was the disappointment on the Jewish side that, years later, Caplan was still defending himself against accusations of responsibility for the break.[73] On the English side, disappointment was mingled with exasperation. Midsummer found the tailors in deep distress. Unorganised, they faced an immediate counter-attack by the masters in the shape of a wage cut. On 24 June 500 workers struck[74] but were forced into submission within the week.[75] The *Factory Times* remorselessly rubbed in their situation. Having been members of the Gasworkers' Union, they were now in 'a very foolish and weak position'. They thought it useless to pay twopence a week 'when nothing was up'. The likelihood was that they wished 'they had remained under the leadership of Cockayne, Paylor and Co.'.[76] In its report for 1892 the Trades Council expressed regret that, where the Jewish tailor was concerned, 'no good results' had been achieved.[77] Leeds trade unionists could look back on some years of fruitless support of Jewish labour organisation. In 1893 – a year of heavy unemployment – attitudes stiffened. In February the Trades Council decided that 'it was a matter they could not ignore' when 'hundreds of Leeds girls had been standing idle', and passed a resolution against 'the continual influx of Jews'.[78] Two months later the Council of the Amalgamated Society of Tailors met in Leeds, where the complaint was made that the English tailors had received no advance on their Log of 1872, and that most Leeds firms were paying below this rate.[79] This event signalled a second attack by the Trades Council on the aliens, upon whom the blame was squarely laid.[80]

There was adverse publicity, too, from the more intimate English friends of the Jewish tailors, who had laboured hard and seen their apparent triumph dissolve away. The patient Maguire perceived that, at this stage of the industry's development, there was division of labour between the Christian and Jewish clothing workers, the latter tending to concentrate on the coat trade. Too much, he thought, was being made of the impact of the aliens and too little of the Englishman's capacity for reducing his own standard of living. Nevertheless, he thought,

> The Leeds alien is the helpless victim of the sweater and the unscrupulous employer, and, as such, he is a hindrance to trades unionism ... The Jews (an eminently unorganisable people in the absence of a Moses) are therefore reduced to terrible straits.[81]

The disappointment of the general public was also expressed in a series of more or less virulent letters to the press extending throughout most of 1893. Writers less thoughtful than Maguire saw the alien – rather than the slump – as the cause of the prevalent unemployment and low wages, complaining that the Jews refused to join a union and ignored 'the legitimate claims of labour upon capital'.[82]

The sensitive situation of the tailors within the hostile environment generated by their secession from the gasworkers, and by the subsequent slump, was aggravated by the 'deep distress' within the alien community recorded by the Jewish Guardians in 1893.[83] Adverse long-term changes were already being detected in the Jewish tailoring trade. As early as 1891 Caplan had noted that, whereas losing one's job had once meant no more than switching from one shop to another, it now meant 'an indefinite period of idleness because there are more hands than are needed'.[84]

The rapid reorganisation, in 1893, of an independent Jewish union occasions little surprise. The new union, The Leeds Jewish Tailors, Pressers and Machinists, maintained a continuous existence until its absorption into the National Union of Tailors and Garment Workers in 1915. Such continuity was unique in the history of Jewish labour, and much has been made of it by writers in support of 'special' theories of Leeds tailoring. There is, indeed, some temptation, in the context of the Jewish movement, to equate continuity with a steady accession of strength; but close consideration of the final two decades of the period reveals merely an intensification of the arduous battles of the early years, and a discouraging background of slump with a deterioration of conditions in the alien trade. Union gains were, therefore, fitful, limited and often subsequently lost. These points are reflected in the volatile levels of membership. Following the devastation in the wake of the parting from the gasworkers, it was with great difficulty that 200 could be enrolled by 1893.[85] Two years later, in the reaction to the anti-immigration resolution of the T.U.C., membership leapt to 1,000.[86] Sixteen years later, this figure had not yet been exceeded (though it had risen to 1,250 in 1901 and fallen to 700 in 1904) and it was not until 1913, under the influence of the Trade Boards for wholesale clothing, that the union could begin to count its members in thousands.[87]

Much had been derived from past experience which was to lend strength in a bleak environment. Mass action was never again undertaken unless provoked by a general lockout, as in 1911. Strikes were prepared more carefully, and every effort was made to limit their scale to individual shops or groups of shops. Paid secretaries were a steadying influence. Of Sam Freedman – appointed in 1895 – the *Factory Times* wrote on his tenth anniversary in office:

> He is not a demagogue. He does not enter into long diatribes and orations. He is a calm, business trade union secretary and best serves the cause by that policy ... When Sam became general secretary the union became more stable and less liable to fluctuations.[88]

The impression given here is of an era of 'responsible' trade unionism. The union had certainly acquired knowledge of English procedures by 1895, and in 1906 it was to engage an official of the Amalgamated Engineers in the person of Moses Sclare, who was at ease in the highest counsels of the T.U.C. Union routine was more regular and policy more deliberate. Study of the internal tensions of the union, however, especially in the Yiddish sources in which they were most completely exposed, and of the ceaseless workshop conflict, points to the conclusion that the final years constituted an epoch of undiminished militancy and political strife. The threat to the union posed by the profound political divisions was neutralised only by the increasing requirement of unity against the masters and the continuing anti-alien manifestations of the later period. The copious debate emanating from Leeds in the 1890s shows why the union remained poised between 'responsibility' and revolutionary militancy. The latter tendency was, perhaps, best expressed by a Leeds worker in 1895:

When many people feel a certain oppression, people who have insufficient to eat ... at a time when they work to the limit of their strength, people whose honour and finer feelings are trampled beneath the feet of an ignorant sweater, they come together to discuss the bitterness of their hearts and follow this by uniting to find ways and means of ridding themselves of their troubles. This is what a trade union should be, but, unfortunately, this is not what it is.

Within the union, instead of attention to the real problems – capital, competition and machinery –

Ceremony follows ceremony. Straight away, there is a stream of 'propositions' and 'seconders' and 'supporters' and 'Mr Chairman' ... If, perchance, one forgets to say 'Mr Chairman', one has already broken a rule ... Books of rules are written just for their own security.[89]

In opposition to this, there was no quarrel as to the three sources of the worker's troubles, but, in other respects, Leeds Jewish workers had learned the need for discipline. As one respondent expressed it:

I see nothing wrong in the act of saying 'Mr Chairman'. If there are simple people who know nothing of trade unionism, is it not a way to teach them more respect for the union by showing respect for the leaders? ... What the honour of being chairman means is quite familiar to us. He has to put up with the many false arguments ... and, afterwards, he gets boycotted from his work whilst his own union fails to stand up for him.[90]

Another cross-current of importance, since the most capable men were involved, was the deepening division between anarchists and social democrats. By 1893 political workers who had once seen fit to share the same club had drifted poles apart. Caplan's denunciation of the social democrats in that year makes this clear:

People ... travel to conferences paid with hard-earned pennies from the labour unions to represent the workers' interests and all they do in the end is to make a place for their lowly intrigues. Such goings-on are pursued by the Parliamentary Social Democrats in the eyes of thinking people, and it is impossible not to accuse them of parasitism and swindling ... We do not see any difference between a Liebknecht and a Gladstone, between a Bebel and a Balfour.[91]

Thus the union remained a hybrid. On the side of organisation, the anarchist influence was apparent in the 1896 decision to elect officers biannually and to appoint a council of delegates from every workplace to oversee the executive.[92] Men of the extreme left such as Isaac Taylor and Louis Ellstein held office and many were Trades Council delegates.

On the other hand, reports indicate that the tailors welcomed lecturers of every persuasion. In its industrial outlook the union hesitated between its old ambition to eliminate the masters, and piecemeal gradual gains.

Interaction with English labour remained as significant as the work for economic gains during the independent years. In spite of the failures under English leadership, the union intensified its identification with the English working class. As the latter came to realise that at least one group of Jewish workers was determined to disprove the general theory of alien unorganisability, there was a ready response. Modest in size and in gains, the union nevertheless delighted friendly English interests by its continuity, especially where, as the roll-call of a Jewish labour conference in 1901 indicated, there were 10,000 Jews in the London wholesale clothing trade, and only 120 organised.[93] Of national figures, Mahon, whose valediction in the split with his union in 1891 had been 'We reckon we are going to have no more to do with you Jews,'[94] was being welcomed back as lecturer and agitator by 1895.[95] James Sweeney, their former secretary, also reappears in union reports of this period as a welcome speaker and lecturer, whilst the Trades Council signalled a *rapprochement* by joining in the union's programme for education in trade unionism.[96]

These reappearances were not random events. With the upturn in industrial output from 1895, union activity quickened. In 1896 there was a series of violent strikes for limitation of Sunday hours and against sackings in the slack season.[97] These brought the comment from the *Factory Times* that 'the Jewish tailors, with Dyche, Freedman and Ellstein, are active at all hours'.[98] It was not until its first major crisis in the following year, however, that the new union established its firm reputation. During a series of minor actions against piecework in certain shops[99] the masters threatened a general lockout on 2 March with the intention of imposing the system throughout the trade.

With the return of heavy unemployment in the trade that year, conditions for resistance were at their worst. 'Privation, want, and the persecution of the sweater,' observed the *Jewish Chronicle*, were still prevalent in Leeds.[100] This was no empty rhetoric. In January the union was organising special collections for distressed members. Many had been reduced to working in the dreaded Jewish bakeries, where the union vowed to do everything possible 'to see that they should not be so sweated eighteen hours a day for such tiny wages'.[101] Women's competition was increasing. Of the immigrant girls, Louis Ellstein wrote that all but 2 per cent had entered the trade, and that many had become 'fully fledged tailoresses' capable of doing hand-made clothing as well as the men. In the English warehouses, he claimed, thousands of suits were made entirely by women as adept as men in all classes of work but earning far less.[102]

The response of the tailors – that they stood ready to strike against piecework – was thus courageous in the extreme.[103] At this, the masters withdrew their collective notice. Piecework, however, had already entered into a large number of workplaces,[104] and the union went on to an immediate offensive aimed at its total abolition. The campaign marks a major turning point in the evolution of the union and its methods. The leading proponents of the action were the socialist Brandstein and the anarchist Ellstein, at a meeting on 6 March 1897. They were closely supported by Sweeney and Arthur Shaw, the Trades Council president. A new system was carefully applied. Offending workshops were struck piecemeal. Each separate group of strikers was taken in hand, instructed as to procedure, and paid five days' wages whilst out of work. To protect funds, a special dispute levy of sixpence per week was imposed on members at work.[105] Such well ordered methods were unknown in Jewish labour movements, and they proved to be of great significance for the Leeds union. In the 1897 piecework campaign it established its authenticity and its claim to the permanent loyalty of a nucleus of significant size – the real basis of its unique continuity in later years.

Whilst the campaign marked a procedural point of departure, in action no new attitudes on the part of the protagonists are discernible. The year may, rather, be regarded as inaugurating a bitter industrial warfare extending almost to the outbreak of the Great War. Early in the campaign the union decided – not merely to abolish piecework – but that 'those shops which operated piecework should be done away with'.[106] Many stubborn masters were thus put out of business. At the same time, some warehouses, exasperated by the incessant disorders in the Jewish branch, offered their work to the union, which promptly opened up two co-operative workshops.[107] Again unsuccessful in the long run, this gesture was a clear indication to the masters that the vision of the earlier unions had not faded. The piecework issue merely sharpened the focus of the class struggle, causing the tailors to reject suggestions of co-operation with the masters against the large firms in pursuit of better making-up prices. On this question, *Arbeiter Freund* warned at the opening of the campaign:

The Leeds tailors ... are informed that there is a dividing wall between their interests and those of the sweaters ... They should know that the boundary between the two classes is sharply drawn and that the struggle must be radical, direct![108]

The attitude was not confined to the Left. The centrist *Yiddisher Ekspres* also fulminated against the evils of piecework, advising that it was for the masters alone to obtain better prices, 'instead of fighting the workers'.[109]

A neglected, but supremely important, aspect of the new union is the impact made on the world of English labour – a process dating precisely from the events of 1897. The movement, so far as the aliens and immigration were concerned, was timely in the extreme. The new union had already reacted to the anti-alien resolution of the T.U.C. in 1895 by attempting to set up a federation of all the Jewish unions of Britain, and by exploiting the dawning favour of the Leeds Trades Council and the Independent Labour Party. Two years after its own resolution on the same theme, the council president, Arthur Shaw, voiced good Liberal sentiments in his disagreement with those of the T.U.C. As long as the aliens joined a union, said Shaw, there was no desire to restrict immigration.[110] In the wake of its resolution in 1895, however, the T.U.C. had sent a deputation to the Home Secretary, who announced that the government were 'certainly determined to legislate' against further immigration.[111] Lord Salisbury confirmed these words, and the Queen's Speech in February 1896 included reference to such legislation.[112] The Leeds union again took the initiative in a renewed federation effort at the end of the same year – a failure owing to the chaotic state of the London unions.[113]

With complete organisational failure in the chief centre of Jewish labour, the Leeds union became the sole repository of whatever good name the Jewish worker might earn in Britain, against so hostile a background. That this responsibility – so self-evidently and successfully taken up by the union – has attracted no attention occasions small surprise in an immigration literature whose concept of 'alien defence' is the state of preparedness of the Jewish bourgeoisie to 'receive' the alien, and which assigns no class role to Jewish unions, but treats them merely as transient and insignificant curiosities.

The front line of battle was paramount. Early in the 1897 struggle the *Yorkshire Factory Times* noted that the tailors were 'fighting a good fight'.[114] The tailors did not suffer either when the same paper, with its circulation in the heavy north-country concentration of English workers, made a hero of a Jewish leader, David Policoff, on his one-month goal sentence for intimidation during serious rioting against scabs.[115] Its opinion later in the same year, that the Jews had 'furnished the Gentiles one example in combination, and another useful point in the abolition of that pernicious system, piecework', was at once startling in view of the subject and calculated to impress English workers deeply.[116] By September the paper was able to announce that the tailors had 'won hands down', obtaining agreements on the closed shop, weekly payment of wages, free entry to workshops by union officers, and the withdrawal of legal cases by the masters. The men obeyed Sam Freedman's orders 'with the nicety of a well-drilled army', and sick, dispute and accident pay were established features of the union.[117] Before the same month, the whole executive of a delighted Trades Council had appeared at a union meeting to congratulate them on their success.[118]

The final years brought the test of further anti-alien crises, culminating in the Aliens Act of 1905. Settled aliens also required means of social survival and signs of acceptance by the host community despite the odd minimisation, in certain places, of the enormous dangers to the Jewish worker emerging in British society in the 1900s.[119] These are apparent not merely in the *Judenhetz* associated with the Royal Commission and the Aliens Act but in the sinister mass demonstrations of the English unemployed in 1908, and in the hysteria generated against anarchism by the assassination of President McKinley in 1902 and the Siege of Sidney Street in 1911.

Across these years, and the events which brought no rest to the alien tailor, the bitter class struggle was closely interwoven with a deepening relationship with the English workers, resulting in the 'normalisation' of the position of the Leeds union, and its full acceptance by English labour. The process is clearly discernible in the pages of the *Factory Times*. 'Mr Freedman and his union,' it observed in 1899, 'work well with the other unions of Leeds.' Two years later came the open acknowledgement that 'the alien Jew, when once he embraces the principles of trade unionism, is one of the staunchest adherents to its principles' – the precursor of similar testimony in 1904, 1906 and 1908.[120] In 1903 the paper crossed swords with the Trades Council when there occurred the omission to inform the Aliens Commission that its anti-alien resolution had been passed a whole decade before.[121] It pointed out that since the resolution much had taken place. The Jews had 'one of the strongest, one of the most prosperous, and one of the most philanthropic of Leeds unions'. It therefore warned the English workers not to approve an Aliens Act which would 'not keep out the German-Jewish financier' who would 'drain the workers dry'. The Jewish tailor, on the other hand, was to be regarded in quite a different light. He was 'a man' and 'was not as easily sat on as he used to be'.[122]

The Jewish tailors were far from passive in the formation of these altered views. They clung to the Trades Council in spite of the affront of 1903, affirming that they would 'show themselves disciplined trade unionists'.[123] In the same year news of their progress from a Leeds delegate caused the failure of a motion against immigration at the Independent Labour Party Conference.[124] To the rival craft tailors of the Amalgamated Society, the 'grimy aliens' of 1899 had become the acknowledged leaders of tailoring labour organisation by 1903.[125] Whilst no other Jewish union, as the *Chronicle* complained, felt it worth while to attend the annual Trades Union Congress, the Leeds tailors were regularly represented by their paid secretaries. Freedman was active on committees against homework, and influential in persuading the Congress to pass a resolution in 1902 in favour of a reduced naturalisation fee for aliens with trade union membership of five years. At the Leeds Congress of 1904 meetings were held at the tailors' club, where many delegates might see the work of the union. Moses Sclare, considering the relatively small scale of his union, played a prominent role in the T.U.C., leading a deputation which included Will Thorne to the Home Secretary on the homework question.[126] The Leeds Jewish Tailors' Union also joined the General Federation of Trade Unions in 1899, being the sole Jewish body to do so; whilst solidarity with English unions was also expressed in a long list of contributions to strike funds. The outlook of the Leeds union is supremely epitomised by Sam Freedman's angry letter to the *Jewish Chronicle* in 1900, when that journal had carried an advertisement for blackleg labour in a Dublin strike:

When we have tried our best to organise ourselves and succeeded in coming into nearer relationships with the English workers, you come out with such advertisements, trying to make the Jews into blacklegs.[127]

In 1903 *Arbeiter Freund* enjoined:

The Jewish worker has a double interest in uniting himself with his comrades-in-suffering in powerful organisations: firstly, to defend his material existence, and, secondly, to avoid arousing the hatred and detestation of his English class-comrades.[128]

It is clear, however, that by the time this was written the Leeds tailors had gone far towards the fulfilment of these dual responsibilities, which lay uniquely upon the alien worker.

The material gains of the 1900s were meagre. The widespread dissolution of the alien sector of the trade into smaller units, the severe unemployment even in periods of normal trade, falling prices and the immense distress of the major slumps, together constituted a strong tide against which the union expended much strength for little more than survival. That they were 'no worse off despite bad trade, emigration of large numbers of their members, and a heavy drain on their funds', was a matter of congratulation by the *Yorkshire Factory Times* in 1909.[129] Isaac Taylor, arguing for participation in the Trade Boards in 1910, presented further good reasons for the desperate situation of his union:

What chance have we trade unions of improving our position when so many workers do not want to hear of our demands? They never come to us and we have no chance of organising them. Do you know why the tailors, machiners and pressers of Leeds, London and Manchester are unable to get work direct from the warehouses? Some say, because they are Jews, but that is not true. It is because, in Leeds alone, 20,000 women and girls . . . are working for a wage of 4s 0d and 5s 0d a week . . . The Leeds Trades Council has declared that the women in the tailoring trade are working for a penny an hour, and I am of the opinion that, as long as we remain unorganised, we cannot get what we seek because of the terrible competition of the women, who will never in this life organise themselves.[130]

Under such conditions the struggle was intensified, and the 1900s may well be regarded as an Age of Strife in which, with few intervals of significance, industrial action was a normal state of affairs. The issues arising during these years demonstrate the exasperating difficulties besetting the union, and account for its slow progress. Questions apparently settled recur in later disputes as if devoid of previous history. Thus strikes against piecework recurred in 1899, 1900 and 1908, despite the nineteenth-century struggles on this score, whilst the matter survived to haunt the major settlement occurring in 1911. Similarly, 'settlements' on sub-contracting, the closed shop and working hours – many made before 1900 – by their recrudescence were clearly impossible to enforce on a permanent basis.

With the replacement of Freedman by Sclare in 1906, a wave of militancy spread through the union, and subcontracting became the object of a new campaign. The wave of strikes in 1906–07 was described by the *Jewish Chronicle* as 'an epidemic of strike fever' in which 'harmony was looked upon as a monotonous state of affairs'.[131] The masters reacted by forming a new Master Tailors' Union of 100 members,[132] and by 1908 they were actively spreading both the piecework and subcontracting systems widely.[133] Thus the hopes of the *Jewish Chronicle* for 'the end of bad feeling', so often expressed, went unfulfilled.[134] As the *Yorkshire Evening News* pointed out, piecework had earlier been practically abolished.[135]

Other polarising forces were at work. Whilst the union struggled with old problems, it had in some other respects paradoxically advanced its control. This was particularly true of what Jewish circles named the 'compulsory labour system', under which the union claimed to have a say in the dismissal of their members. Secondly, as the Trade Boards Act came before the Commons both sides prepared for the revolution of State intervention on wages, and sought to strengthen their organisation. The union organised demonstrations against their conditions, with wholesale propaganda against the masters, and, for the first time, succeeded in 1910 in effecting a stable federation of Jewish unions outside London.[136] The masters, for their part, extended the scope of their association to include trousers and vest makers as well as coat makers, to ensure proper 'representation upon the Boards to safeguard their interests'.[137]

Though Sclare was appointed to the National Board for Tailoring in 1910,[138] he had already placed before his union late in 1909 the plan for 'a drive for better conditions'. Under this, not only piecework but daywork was to be replaced by uniform hourly rates, since 'hundreds of different rates' were being paid under daywork. Hours, too, were still irregular, and the working day of 6 a.m. to 10 p.m. was not uncommon.[139] These demands produced such a wave of strikes throughout 1910 that, early in 1911, the masters decided upon a final stand, declaring a general lockout.[140]

Arbeiter Freund described the ensuing struggle, correctly, as 'the most important battle in Jewish trade union history'.[141] Its settlement under arbitration represents the summit of the union's achievements before incorporation into the National Union of 1915. Under its terms, 'compulsory labour' was abolished. Workers were not to be victimised for being union members. Piecework was to be the subject of an agreed Log Statement and yield wages no lower than could be earned on a time basis. Internal subcontracting was abolished, and working hours were to be reduced by stages to nine per day by 1 January 1912.[142] It had, in effect, required thirty-five years of struggle before the Jewish hours approached parity with those of the English trade.

From these gains to the end of the period, the union's stature increased. Its *Report* for 1913 was described by the *Jewish Chronicle* as 'a comparative *résumé* of the activities, not only of the central organisation in Leeds, but also of the Trade Union movement throughout the Jewish tailoring industry in the Midlands and in the North'. It was 'a remarkable record for a Jewish Trade Union to have a continuous existence of twenty-one years'.[143]

That remarkable continuity, it has been suggested, was not the consequence of any capitalist 'gift' of specially favourable conditions in the Leeds trade; on the contrary, it has been viewed as a class response to harsh and deteriorating economic circumstances. Close appraisal of the class interaction between Jewish master and worker not only contradicts the optimistic conclusions so widely canvassed concerning Leeds but amply demonstrates that the paradox existing between the bitter battles of the tailors and their 'favourable' environment is entirely illusory. The apprehension of the master as a class enemy, and the reactions of the unions – inasmuch as they were conditioned by external criticism from the host society – were based on the reality that much of that criticism was only too appropriate. It has been shown, through an examination of the *dialectical* processes in the tailoring industry, that much of the exoneration of the aliens from charges associated with their industrial impact is misplaced; and that many of the charges made by Englishmen were entirely rational. Thus the achievements of the Leeds tailors – limited as they were – were the fruit of a more arduous struggle than might be supposed necessary, given the conventionally favourable picture of their industry; and their eventual reputation in the English labour movement formed a contribution to the alien movement of incalculable value.

NOTES

1 *J.C.*, 17 January 1911.
2 *Ibid.*, 8 February 1907.
3 Gainer, *Alien Invasion*, p. 96.
4 Parkes, 'Anglo-Jewish community', pp. 49–50.
5 *Committee on the Truck Acts*, q. 5950.
6 *J.C.*, 8 February 1907.
7 *Aliens Commission*, q. 14111.
8 Lerner, 'Jewish immigration', p. 14.
9 *A.F.*, 23 October 1908.
10 *Ibid.*, 31 January 1896.

11 Gainer, *Alien Invasion*, p. 101.
12 *Ibid.*, p. 30.
13 Gartner, *Jewish Immigrant*, p. 138.
14 *A.F.*, 25 September 1908.
15 Mendelsohn, *Class Struggle*, pp. 82–115.
16 *A.F.*, 10 July 1903.
17 *Ibid.*, 23 October 1908.
18 *Ibid.*
19 *D.Y.E.*, 5 November 1897.
20 *Ibid.*
21 *A.F.*, 6 October 1905.
22 *Ibid.*, 14 January 1910.
23 P. M. Raskin, the Jewish Inspector of Nuisances, and David Policoff, union leader, former radical turned Zionist.
24 *A.F.*, 6 November 1903.
25 *Neue Tsait*, 3 June 1904.
26 *Ibid.*, 1 July 1904.
27 *Ibid.*, 14 October 1904.
28 J. Thomas, 'A history of the Leeds clothing industry', *Yorkshire Bulletin*, Occasional Paper, I, 1955, p. 30.
29 M. Stewart and L. Hunter, *The Needle is Threaded*, London, 1964, p. 118.
30 *A.F.*, 18 January 1889.
31 *Ibid.*, 25 January 1889.
32 *Ibid.*, 12 April, 5 July, 12 July 1889.
33 *Y.F.T.*, 6 September 1889.
34 *A.F.*, 29 November 1889.
35 *Ibid.*, 13 December 1889.
36 *Ibid.*, 20 December 1889.
37 H. A. Clegg, *General Union in a Changing Society*, Oxford, 1964, pp. 11–13.
38 Lerner, *Breakaway Unions*, p. 90.
39 *Commonweal*, 26 June 1888.
40 *A.F.*, 11 December 1891.
41 *Ibid.*, 21 March 1890.
42 *Ibid.*, 2 May 1890.
43 *Y.F.T.*, 9 May 1890; *A.F.*, 9 May 1890.
44 *A.F.*, 27 June 1890.
45 *Y.F.T.*, 29 August 1890.
46 *A.F.*, 29 August 1890.
47 *Ibid.*, 5 September 1890.
48 *Y.F.T.*, 5 September 1890.
49 *Ibid.*, 29 August 1890.
50 *A.F.*, 19 September 1890.
51 *Ibid.*, 17 October 1890.
52 *Ibid.*
53 *Ibid.*, 3 April 1891.
54 *Y.F.T.*, 31 October 1890.

55 *Ibid.*, 19 June 1891.
56 *Ibid.*, 26 June 1891.
57 *Commonweal*, 28 June 1890.
58 *Ibid.*, 6 September 1890.
59 *Labour World*, 1 November 1890.
60 *The Workman's Times*, 7 August 1891.
61 *Y.F.T.*, 14 August 1891.
62 *Ibid.*, 25 September 1891.
63 *Ibid.*, 30 October 1891.
64 *J.C.*, 17 June 1903.
65 *A.F.*, 11 December 1891.
66 *Y.F.T.*, 24 October 1890.
67 *A.F.*, 8 May 1891.
68 *Ibid.*, 11 December 1891.
69 Caplan's pun on the Yiddish words *fiehrer* and *euberfiehrer*. *Ibid.*, 25 December 1891.
70 *Ibid.*
71 *Y.F.T.*, 18 December 1891; 8 April 1892.
72 *A.F.*, 21 August 1896.
73 See, for example, *ibid.*, 1 September 1893; 31 July 1896.
74 *Y.P.*, 24 June 1892.
75 *Report on Strikes, 1892*, P.P. 1894, LXXXI, pt i, C 7403, p. 216.
76 *Y.F.T.*, 1 July 1892.
72 *Ibid.*, 8 July 1892.
78 *Ibid.*, 8 February 1893.
79 *L.W.E.*, 22 April 1893.
80 *Ibid.*, 6 May 1893.
81 *Labour Chronicle*, 6 May 1893.
82 See, for example, *L.W.E.*, 7–21 January, 18–25 February, 4 March, 21 October 1893.
83 *Annual Report of the Leeds Jewish Board of Guardians, 1893*.
84 *A.F.*, 9 October 1891.
85 *Ibid.*, 26 April 1901.
86 *Y.F.T.*, 13 December 1895.
87 *J.C.*, 27 January 1911; *Report of the Registrar of Friendly Societies, 1913*, P.P. 1915, LXXVI, 121–iii, pt C, p. 61.
88 *Y.F.T.*, 28 April 1905.
89 *A.F.*, 15 November 1895.
90 *Ibid.*, 29 November 1895.
91 *Ibid.*, 1 September 1893.
92 *D.Y.E.*, 22 January 1897.
93 *A.F.*, 17 April 1901.
94 *Ibid.*, 1 September 1893.
95 *Ibid.*, 27 December 1895.
96 *D.Y.E.*, 4 December 1896; *A.F.*, 8 May 1896.
97 *Y.F.T.*, 1 May 1896; *D.Y.E.*, 18 December 1896; *A.F.*, 23 October 1896.
98 *Y.F.T.*, 4 December 1896.

99   *D.Y.E.*, 5 March, 26 March, 2 April 1897.
100 *J.C.*, 5 March 1897.
101 *D.Y.E.*, 15 January 1897.
102 *A.F.*, 4 September 1896.
103 *D.Y.E.*, 5 March 1897.
104 *L.W.E.*, 6 March 1897.
105 *A.F.*, 12 March 1897.
106 *D.Y.E.*, 12 March 1897.
107 *Ibid.*, 26 March, 16–30 April 1897.
108 *A.F.*, 5 March 1897.
109 *D.Y.E.*, 16 April 1897.
110 *Leeds Mercury*, 9 September 1895.
111 *The Times*, 6 February 1896.
112 *The Standard*, 30 March 1896; *The Times*, 30 July 1896.
113 *D.Y.E.*, 27 November 1896.
114 *Y.F.T.*, 26 March 1897.
115 *Ibid.*, 16 April 1897.
116 *Ibid.*, 23 July 1897.
117 *Ibid.*, 3 September 1897.
118 *D.Y.E.*, 9 July 1897.
119 See, for example, Parkes, 'Anglo-Jewish community', pp. 49–50, where this complex phenomenon is narrowed down to nothing more than the reactions of poverty-line English neighbours of the aliens.
120 *Y.F.T.*, 8 December 1899, 30 August 1901, 25 March 1904, 20 June 1906, 14 August 1908.
121 *Aliens Commission*, q. 14998.
122 *Y.F.T.*, 3 April 1903, 25 March, 29 April 1904.
123 *J.C.*, 10 April 1903.
124 *Y.F.T.*, 17 April 1903.
125 *Journal of the A.S. of T.*, September, 1899, p. 119; September, 1903, p. 67.
126 *J.C.*, 9 May 1913.
127 Quoted in *Y.F.T.*, 25 May 1900.
128 *A.F.*, 10 July 1903.
129 *Y.F.T.*, 25 February 1909.
130 *A.F.*, 14 January 1910.
131 *J.C.*, 9 November 1906, 31 May 1907.
132 *Report of the Registrar of Friendly Societies, 1911*, P.P. 1912–13, LXXXI, 123-xv, pt C, p. 58.
133 *A.F.*, 24 January 1908.
134 *J.C.*, 10 May 1907, 18 December 1908, 21 May 1909, 18 February 1910.
135 *Y.E.N.*, 16 January 1908.
136 *J.C.*, 1 May 1908; *A.F.*, 8 April 1910.
137 *J.C.*, 1 July 1910.
138 *Y.F.T.*, 22 December 1910.
139 *A.F.*, 22 October 1909.
140 *Y.E.N.*, 27 February 1911.

141 *A.F.*, 3 March 1911.
142 *Ibid.*, 14 April 1911.
143 *J.C.*, 1 May 1914.

Chapter 5

THE ALIEN SLIPPER TRADE: A STUDY IN HEROISM AND DECAY

As an immigrant occupation, footwear ranked second only to tailoring. The typical Leeds alien footwear worker was to be found in the slipper trade where his impact on the native workers was to have undesirable repercussions on the immigration movement as a whole. It is barely surprising, therefore, that the apologist historiography pervading recent work on immigrant industry has awarded the subject scant treatment. Similarly, models of alien economy which, in their typical eclecticism, convey images of classless serenity in alien communities, are unable to accommodate either the slipper-man victim of the sweated capitalist order at the extremity of its anarchy, or the intra-ethnic struggle which was its dialectical counterpart. Gartner, typically, allows the trade little significance in the Leeds context, dating its appearance as 'early in the present century', and eliminating at a stroke two decades of industrial history, working-class struggle and the pernicious influence it had exerted upon the alien movement well before 1900.[1] As early as 1884, in fact, it was noted in Leeeds that the aliens were turning from trafficking to manufacture, and that hundreds had entered the local footwear industry. A union had also been formed to fight the 'long hours and small wages'.[2]

During the early years of the period Leeds was arguably the largest leather town of the kingdom. In 1870 it housed no fewer than thirty-four tanneries, 700 shoemakers and 100 boot and shoe manufacturers. The labour force in that year was 5,000 strong, increasing to 11,500 by 1893.[3] Despite this, the footwear manufacture was in a condition of long-term decline, from 144 firms in 1886 to fifty-four in 1911. Jews were not prominent in this branch. Directories list nine recognisable names in 1886 and a mere three in 1911. The slipper manufacture was always secondary to the town's boot and shoe trade. In 1882 twenty firms are listed, rising to a peak by 1904, when thirty-eight names appear, followed by a decline to twenty-one in 1911. In this branch, however, Jewish names were more prominent from the 1880s; whilst, from 1900 to the end of the period, all listed slipper manufacturers bear Jewish names.

The stage of development reached by footwear manufacture at the commencement of Jewish immigration rendered it prone to incursion. Whereas machinery had been applied only in the closing and attachment processes before the 1880s, it spread more widely from this time to the early twentieth century. As in tailoring, the machine laid the foundations of subdivision of labour. Mechanisation was slow and uneven, however, and, where it was still considered uneconomical, outdoor hand manufacture persisted. During the 1880s, and contemporaneous with the first immigrant waves on a large scale, there remained a number of processes — notably lasting and finishing — which were highly amenable to the handwork system of the alien team. This form could be no more than interim, however, since, by the mid-1890s, lasting and finishing machinery had been introduced. By the turn of the century machinery had also been applied to welting and nailing. Mechanisation signposted a predictable concentration of capital, and firms of up to 200 workers became more common.

The disturbing experience of mechanisation created predictable distress. The labour supply, already swollen by the employment of juveniles, and by an influx of the rural unemployed, was further augmented by the facility with which machinery allowed the trade to be learned. The supply of footwear masters also rose rapidly in the 1870s and 1880s as English workmen demonstrated, by crowding into the trade, that entrepreneurship ambitions were no monopoly of the aliens. Equally predictable were the cheapening of products and declining profit margins. Manufacturers sought cost reductions by the substitution of capital for labour, or, in appropriate circumstances, by the employment of ever-cheaper labour in the form of the outworker. In many cases, therefore, market conditions generated a counter-tendency towards the domestic system. Relations between the outwork sector and the wholesale firms closely paralleled those in the Leeds tailoring industry. The supply of work was irregular, and the burden of the seasonal and other cycles was borne by the outworker. Bribing and tipping were required to ensure a supply of work. Footwear was cut indoors and sent out for completion, in which processes the outworker often employed his own family.[4]

In sum, the dawn of Jewish immigration saw the industry in a classic Marxian state. Owing to the catalyst of mechanisation, writes Marx:

England is at present experiencing ... the conversion of manufacture, of handicrafts, and of domestic work into the factory system, after each of these forms of production, totally changed and disorganised under the influence of modern industry, has long ago reproduced, and even overdone, all the horrors of the factory system, without participating in any of the elements of social progress it contains.[5]

The pattern of alien participation in the Leeds slipper trade was far from uniform. Garrard considers that the alien tended to delay the introduction of the factory system,[6] but it is clear that, as in tailoring, the outside slipper workshops were equally the reflection of the large existing English houses from which they drew their irregular sustenance. Some aliens, furthermore, manufactured on their own account for sale by hawking to retailers and market traders. Reminiscence of the tailoring trade is also aroused by the variety of workshop size. At least four Leeds aliens employed ninety workers on the basis of large orders from multiple retailers. In these instances the alien workshop organisation resembled that of the factory, since the complete slipper was manufactured.[7] In this group there were some very active aliens. One, who came to Leeds in 1880, commenced the manufacture of slippers and was in a position to purchase a factory in the Leylands for £1,140 by 1889. By 1900 he was also the owner of eight houses, whilst his wife dealt in property, took in lodgers, and machined slipper-tops in her spare time.[8] With the increasing elaboration of slipper patterns, these larger manufacturers diversified into the market for ladies' single-strap shoes, which remained popular until 1914. This article was simpler to produce, required fewer skilled hand-workers, and, with machinery, costs could be much reduced. The latter became increasingly urgent, since the power of the multiple retailer to place bulk orders was great, and competition had forced down the making price of slippers to 1s 0d per pair. Such men survived only by grim economies, long hours, and the plentiful use of cardboard and paste in place of genuine materials, to become large manufacturers in the twentieth century.[9]

Smaller shops were more characteristic of the trade. Some might employ up to thirty workers, as the proceedings of the Labour Commission of 1892 indicate.[10] Most alien units, however, were smaller than this, being confined to riveting, lasting and finishing, chiefly under dwelling-house conditions. Thus the typical Leeds slipper master worked for a large house, conveying the goods from the warehouse on a handcart for making-up either in his own home or in a 'converted' residence used as a workshop.[11] 'The inspectors seldom visit these places and in fact seldom find them,' complained the *Yorkshire Factory Times* in 1891 – a truth well borne out by the utter inspectorial silence on the subject over the whole period.[12]

The work – at least in the transitional sense – was readily available to aliens in Leeds, and the capital demands, in the shape of a sewing machine and a number of wooden lasts, were modest. Even where complete manufacture was carried out, however, little more was required. Materials were little more than ready-cut soles and remnants from carpet manufacture. For the popular cashmere slippers of the period, remnants were obtained from the cloth mills of Bradford; whilst patent leather pieces for toecaps were the remnants of the ladies' shoe manufacture of Leicester.[13] As to the organisation of work, the three 'alien' processes were well suited to the outdoor team system within which one man applied the highest skill, whilst the rest of the work was carried out by men at the lower levels of the hierarchy.[14]

Where the domestic system was involved, directories give little aid in assessment of the number of alien slipper workshops in Leeds. To the firms listed must be added numerous unrecorded bedroom and cellar units. The number of workers is also mysterious. The 1891 census records 313 Jews in this occupation.[15] In 1903 the *Yorkshire Factory Times*, always a close observer, suggested a figure of over 1,000.[16] No estimate is likely to be satisfactory. The ill-defined status of the alien slipper master, with his small investment, point to a high mobility. The industrial standing of the slipper worker is even less clear. In footwear generally, riveters, lasters and finishers had a reputation for indiscipline and waywardness,[17] and, as labour organisers discovered, the alien was hardly different in this respect. Conditions were such that every intelligent worker wished 'to get out of the cellars'.[18] Many were of a less intelligent type or uncommitted by their nature to a given trade. The spasmodic state of demand, especially where production was for hawking to retail shops, encouraged the feeling that the trade was basically casual to a degree. Thus, apart from the skilled operative, most men tended to spend only six months of the year in it. Many also made the annual move into the Jewish bakeries in connection with the extra demand for the special Passover cake. It is thus clear that the labour force was quite unstable and that the image of the slipper maker as a tradesman was unclear.[19]

In spite of the many similarities in the industrial situation of the Leeds alien worker in the tailoring and slipper trades, a fundamental – and even fatal – difference existed. Unlike the tailors, who were auxiliaries of an expanding local industry, the slipper workers simply prolonged, by their ready availability, a hand system which became increasingly anomalous, and which, in face of the concentration of capital implied in the spread of the machine,[20] could provide only the most inhuman conditions. Further, whereas wholesale tailoring was increasingly located in Leeds towards 1914, the slipper trade was being drawn to Rossendale. Changes in fashion also influenced the shift. The *Chronicle* observed in 1911:

> When leather and cashmere slippers were generally worn, it was an important industry, and one which gave employment to a large section of the local working class community. But this has been badly hit by the competition of the Lancashire slipper makers in the Rossendale Valley, who do the bulk of the slippermaking trade today.[21]

The Jewish slipper worker of Leeds had placed himself in a situation in which the anarchy of capitalist competition, aggravated by the interposition of the master between himself and the ultimate employing warehouse, was able to wreak havoc. From inception the industry functioned as if no regulatory legislation had ever been entered in the statute book. Hence it was rapidly enveloped in a characteristic bitterness generated by both internal and external tensions.

Significantly, it was James Sweeney, in his capacity as footwear union leader, who, in 1884, registered the first protest against the alien trade. At a Trades Council meeting he called attention to the excessive hours and filthy shops in which slippers were made, foreseeing accurately that alien competition would oust the English workers.[22] The conditions described by Sweeney received confirmation from a first Yiddish source in a letter to *Arbeiter Freund* from Leeds in 1888:

> Would you kindly publish these few lines concerning the working slippermakers of Leeds? Perhaps these poor workers will consider their bitter and darkened condition and see how badly they are oppressed by the sweaters and bloodsuckers – the masters. Brothers! Poor slippermakers! I understand quite well that many of our workers now feel their tragic situation because hunger-need has been a permanent inhabitant of their poor houses ... Brothers! Just consider the difference between two years ago and today. The price for making slippers was 4s 6d. The good-hearted masters then said that 4s 3d was good enough for us, and, a few months ago, many masters also took off the threepence and now pay only 4s 0d. Now ... the masters have talked amongst themselves and have said that this is also too much – it is not necessary to pay more than 3s 6d.[23]

With the deepening concern over sweating, immigration and unemployment, attacks multiplied. The *Factory Times*, alarmed at the incredible cheapness of slippers, sent its Leeds correspondent on a tour of the alien workshops to find – not only adult Jews – but young girls working until late at night for a weekly 6s 0d. 'These sweating dens,' he concluded, 'are canker worms that require stringent treatment.'[24] In 1891 the *Workman's Times* described the 'hordes of foreigners bundled together making slippers at a price that cannot keep body and soul together'.[25] In the following year the Labour Commission heard that the Jews had 'permeated into the slipper trade' of Leeds, where they worked very long hours.[26] The secretary of the Leeds Boot Manufacturers' Association claimed that he had entered alien bedroom workshops in which ten people were at work late at night. As to wages, he recalled that English workers had received 11s 0d per dozen for slippers, whilst the Jews produced an inferior product for which the pay was 4s 0d to 4s 6d. He was not at all certain that all received money wages, or whether some worked only for their keep.[27] This was a well founded suspicion. Some slipper workers of the lowest grades lived in, working for no wages other than a meagre board and lodging. Even when in employment, such men were to be seen begging in the streets of the Leylands, especially on the Sabbath Eve.[28].

With the progression of the 1890s, the 'slipper scandal' waxed. Prices fell, and the limits to human endurance appear to have been reached. The Mayor of Leeds and his responsible officials, in their annual tour of the Leylands in 1894, encountered hordes of Jewish slippermakers crowding into condemned courts at the foot of Quarry Hill, where high rents were being paid for decayed hovels.[29] Sweeney again proclaimed his own findings at the Trades Council. Conditions in the trade were a disgrace to Leeds, he accused. He knew where eight men and two boys worked sixteen hours a day in a small bedroom. Seven people worked on slippers in another house in which a family of seven also resided. Prices had fallen by 2s 0d to 2s 6d in the previous nine years, he claimed. Harris Levi, a member of the alien trade, readily agreed that conditions were very poor. Average working hours, he affirmed, had risen to ninety-six per week, whilst wages were 17s 0d to 18s 0d.[30] The *Leeds Evening Express* found grim humour in the situation. Harry Kravis of Templar Street, it related, was walking home from work after eleven o'clock at night when he encountered three 'friendly' Englishmen:

As their embraces resulted in forcing the Jew on to his back in the gutter, he is to be excused for thinking that the trio were a little too enthusiastic. But being himself possessed of the exuberance of spirit one expects to find in a slippermaker on account of the small number of hours those in the industry work – a paltry ninety-six per week – he would have been willing to forgive ... had it not been that [one of the trio] manifested a strong desire to borrow his watch.[31]

Although, as John Coyle, the slipper union leader informed Robert Sherard during the latter's Leeds investigations, the slipper trade had always been 'among the starved industries',[32] the English workers retired in haste under the new conditions. The *Express*, confirming the impression of alien monopoly received from directories, reported that a mere fifty Englishmen remained in the trade in 1894, where once there had been 500. Why this had occurred was carefully explained. Jewish slipper shops were chiefly bedrooms with 'a carpet of cloth clippings, bits of leather, dirt and cardboard'. In many cases they were garrets with ceilings open to the roof. Overcrowding was universal. Work began at 6 a.m., and, 'to get on with their work, they dispensed with meal times and left at twelve midnight, sometimes earlier – earlier in the next day'. Every shop had its special 'quick hand'. He was 'a marvel' capable of earning 24s 0d a week, but the ordinary workers earned no more than 13s 0d to 15s 0d. The master himself was no better off, being ground down by the wholesale buyer. Payment by the wholesaler was made half in cash and half in leather, and, in spite of low prices, 5 per cent was deducted from the cash portion as 'payment' for the privilege of retaining the work of the particular warehouse. A pretended discount of $2\frac{1}{2}$ per cent was allowed on the leather, but the master could buy the same material cheaper for himself without a discount.[33] Wages were therefore paid to the alien workman on a highly irregular basis, since the master so often found himself without liquid capital.[34] This was often repeated as the result of unannounced price reductions by the wholesaler.[35] Masters thus compelled to borrow ahead of revenue, to cover wages, often found themselves working for nothing.[36]

As the end of the nineteenth century drew near 'the trend towards large scale production using machinery' continued, along with the construction of the factories in which it could be housed.[37] In view of this, the alien-dominated hand trade could hardly remain in anything other than a wretched condition. The small Jewish factory, wracked by falling prices and dominated by the large buyer, was an equally undesirable workplace. Despite his reputation as an anti-semite, Robert

Sherard's valuable account of the Leeds trade at this epoch harmonises well with other sources, including Jewish ones. John Coyle, his informant, showed how displacement had occurred. Qualities which had earned the English worker 9s 0d a dozen were now being made by the aliens for 5s 0d. In the chief line of patent slippers, Coyle claimed that he had formerly received as much as 14s 0d, as against the alien's 7s 6d. The Christian had lost his hold because the Jews laboured from 7 a.m. to midnight, during which period each man would produce twelve dozen pairs. For this, said Coyle, he received the 'munificent sum of 3s 0d', which was 'wages with a vengeance'. Even at this price, however, the English worker found it difficult to obtain employment. Those few English artisans still clinging to the trade were in no better situation than the aliens. Working under their own domestic system, earnings averaged fourpence an hour for a fourteen-hour day, and they were 'on the verge of starvation'.

In the Jewish sector, Sherard estimated that more than 1,000 'families of foreign extraction' were making slippers. At 11 p.m. he visited a Jewish workshop with a staff of forty workers 'hammering and pasting with such rapidity that it was impossible to follow their movements'. They had been at work since 8 a.m. and expected to continue until after midnight. The 'marvel' spotted by the *Express* some years before and now dubbed 'The Lightning Slippermaker' by Sherard, was also present here. This man, said Sherard, might earn 30s 0d a week, but the ordinary hand averaged only twopence an hour, earning only 16s 0d. Sherard's findings raised a storm, but he insisted upon their accuracy.[38]

Four years later the same writer revisited Leeds only to find that the English workers had disappeared. The sole survivor was John Coyle, who had abandoned the trade. There was now, he stated, no room in the trade for Englishmen, as alien competition had 'definitely killed them out'.[39]

Incredibly, the trade had still not reached its nadir: the worst of its death throes lay ahead. In 1903 the *Factory Times* observed that not only was Leeds slippermaking entirely in Jewish hands but wages had fallen by 50 per cent since 1896. Hours of work remained as high as eighteen per day.[40] Whilst factory-based machinery intensified competition among the outworkers and depressed wages, raw material prices were rising.[41] The prices of slippers also fell, moving counter to the trends of the pre-war years,[42] with the result that increasing pressure on making-up prices was placed by the large wholesalers on their outworkers.

It seems clear that the large manufacturing side of the trade was preparing to disengage itself from the outside branch on technological grounds. With the installation of the first clicking presses around the turn of the century, in fact, footwear manufacture became fully mechanised, and putting-out, though it might persist in desperate areas such as the Leeds Jewish slipper trade, was doomed.[43] The new machines of the early 1900s facilitated the American team system and the further subdivision of processes on a clearly more productive basis than was possible in the outwork sector. Hand-sewn men, in particular, could survive only by the most terrible exertions.

Jewish sources of the 1900s confirm that Sherard had not been airing mere anti-semitic prejudices, and that he had had small need to defend his findings of the late 1890s. The pictures painted by the *Yorkshire Factory Times* and the *Leeds Express* group, too, had, it seems, been sadly genuine. The Leeds correspondent of *Arbeiter Freund* recorded a meeting in 1903 at which Jacob Caplan had 'demonstrated with facts that the average wage of a Jewish slippermaker, riveter and finisher was $3\frac{1}{4}d$ an hour for a sixteen-hour day'. Wages had fallen by 50 per cent in three years: from 3s 6d a dozen to 1s 9d. Nor were matters assisted by the fact that over 1,000 workers still clung to the trade.[44] On the right wing of the Jewish press there was, equally, no concealing the facts two years later, when the *Jewish Journal* reported comprehensively. The trade was much fallen and leather was dear. Prices could not be raised because of competition among the masters. The smaller shops were, therefore, being eliminated, and rising unemployment was the result.[45] By 1906 only 600 Jewish workers remained officially in the industry, but untold numbers worked in the bedroom sector. The eighteen-hour day, reported *Arbeiter Freund*, was the rule, with pay at 3s 0d a day. Even at these rates, wages were often held back for six weeks.[46] The description given by the *Jewish Chronicle* in the same year not only agrees substantially with that of its revolutionary contemporary but underlines clearly the effects of the ultimate drive to mechanisation and the factory. It found that hand-sewn men were working ninety-six hours per week and earning a maximum of 24s 0d. The handful of larger Jewish employers apart, the trade had fallen entirely into the hands of the bedroom master, and was 'in an incredible position'.[47]

One year later a Leeds alien master found it necessary to prohibit his men from working between midnight and 6 a.m.[48]

The Leeds Jewish slipper trade exhibits classically the Marxian conditions arising in the transfer from domestic to factory work. These conditions were familiar enough throughout the English footwear trade, but were experienced in an aggravated and inordinately prolonged form specifically in the Leeds alien branch. The Webbs' view of the footwear transition was naive, with 'new capitalists without traditions, exposed to keen rivalry from foreign competitors . . . eager to take every advantage of each change' as the causative factors in conflict.[49] In Marx's version, whether the capitalist is new or old appears of little moment. Nor is foreign competition either necessary or sufficient to initiate the fatal transition. The problem is technical and relates to the limits to which factors of production — in this case, labour and simple capital — are most profitably exploitable. There is a point, notes Marx, at which the cheapening of labour power by its abuse and 'by sheer robbery of every normal condition requisite for working and living, and by the sheer brutality of overwork and nightwork, meets at last with natural obstacles which cannot be overstepped'. Similarly, the cheapening of goods by these methods — and exploitation in general — cannot be carried further once this point is reached. It is then that 'the hour has struck for the introduction of machinery and for the thenceforth rapid conversion . . . of manufactures into factory industries'.[50] The miserable prolongation of the category of industry, of which the Leeds alien slipper trade was a clear member, is made by Marx a function of the extent to which the market may be satisfied prior to the completion of the transition from the domestic to the factory system. The market itself, however, is first extended to accommodate factory output by exploitation of conditions exemplified by the apparel industries, including footwear:

> The great production of surplus value in these branches of labour, and the progressive cheapening of their articles, were and are chiefly due to the minimum wages paid, no more than requisite for a miserable vegetation, and to the extension of working time up to the maximum endurable by the human organism.[51]

Satisfaction of these Marxian conditions augured for the Leeds alien slipper trade a bleak existence as cynosure of hostile eyes (not all of which were English) and an egregious role in alien society itself. In the trade were embodied every last variable of the anti-immigrationist's model: the endless working hours, the starvation prices and the insanitary attributes readily supposed by many to be an alien monopoly. Furthermore, the serious charge that aliens displaced

English labour – of which the Leeds alien tailor was often exonerated, if not quite accurately – was only too substantial in regard to the slipper workers; even if the market itself was about to perpetrate the deed with the aid of the machine rather than the alien. It was the acceleration and consequent dramatising of the process by the impact of the alien that told.

In his vicious anti-semitic articles in the *Yorkshire Post* in 1903, repeated in the *Standard* two years later, the popular mass journalist, Foster-Fraser, was able to adduce but a single example of actual displacement: the Leeds slipper trade, in which, as he put it, the alien had 'starved the English workers into the workhouse or into the ground'. This sole example, despite the furious anti-semitic paranoia with which the work of this future knight of the realm, with his mass readership, was thoroughly suffused.[52] The work of the Foster-Frasers was nothing more than a journalistic nine days' wonder, however. They inspired *ad hoc* terror whenever there was a Royal Commission on Aliens or a Sidney Street Siege. But, at industrial level, the reality was day-to-day confrontation with the displaced and the threatened – in the shape of their English footwear union.

The impact of the machine had created problems enough without the alien. The National Union of Boot and Shoe Operatives (NUBSO) was founded in 1890 to unite the former Riveters and Finishers with the clickers and pressmen. The union struggled throughout the period in Leeds, London and elsewhere against the very tendencies aggravated by the immigrants. One urgent problem was the establishment of uniform piece-rate lists – the Statement – in an industry of diverse goods and changing fashions, and in which the old rates were profoundly affected by machinery. Thus payment disputes were numerous, culminating in the major lockout of 1895. This resulted in a victory for the employers, especially on the manning of machinery.[53] Another important strand of policy was the drive towards indoor working throughout the industry, with the consequential abolition of outside work. Agreement on this point was reached with the employers of Leicester in 1891, by which time the alien system was in full spate elsewhere. The union's long-term difficulties were exacerbated by the effects of the 1895 lockout, in which the lack of success created disaffection. The dispute itself disabled the finances, and the union suffered a decline in membership from 44,000 in 1895 to 24,000 in 1906.[54]

It was, nevertheless, a major national union with a prominent voice in the labour movement when the time came for its confrontation with the alien system; to which, with its unregulated hours, chaotic wage structure and putting-out, it was bound to react with hostility, even if the English trade was far from cleansed of such impurities. Locally, there were special occasions for additional antipathy. The union had made some progress with Leeds employers on recognition, a joint board, and a uniform Statement[55] when the alien irruption began to be felt. There is evidence in the regular union reports of long-term unemployment in Leeds, and resentment was inflamed by a shift of firms to Bristol – a loss of jobs which the English worker could ill afford.[56]

With the English worker's retreat from the slipper branch, the alien was left to face the hopeless struggle against the machine, and in possession of an undesirable and disreputable monopoly. The trade was also burdened by unwholesome craft memories. The fact that sweating antedated Jewish immigration has, in a number of works, been cited as a defence. It is suggested, however, that the recrudescence of sweating during the alien period contributed to the exasperation of English workers, who had made real advances on some fronts by the 1880s. In this connection the work by E. P. Thompson and Miss Yeo on Mayhew's observations of London trades in the mid-century is invaluable in demonstrating how precisely conditions in the immigration period replicated those generated by foreign labour in the same trades three decades earlier.[57]

It was entirely predictable that the industrial wing of the anti-immigration movement would be led by officials of NUBSO, who influenced opinion widely. Further, their views on the footwear trade – often unexaggerated as they were – could easily be generalised to alien industry, where they were of little relevance, or translated into generalised argument against immigration. William Inskip and Charles Freak, respectively secretary and president of NUBSO, led the attack at the T.U.C. of 1894, the former moving the successful anti-alien resolution.[58] In the following year the same pair were responsible for the second resolution on this theme.[59] Much has been made of the fact that this resolution was never formally repeated in the T.U.C., by scholars seeking to minimise the power of the working-class reaction to the aliens. The Congresses which passed the resolution were by no means the beginning or end of the reaction, however. Freak had already spread the question on to a national platform provided by the Royal Commission on Labour, a year before the Congress of 1894.[60] The latter, and the Congress of 1895, were, in fact, mere milestones marking a long and hostile road, rather than the termini as which they have so often been presented. In any event, the calm evinced by recent scholarship over the T.U.C. resolutions was not shared by the Jewish worker at whom they were directed. How well Inskip and Freak had done their work is clear from the gravity of the reaction within the alien left. *Arbeiter Freund* warned that the government had promised the T.U.C. deputation a law against further immigration, following the 1895 resolution: 'To discover what was meant by 'poor foreigners', one has only to read the words of Mr Freak, who led the way ... to be convinced that it was the poor Jewish worker who was meant.' Comrade Gordon had written from Manchester to say that he was ready to prove that, working alongside thirty-two pressers in a Manchester factory, he had been the only one to walk out when wages had been cut. But, thought the paper:

In our view, cases like that cannot help the Yiddish-speaking workers against the threatening danger, for this danger does not subsist in the fact that a Conservative government will bring in a law ... but, rather, in the unrest which an agitation of this kind will produce in the working masses of England ... who allow themselves to be persuaded by the Freaks and Inskips.[61]

On this view, the NUBSO officials, agitating from the standpoint of their own industry, had clearly broadened the anti-alien front so that it encompassed immigration as a whole. Nor did the pernicious effects of the discord occasioned in the footwear trade terminate with the 1895 Congress and its immediate aftermath. By 1903, when Jacob Caplan published an analysis of the origins of the Aliens Commission for *Arbeiter Freund*, Inskip and Freak were the veritable symbols of anti-alienism. The T.U.C. alone, he stated, had demanded of 'its papa – the State' measures against the unwelcome foreigner. Such few Englishmen as had demanded such a thing 'were simply provoked by agitators such as an Inskip or a Freak'.[62]

Events in Leeds went by analogy, indicating that local union men were well up with the national leadership. NUBSO officials ensured that alien doings were well aired in the Trades Council. Thus the general anti-immigration resolution of the council in 1893 was, in part, the response to a specific report by John Coyle that only seventy Englishmen remained in the Leeds slipper trade out of several hundreds.[63] This resolution did double anti-alien duty, being reported to the Aliens Commission a whole decade later without reference to its date of origin.[64] The council followed its resolution by tendering to the

Home Secretary a statement to the effect that 'slippermaking had been destroyed by Jewish immigration'. One Leeds firm 'now engaged only half a dozen men' when it had once employed 200.[65] Thus the Leeds slipper workers attracted the odium of vocal labour circles in a position to magnify their views to a national scale, and to generalise them so that they seemed sufficient reasons for general exclusionist clamour.

A group so miserably endowed in every industrial sense, surrounded by, and capable of generating, such dangerous turmoil, had also to engage in its own struggle across class lines. Ill-equipped for battle, the prospects for emulation of the tailors appeared bleak. Recent scholarship has treated the class struggle in this industry very lightly, yet, even more than the tailors, the slipper workers existed beneath the dual pressures of appalling industrial conditions and the hostility of the host society. Clearly, the deepest interest in alien slipper unions was going to be that taken by NUBSO – whose members were most often in direct confrontation with them. The attitude of the English union was, at first, patently derived from the general attitude of the English worker, which is excellently summed up by B. C. Roberts:

> The main interest of the British worker was to prevent his position from being undermined by the influx of cheap labour; once the labour was here, the trade unions wanted for their own protection to ensure that it enjoyed the same standards of living, and possessed the same rights as their own membership.[66]

Whilst this describes NUBSO attitudes well, failure to achieve its objectives in regard to the Leeds aliens was, in time, to lead to outright rejection of any paternalistic tendency.

Thus the Leeds alien slipper unions passed a dual existence within a system of close, if ambivalent, relationships with NUBSO on the one hand, and in strife of unrelieved bitterness with the Jewish masters on the other. The dispositions were more complex than this, however. Given the haunting presence of NUBSO, it could also be assumed that a wider spectrum of labour and political interests would be drawn in, and that a high degree of emotionalism would characterise the affairs of the slipper unions. An important example is the intense and busy concern of the Jewish left. 'International' working-class solidarity was at stake in the poor industrial performance of the alien slipper worker, and in the English reactions it provoked, so that the Leeds unions would never lack for leaders in the revolutionary mould. Even more than in the tailors' unions, Jewish anarchists and social democrats were deeply involved in the slipper unions, leading as well as reviving them upon their frequent failure.

Though the press gave the first wide public intimation of an alien slipper problem in Leeds in 1884, within the trade anti-alien momentum had been generated as much as six years earlier, and a handful of years prior to significant immigration into Leeds. In 1878 the report of a conference of the old Operative Riveters' and Finishers' Union contained a protest at the inroads made by the Jews into their trade, accusing them of undercutting. They were able to do this, it was claimed, as their standard of living was below that of the English workers.[67] This has great interest not merely by virtue of its early date but by its presentation of the shape of grievances and complaints to come. The slipper union of 1884[68] undertook strikes at Jewish workshops in the next two years, but, presaging future procedures, it collapsed in 1886.[69] Drawing its own conclusions, NUBSO foresaw that 'the pernicious practice of employing large numbers of Sweaters' was likely to create great difficulties for its Leeds membership.[70] Within a few years, prophecy had become certainty.

The chief preoccupation of the English union in the later 1880s was the wave of technological change which allowed lasting and finishing by machine, and which was accompanied 'by a greater use of boys, a more elaborate subdivision of labour, and a fuller use of subcontracted work'. The union reacted by instituting policies of opposition, including the abolition of outwork, the prevention of further subdivision, and an attempt to discourage mechanisation by the restriction of output and demands for high piece-rates.[71] Most of this was instantly antithetical to the typical practices of the alien slipper trade. In Leeds, too, the alien worker's proclivity to remain at his work for ninety-six hours a week was an added motive for concern. Thus definite policy towards the aliens was enunciated by Freak at the NUBSO conference of 1888. Whilst admiring their Victorian virtues of thrift and sobriety, the Jews, he thought, were 'ignorant'. Therefore he hoped that both 'sweaters and sweated' could be got into the English union.[72] Like many modern bourgeois scholars, Freak overlooked the class-divided nature of Jewish immigrant society, viewing its footwear sector as a homogeneous social entity based on Jewishness and common geographical origin, and devoid of social separateness between master and man. He was thus able to view the alien sector of his industry as an undifferentiated mass which might be swept whole into a trade union without reference either to its internal class problems, or the respective socio-economic functions of its different strata.

Class formation was, in fact, taking a predictable course, with a revival of Jewish action prompted by the socialists, even as Freak spoke. Prices for making-up – and therefore wages – were falling, and the labour supply was being swollen by newcomers. The need for a new alien union was great, and the call was led by a Leeds slippermaker:

> Brothers! Accept the advice of a young wage-slave, a slippermaker. Let us unite ourselves and form a society. If we become united we will be able to battle against the masters ... A few idlers hold sticks in their hands and beat us and we, such a great mass of workers, are unable to snatch the sticks from their filthy hands. It is a shame for us![73]

This agitation saw the slippermakers into the same movement as the tailors in the revolt of 1888, backed by Maguire, Paylor and Sweeney. A new union, the Leeds Jewish Slippermakers, was quickly formed and regular meetings were established at the Barleycorn Inn, Hope Street, Leylands.[74] The masters attempted to persuade the men that a union was no good for them, and promptly sacked its chairman, Jack Matlovsky, who was boycotted and forced out of Leeds.[75] The union, bolstered by the socialist enthusiasm sweeping through Leeds and into the alien industries, and guided by Maguire and the Socialist League, held together. When the tailors blundered into their disastrous general strike in May, the poverty-stricken slippermakers supported them with strike contributions.[76] With the collapse of the tailors, however, and in the baleful aftermath of a master-dominated Leylands economy, unionism in both trades dissolved in a welter of recrimination and strife.

Union revival in the slipper trade was the product of a complex alliance of forces and reflected once more the movements in the tailors' unions. In 1890, when the latter made their remarkable alliance with the Leeds gasworkers, the slippermakers were drawn into the same movement. The advantages seen by the tailors appeared equally applicable to the footwear men; whilst, to the socialists of the League, the prospect of control of alien labour doings at their worst appeared outstanding. With the strong and understandly ready support of a Sweeney concerned for his trade, Maguire, Paylor and Cockayne, aided by Caplan, rapidly formed a union which duly became a branch of the Gasworkers' Union, and with a socialist leader, Morris Rudman.[77]

Realising that the direct recruitment of more than forty Jewish members was proving a task beyond its powers,[78] the local policy of NUBSO shifted away from Freak's call for the comprehension of all alien footwear workers. Instead it supported the amalgamation with the gasworkers, holding itself ready to assist wherever possible. In June 1890 Rudman wrote to *Arbeiter Freund*:

> With joy I am able to report that the Slippermakers' Society now stands, so to speak, at the head of the Leeds Jewish labour movement. Socialism does not frighten them. On the contrary, the Socialists are very busy amongst them and their speeches are heard with great attention ... Members are joining weekly ... and now we are working hard to maintain the unity between the Jewish and the English slippermakers.[79]

The euphoric tone had, as its just cause, a fine, if typically temporary, victory in March, in which, with the aid of NUBSO, a strike had seen the enforcement of a uniform Statement at twenty Jewish shops.[80] Actions of this type represented the 'alien phase' of wider NUBSO policy, which aimed to protect the wage rates of clickers and pressmen. This had attracted them into the union, adding to strength (and changing its name) by 1890.[81] The central problem was to enforce the Statement where there was no national uniformity, and where, indeed, the single-shop Statement was not unknown.[82] In the alien sector of the Leeds slipper trade this policy was reflected in an effort to impose a uniform list on groups of Jewish shops, in which, as the *Factory Times* put it, the masters paid 'any way they liked'.[83] The urgency of the attempt was manifest. By 1891 the Leeds branch of NUBSO had won a week of fifty-four hours, and an average wage of 23s 0d — a standard with which the aliens could tolerate no comparison.[84]

Rudman's report of increasing membership was no idle boast. In the enthusiasm running parallel to that among the tailors, membership rose to 500.[85] In June a second agitation for the uniform Statement was opened with the support of the gasworkers. As Rudman reported, confirming the impression of chaotic rates given by the *Factory Times*:

> As the wages in the slipper trade are not equal (the usual price per dozen is 4s 3d and 5s 3d but almost half the masters pay no more than 4s 0d and 5s 0d) the slippermakers have decided to strike to level out prices ... In this manner, we seek shortly to equalise all prices and then we will prepare for a general strike next season.[86]

Under the gasworkers, the slipper trade became as active as the tailoring trade, and a number of successful strikes for the uniform Statement ensued, the largest involving 230 workers from twenty workshops.[87]

The external relations of the slipper workers were fraught with sufficient problems: low wages, long hours, ruthless masters, and the close proximity of a powerful English union, had served to focus fierce attention on their trade. This did not prevent the internal problems of the alien union from gaining the upper hand, however. In spite of their strike successes, this promising union soon disintegrated, leaving the tailors as the sole alien Jewish branch within the Gasworkers' Union. The slipper workers had not been popular with the English trade unionists, to whom they had seemed impatient and intolerant. They 'carried on like wildfire' when John Judge, the NUBSO secretary, ruled against them in an arbitration. No wonder the Jewish masters were such demons, thought the *Yorkshire Factory Times*, when they had such demons working for them.[88] The alien union fell away so rapidly that, by September, a revival was being joyously hailed.[89] This was to prove impermanent, however, despite the hard work of the gasworkers and the Jewish socialists, to prevent secession. Caplan persistently urged the need for 'solidarity with their English brothers', and advised participation in the gasworkers' demonstration for the eight-hour day in October.[90]

By this time, however, Caplan was preaching to no more than a socialist remnant, split off from the 500 who had entered the gasworkers' movement. Socialism disturbed the older men, who failed to share the enthusiastic visions of the younger workers. The latter, on their part, were often impatient, and tended to stop paying their contributions and attend meetings on little provocation.[91] Of the intractable conditions beneath which the building of a union was being essayed, little need be said. With little money and less energy, the establishment of a permanent organisation was doubtful. New immigrants, as even Jewish witnesses asserted, negated the work of loyal unionists by their amenability to private wage bargaining outside the scope of agreed price lists. As wages fell those insisting on Statement rates were put to the boycott, and, in this manner, much leadership ability was lost to the group of slipper workers.[92] In the significant fraction of the trade carried on in the bedroom workshops, and quite unorganisable by the unions, the price list was sterile as a regulator of wages. In the small Jewish factories and non-domestic workshops with organisational potential, apart from the generally discouraging conditions of the trade, union agitation had to contend with the low intelligence of the average slipper worker. One problem for the union educator was the widespread illiteracy in Yiddish, which prompted *Arbeiter Freund* to advise the slipper workers to get their secretary to read articles out to them at their meetings in 1890.[93]

The immediate effect of these problems upon external relations was the abandonment by the final remnant, in 1891, of the Gasworkers' Union.[94] An independent union of sixty members was soon formed, but this did nothing to assuage the disappointments felt on the English side. The *Yorkshire Factory Times* taunted the slippermakers – as it had the tailors. When, shortly after the final break, an approach was made to the Leeds Co-operative Society to propose the setting up of a workshop for the aliens, their statement as to working hours, wages and conditions 'was dreadful to listen to'. Thoughts of social improvement, it appeared to the paper, had 'been completely crushed out of them'. Hordes of foreigners were 'every day making slippers at a price that could not keep body and soul together'. The Jews had made 'a bad mistake' in leaving the Gasworkers' Union, and their new union was 'now nowhere'.[95]

Within NUBSO, where disappointment was extreme, reaction was volcanic. Leeds, said a union report of 1892, swarmed with aliens, and the British workman would not always submit patiently. They were put in cellars where daylight never penetrated, and 'in sheds not fit for horses or dogs'.[96] In the same year Inskip took the opportunity afforded by the Leicester conference with the footwear manufacturers to single out Leeds and Manchester as places where 'pauper aliens' flooded into the footwear trade in large numbers.[97] The Leeds Trades Council resolution against aliens and the national publicity on the T.U.C. platform were soon to follow. Yet economic pressures and the established NUBSO policies ensured that, alongside hostility, the efforts of the English union to control alien slipper work were unexhausted.

There was excellent justification for the revival initiated in 1893. The tailors were re-forming – and in a manner which was to yield them a continuous existence thereafter. Isolation faced the slipper workers. Complaints of falling prices in the trade were on the increase. The severe slump of 1894 raised the temperature of local criticism and activated the Trades Council plus more remote parties. The new union was again the fruit of socialist work. 'Comrade Sweeney', as he was known to *Arbeiter Freund*, addressed numerous meetings, explaining to the slipper workers 'the necessity of a society for the Leeds workers as well as for all workers'.[98] The *Leeds Express* newspapers opened a comprehensive attack. In times of depression, it was said, people searched for the causes. One of these was 'the concentration of Jewish workers in one particular locality'. The English worker in Leeds had 'seen the slippermaking industry gradually passing into the hands of the aliens, each successive step entailing a reduction in wages with a certain increase of hours'. He had seen 'batch after batch of greeners imported and set to work all the hours that God sends at next to no wages' until their hearts had 'grown sick'.[99] The Trades Council, stung into action, invited the new slipper union leader, Bernard Mendelsohn, as a delegate in April in an effort to prevent further price reductions and strengthen his union.[100] The council president, Arthur Shaw, and secretary, Owen Connellan, went out into the open air to address mass meetings 'to encourage the Jewish slippermen' and to publicise their condition.[101] For answer, the Jewish masters proposed a reduction in the price for cashmeres from 4s 0d to 3s 9d, backing this was a lockout threat. 'Acting at the instigation of their British fellow-workmen', the aliens decided to resist, and, by early May, a strike was 'in full spate'.[102]

It is clear that English circles regarded this occasion as a major test of Jewish labour character, and the aliens were supported widely. Sweeney's motion of support was rapidly carried in the Trades Council and fund-raising credentials were granted.[103] NUBSO made a grant of £4 to the strike fund, hoping that 'these downtrodden Jews would be able to make a good sound union in Leeds'.[104] The *Yorkshire Factory Times*, reporting widespread support, had 'never been more sorry' than it was for the strikers. 'They looked ready for dying. Hunger, languidness, sorrow and dullness, consequent upon long hours and low pay, were upon them.'[105] In the following issue the paper warned the strikers to stick together, for they had 'plenty of dodging'. Further, 'they had a Jewish price and an English price, and want of knowledge of English told against the Jewish workers very much'.[106] The strikers were supported by a campaign of public meetings, at which Sweeney, Coyle and the Trades Council executive spoke alongside the Jewish socialists. There were also delegates from the Newcastle slippermakers, as well as from non-labour organisations such as the Society for the Propagation of the Gospel to the Jews.[107] Thus supported, the aliens held out, and, by mid-May, thirty-four masters had agreed to a new Statement and code of working rules.[108] A striking aspect of the victory, as it appeared to the *Factory Times*, was the submission of a large number of small masters whose unregulated competition had made it impossible for larger firms to pay Statement rates.[109]

The aftermath of the strike throws much light on the Leeds alien slipper trade, and on the exasperations facing NUBSO officials in their efforts to grapple with both alien masters and workers. Many small shops may have been 'conquered', but any abuse still appeared likely.

On returning to work at the agreed list rates, which covered fifteen items,[110] the men were informed that there was no work for them at these rates, but plenty at the old. 'The whole thing,' fumed the *Leeds Evening Express*, 'seems to be a mere farce.' The agreement, it considered, had been nothing more than a trick to lure the men back to work. On checking, the paper found the masters doing their own stitching, and prices lower than before the strike. It also published a full-scale protest at 'this hideous system of slavery', signed by an alliance of Trades Council and NUBSO officers.[111] This stung the workers into a fresh strike, during which a group broke away and began the making of slippers on their own account. They were working 'the usual number of hours' and the leaders feared others would follow their example.[112] A new agreement was, nevertheless, reached with the masters,[113] but late June found the Jewish union, John Coyle in attendance, passing impotent resolutions against masters paying below the agreed rates, and against the workers who were accepting them.[114]

The special problems of the slipper trade were clear. Though the struggles of 1894 hint at the presence of a loyal nucleus, the potential union membership of over 500 was nowhere attained. Between 1894 and 1898 no more than ninety members joined,[115] though the official estimate of 100 strikers in 1894 appears understated in view of the large number of shops involved.[116] The conduct of masters and men was, to English eyes, eccentric and treacherous. Agreements and fidelity to one's fellows appeared to have little meaning at this level of the Leylands struggle for survival. Any advantage gained by the union was evanescent – the result of a temporary 'prosperity'. Thereafter, conditions characteristic of the long-term decline of the trade reasserted themselves, and the struggle for the Statement was perforce renewed. In the depressed year of 1894 the Jewish strike had been the chief labour event in Leeds,[117] and the union had held out heroically for several weeks on strike pay of 3s 3d per week for married men.[118] In the slipper trade, however, even this depth of devotion was insufficient to ensure continuity, and the union had dwindled away by the end of the year.

Under the worsening conditions encouraged by the advance of the machine in the later 1890s, Mendelsohn – himself a slipper worker who was occasionally sacked for his pains[119] – worked to establish a strong union over a period of several years. The reports of this period, however, suggest indifference.[120] In 1897, in an effort to rescue the aliens from the worst workshops, Sweeney and the Jewish tailors, with Shaw and Connellan as directors, organised a co-operative workshop.

This project failed from lack of financial support, though the *Yorkshire Factory Times* considered it 'the best move they made'.[121] Precisely why this attempt was made in that year is clear from the letter of appeal written by Saul Ellstein, the Leeds social democrat, to the *Factory Times*. 'You can see,' he wrote, 'slipper workers going to work at six in the morning and coming home at eleven at night, having earned 4s 0d or even less.' The main problem of the union, he thought, lay in the numerous shops of three to five men, where, since the 1894 agreement, prices had fallen to the point where the longest possible working hours no longer yielded a living.[122] The power of the masters had been reinforced by the formation of an employers' union which the workers found sinister. As the same writer reported to *Yiddisher Ekspres*, the progress of the masters' union had produced twenty recruits for the men's union, but he would have been far happier if the men had united themselves from motives other than 'fear of the whip'.[123]

NUBSO continued its efforts to enforce the Jewish Statement of 1894, and to encourage organisation.[124] The English union was encouraged in these policies by new abuses in the alien branch. Jewish masters would pay agreed union rates and solemnly enter them in wages books, following which the worker would surreptitiously return sums to the master. The net effect was a return to pre-1894 wages.[125] There was additional encouragement to the English union in its attitudes in that it had begun to attract some of the skilled Jewish riveters into its ranks.[126] In the last years of the century this promising development was much pursued by NUBSO, since, in 1897, Jewish members under the supervision of the English union had succeeded in establishing Statement wages in the larger shops.[127]

During 1898 NUBSO officials, backed by the Jewish tailors, made heroic efforts to counter the difficulties of the alien slipper branch, and, especially, the problem of wage control and union recruitment against the background of falling prices and worsening conditions. The tailors lent their hall for numerous meetings,[128] of which NUBSO officers addressed over fifty in six months, endlessly touring the Jewish shops 'informing the masters that the lists would have to be kept to'.[129] Much of the effort was devoted to the recruitment of the Jewish workers into NUBSO itself, but there was little to show for all this labour. Reference has already been made to the fewness of alien recruits to the English union during the period as a whole. The Jewish union fared no better. Seemingly defeated by economic conditions, its membership slumped to twenty-six in 1898. When, in the following year and under a new and vigorous leader, Abraham Schleich, this was raised to 150,[130] it seemed to the English union that all the Jewish workers in any way inclined to unionism were equally inclined to remain independent.

This was confirmed by the disquieting news that Schleich had applied to the Trades Council for credentials and organisational assistance.[131] In this forum, he encountered the full weight of all the bitterness and hostility manufactured by the alien trade in the previous two decades. The English officials opposed the application, arguing that the Jews had persistently accepted wages below Statement. They condemned Jewish workers who aided the masters in this by handing back money after it had been paid, or who accepted wages lower than those entered in wages books. What hurt most keenly, they alleged, was that Schleich's new union had begun to take in men who had been recent members of NUBSO. All these men, skilled riveters, were now working below price, they alleged. The courageous Schleich admitted these charges freely, but assured the council that the Jewish workers were 'anxious to reach the high level of the English workmen'.[32]

The Trades Council, for its part, refused assistance. Nor would the new union be recognised, as its members had undercut NUBSO rates, and they would first have to 'make their status as a trade union above reproach'.[133] Simultaneously the English union accused the alien leaders of 'endeavouring to suborn' its Jewish members. The Jewish union had requested mutual recognition of members within the same shop on production of a union card. This might have been in order had it not been found that the Jewish workers had based their list threepence per dozen below the agreed rates for the trade as a whole. Mutual recognition by NUBSO would, therefore, involve blacklegging their own Statement.[134] The Trades Council set 24 April 1900 as the date by which the alien union should be in receipt of Statement wages if recognition were to become a fact.[135]

The Jewish response was positive, confirming the earnestness of Schleich's assertions. Following an abortive conference with the masters, an unfunded strike of 200 men was undertaken, at the end of which the Statement had been widely conceded. 'The men have been loyal,' reported a surprised *Jewish Chronicle*, 'and they have won all along the line.' The assistance of the English unions had also been 'gratifying'.[136] Support had, indeed, been received from many quarters, illustrating once more the power of the alien slipper workers to generate intense feeling.[137]

Less gratifying were the feelings of NUBSO, which had also

supported the strike. The hope had been that, with the achievement of uniform rates, and with the close relationships of the strike, the aliens would terminate their own small organisation and seek to merge with the English union.[138] The aliens were, in fact, 'heading for trouble', as, by September, not only were they not joining NUBSO but their own union was again in process of disintegration, and the members were 'reverting to old practices such as evading standard lists'.[139] In 1901 John Buckle persuaded some few Jewish members back into the fold,[140] but Jewish membership remained stubbornly below fifty,[141] whilst independent Jewish unionism disappeared from the trade for several years.

The condition of the trade, the malpractices in the alien branch, and the intractability of the alien slipper worker, induced responses of even greater severity in the 1900s. The Jewish anarchists and socialists proved faithful supporters, but, even here, disappointments were conducive to second thoughts and the social democrats, at least, would conclude that integration with NUBSO was the only solution to the problem of the Jewish slipper worker in Leeds. *Arbeiter Freund* indicates that the anarchists were working for yet another revival of the union in 1903 – a critical year of anti-alien agitation:

A new spark of life has shown itself. The Jewish slippermakers, riveters and finishers have, it seems, at last begun to grasp that their outgoings are growing longer daily and their income ever shorter. Who can picture the bitter life, the tragic fate, the hard and dirty labour, the tiny wages and long hours, and the lowly treatment of a Jewish slippermaker working for a Jewish sweater?

Case studies supplied by the paper's Leeds correspondent, 'Ben Hilel', confirm – not merely the savagery of exploitation – but also that the ire of the English footwear union was far from misplaced:

A worker had been sacked by a master ... After being idle for two weeks this man went back to the master and offered to do eighteen dozen more pairs by machine for the same wages. The master agreed and took the man back. The man kept his word, and, on seeing this, the master decided to demand that all his workers do the same number of pairs. Those who would not or could not were forced to leave their place ... Another case, a regular one, a certain slippermaker master paid the 'trade union prices', but only on paper. He discovered a remarkable mathematical calculation. You will certainly wonder how bread, clothing, rent and everything else gets dearer whilst, at this shop, everything gets cheaper, and this is why. Every worker knows quite well that the price in the book is 2s 3d a dozen, but, for his wages, the worker gets no more than 1s 9d a dozen. You may ask where the other sixpence goes. But that is only the master's business!

They ought to have revolted and created a strong union, thought this correspondent, but this did not appear to be the case. Of the thousand-strong slipper work force, many had not bothered to attend a revival meeting addressed by Jacob Caplan. Of those present, many left early to catch the second race. When an appeal was made to cover the expenses of the meeting, 'all the slippermakers got up and ran away cursing the chairman for making a collection on the Sabbath'. Such was the intellectual level of this *lumpen* stratum of Leeds alien society that the writer could not forbear asking whether it was 'worthwhile wasting a word on these lowly slaves. Was it not preferable to let them go under altogether?'[142]

The final phase of trade unionism in the Leeds alien slipper trade was ushered in by a more significant loss of goodwill than this, in the official rescinding by NUBSO of its policy of attempting to raise up Jewish conditions. By 1900 the gap was enormous. In that year the Leeds minimum wage for English riveters and finishers was 28s 0d for fifty-four hours,[143] whilst the Jewish operative would need to work almost twice as long to earn this sum. The Gentiles, announced the national union in 1904, were disgusted, and refused the aliens further assistance. At one time 'these workers had a good many labour friends', but their neglect and apathy had alienated them.[144] This new phase of overt hostility coincided with increasing contact in the larger Jewish workshops, in which national union members came increasingly to be found. With the added ingredient of yet another new and independent alien union, founded in 1904 under Benjamin Grossbart, this was an explosive mixture.

Paradoxically, the union which witnessed the termination of unionism in the Jewish slipper trade of Leeds, was, by earlier standards, a well led, idealistic and determined body, holding fast to the leadership and trade union principles. A capable organiser and propagandist, Grossbart was secretary of the Leeds social democratic club, and it is from his reports in the party organ,[145] *Die Neue Tsait*, that the new spirit of the union may be divined. In December 1904, he reported that his union, small and poor, had done deeds which merited a place in history:

On the 5th of November a group of workers came to the union to complain that, after eight or nine years' service at one shop, the master had suddenly forced them out because he had considered he was giving them too much to eat ... It is tragic enough when a slippermaker working from 7 a.m. until midnight ... gets 24s 0d. Along comes the sweater and says, 'No! That's too much for you. I want another sixpence a dozen for myself. For you, 19s 0d a week is enough ... for 110 hours.'

Grossbart pointed out that, although these men were non-unionists, a victorious five-week strike had been undertaken on their behalf without external assistance. In spite of the terrible slack time prevailing in Leeds, simple workers had contributed 1s 6d each per week to support the strikers' families:

> From this case, one may clearly be persuaded of the power of solidarity. Leeds footwear workers, who were condemned by other classes of workers, have, on this occasion, demonstrated that they are not the worst; that, in this strike, they have fought like heroes.[146]

Further strikes followed in which, once more, heroism was uppermost. In appealing for support for a further strike in the next year, Morris Meyer, the editor of *Neue Tsait*, presented a picture of the slipper workers in battle which very strongly emphasises the new spirit:

> I have had the opportunity to see the striking slipper workers of Leeds, but, in truth, I did not see any strikers – only ghosts, shadows without life, without strength ... Not a spark of the spirit which should be present during strikes, when one is in battle with the enemy, could be observed. But can one lay any of the blame on these unhappy ones? Certainly not! Who are they, these slippermakers? Poor sweated-out workers; people who work, as in the good old days, twelve to fourteen hours a day, and who receive – as Winchevski expressed it – 'too little to live, too much to die'.[147]

Characteristically, the union had passed from social democratic to anarchist leadership by 1906, when the correspondent of *Arbeiter Freund* vividly revealed the depths to which the trade had sunk:

> It is self-evident that the sweaters have taken the opportunity ... to enslave their workers in the most shameful way. It is very difficult to do justice fully to the lowly and base treatment these footwear workers have received at the hands of their sweaters. They have worked from 6 a.m. to midnight and their wages have been 3s 0d a day ... But that was not enough for the sweaters who used to hold back wages for six weeks, and, should any of the slaves complain that he could not wait for his money as there was a danger of starvation for himself and his family, he got the sack.

A proposal by the masters to raise the wage-payment period to twelve weeks produced an immediate strike in several of the largest shops, and, with the aid of the tailors, agreement on recognition, weekly payment and higher rates was obtained.[148]

In November the slipper workers walked out at one of the largest Jewish shops – and into a fatal collision with the English union. The events were to prove decisive for alien unionism in the Leeds footwear industry. By the date of the dispute the Leeds branch of NUBSO had made good progress, whilst the union nationally was on the eve of revival from the defeat in the lockout of 1895. One aspect of its revival was the wider organisation of new classes of workers.[149] In the Leeds dispute of 1906, therefore, NUBSO attitudes reflected – not only past disappointments in regulating the Jewish trade – but the outlook of a union determined to countenance no rival.

Apart from the fact that the trade was in an advanced state of decay, and that wages had fallen 'to the minimum', the masters persisted in refusing to honour wage agreements, thereby wiping out the gains from past strikes. The master at the centre of the November dispute was described by *Arbeiter Freund* as 'the cleverest in Leeds at knowing how to use the slave status of his men to pay sixpence to ninepence below union rates', and accused of causing his competitors to reduce wages by undercutting them at the warehouse. The demands of the union were recognition and Statement rates. The master agreed, but insisted on the dismissal of two men. This caused a general walk-out, which was joined by NUBSO members at the same shop.[150] To the consternation of the Jewish union men, NUBSO ordered its members back to work, thereby laying the foundations of an immense furore and sounding the death knell of alien footwear unionism in Leeds.

The *Jewish Chronicle* observed:

A leading feature of the dispute is that no sooner had the men ceased to work than men belonging to the National Union of Boot and Shoe Operatives – both Jews and Gentiles – entered into agreements, and are now working under the protection of the police.[151]

As the detailed and often hilarious account in *Arbeiter Freund* indicates, this was perfectly accurate. On the morning that ten NUBSO men were observed entering the workshop, a crowd of over 200 gathered and threatened a riot. The master called the police, who, being too few to control the crowd

and also fearing for the bones of the scabs, began to blow on their whistles nervously. This brought a great number of fat bobbies in blue caps and coats which made them resemble bloodthirsty ravens in the midst of a flock of excited sparrows.

The shaken master agreed to a settlement, but the union demanded the sacking of two of the scabs. The master replied that he had made agreements with them and, besides, they could not be scabs, since they had been sent in by the English union. What was more, the latter had promised to supply a full set of workers if the dispute were not quickly settled.

The strike committee thus addressed itself to NUBSO, seeking an explanation. The report in *Arbeiter Freund* preserves some of the actual conversation, which is self-explanatory:

'Seeing that we are the organisers of the workers in the footwear trade,' began Herr Buckle, 'we cannot permit the formation of any union anywhere in England which does not belong to our federation. For that reason, we do not recognise you as a union, and, naturally, we have the right to send workers to fill vacant places.' Concerning the agreements, they knew nothing . . . and did not permit themselves to be questioned further on this score.

Further conversation pointed to fundamental differences in attitude to trade union methods, and to a decided absence of militancy in the Leeds branch of NUBSO:

'What kind of union do you think you are?' they asked. 'You are an undisciplined lot. With you, the members rule the roost. Whenever they feel like it, they go out on strike. That's not a union! With us, the officials consider every dispute and we usually avoid every occasion which may lead to a strike. We teach the workers that they must see things the same way as the masters. After all, they create the work and the money with which to pay wages.'

The strike soon collapsed, but the circumstances which were to ensure that this was not the end of the matter were described by the correspondent. The result, he wrote,

is that the scabs remain at their work. This was devised by the secretary of the English branch. The workers are very upset at having to work alongside scabs in the same workshop, but, in the meantime, there is nothing they can do against such a strike breaker.[152]

As Morris Hyman, the alien union secretary, complained in *Arbeiter Freund*, this was 'trade-unionistic' strike-breaking on the part of the English union. Outrage was to follow. On checking the statutes of the Leeds branch of NUBSO, it was found that no member was to enter into private agreements with masters under penalty of expulsion. 'Under this rule as it stands,' claimed Hyman, 'the "contract workers" of the English branch ceased to be union members and should have been considered scabs immediately they made agreements with the master.' What could be more natural, he asked, than that the Jewish slippermakers should not take up the struggle anew? This time, however, it was not to be against the master, but the English union which had 'trampled with its own feet on its own rules, and forced the Jewish footwear workers to work with scabs'.[153]

Leeds was astonished at the spectacle of a struggle between the notoriously unorganisable slipper workers and a national union, on a matter of principle. The *Leeds Mercury* reported sympathetically 'the ring of genuine trade union sentiment' at a Jewish protest meeting,[154] and it is clear that the slipper workers had, after long years of struggle, succeeded in establishing a genuine union organisation, paradoxically when their trade was at its lowest ebb, and when powerful forces were ranged against them. Among the many participants in the controversy, opinion crossed religious lines. The union also became something of a pawn in the political battles within the community.

The *Yorkshire Evening News* drew on the past reputation of the slipper unions. As there were Jews on both sides in the dispute, it observed, and as membership of the English union was open to all, the utility of an independent Jewish union was doubtful, recalling that so many such unions had come and gone in the past fifteen years.[155] The alien case, as stated in *Yiddishe Wochentliche Tzurnal*, was that the last union had been solid, making gains in wages and in greater humanity of treatment. The actions of the English union had undone all this. Much hand-sewn work remained in Jewish hands, and these workers were, in fact, ineligible for membership of NUBSO. The aliens also felt that, as the slipper trade had fallen entirely into their hands, there was latent anti-semitism in the English union. Thus their situation was awkward and an independent union essential.[156]

Closer to home, important supporters were falling away. Morris Meyer, the social democratic editor of *Neue Tsait*, had altered his mind, and, in place of appeals in aid of the union, he substituted his view that, after all, the Jewish workers would be better off in the English union. Whilst conservative Jewish journals such as the *Jewish Chronicle* and the *Wochentliche Tzurnal* had not been offended by the politics of the strikers, the disciple of Kautsky now discovered them to be to his distaste. The extremists, he argued, were leading the strikers into a swamp. As *Arbeiter Freund* reported him, in a speech at Leeds before a large audience:

he traitorously slandered the strikers and justified the behaviour of the English union. This 'fine' person did the same thing in Manchester ... Further comment on this is superfluous.

The English union was the parent, philosophised Meyer, and the Jewish union the child – and the child should not go against the parent. This puerility provoked *Arbeiter Freund* to a bitterly sarcastic response. Nevertheless, the social democrats seceded from the group of parties which had gathered around the union in aid of the strike. When the Jewish tailors, anxious for a settlement and nervous about attacks on NUBSO, shortly followed the social democrats, the union was left with the support alone of the Anarchists, the Jewish cabinetmakers and the Zionist labour group, Poale Zion, to struggle 'against master, scab, hunger and cold'.[157]

By the end of 1906 the Jewish slipper workers had widened the struggle by calling strikes wherever NUBSO members entered a workshop. In its situation, almost isolated, without funds, and in the cold season, this was an incredible display of courage and principle by a union whose predecessors had so regularly disintegrated. With things 'very bad', and the workshops 'full of scabs', and with their 'families suffering cold and hunger', the union presented its case to NUBSO headquarters at Leicester, only to be informed that they did not wish to consider the matter.[158] In January 1907 the national union gave permission for members to enter into agreements with masters, 'though cognisant of a dispute pending'. To publicise this bitter blow, a procession of 2,000 workers was held, but it altered nothing. The reasons were frankly given by the *Jewish Chronicle*, whose regard for the strikers had waxed with time. The supply of English labour was welcomed by the Jewish masters, whose interest in the Jewish worker lay only in the latter's acceptance of the lowest wages. If union rates were to be paid, the preference was for the English operative.[159]

In the face of this sign of universal Jewish brotherhood, most strikers were forced back to work by April 1907. Further outbreaks occurred at the reduction in piece rates which followed at some shops,[160] but the union could not survive what had become an alliance between NUBSO and the Jewish masters. On 13 April the Anarchists held a meeting in Leeds on the theme 'The End of the Slippermakers' Union'.[161] A year later membership had fallen to fifty, and by 1910, when it was registered for the last time, a mere sixteen members remained.

The termination of the struggle was, in many ways, a blessed release. The cellar workshop would shortly give way to the mechanised factory, and, of the Jewish trade, only a cluster of fairly substantial manufacturers would remain. The tailors were shortly to be absorbed into the great national union forming in their trade. Little remained of the slipper trade in Leeds, however, and few Jewish slipper workers to be added to the ranks of NUBSO, with the termination of their independent union.

NOTES

1. Gartner, *Jewish Immigrant*, p. 94.
2. *L.E.E.*, 19 March 1884.
3. J. Buckman, 'Later phases of industrialisation to 1918', in M. W. Beresford and G. R. J. Jones, (eds), *Leeds and its Region*, Leeds, 1967, pp. 162–3.
4. This outline relies heavily on the definitive work: A. Fox, *A History of the National Union of Boot and Shoe Operatives*, Oxford, 1958, especially pp. 10–26, 53–5, 85–93, 260–2.
5. Marx, *Capital*, p. 519.
6. Garrard, *Immigration*, p. 159.
7. See *Y.F.T.*, 8 April 1892, for a complaint that some alien shops themselves sent work out for finishing under bad conditions.
8. *Leeds Daily News*, 27 August 1900.
9. Oral information conveyed to the writer by 'M.L.' of Leeds, who was the son of a member of this group, and who spent a long working life in the trade. Multiple retailing on a large scale began before 1875. On this, see J. B. Jeffreys, *Retail Trading in Britain, 1850–1950*, Cambridge, 1954, pp. 354–6, 370.
10. *Labour Commission, 1892*, P.P. 1892, XXXVI, C 6795-iii, p. 63.
11. *NUBSO Report*, November 1886, p. 9.
12. *Y.F.T.*, 30 October 1891.
13. 'M.L.'
14. Fox, *History*, pp. 93–5.
15. Quoted in *Recent Immigration*, p. 156.
16. *Y.F.T.*, 18 September 1903.
17. Fox, *History*, pp. 20–5.
18. Oral information conveyed to the writer by 'D.R.' of Leeds, a slipper worker of the period.
19. 'M.L.'
20. By 1903 some slipper firms employed as many as 1,200 workers, and could produce at the rate of 100,000 pairs weekly. See *Men's Wear*, 12 November 1903.
21. *J.C.*, 12 May 1911.
22. *L.E.E.*, 3 May 1884.
23. *A.F.*, 27 January 1888.
24. *Y.F.T.*, 4 October 1889.
25. *Workman's Times*, 31 October 1891.
26. *Labour Commission*, q. 11994.
27. *Ibid.*, qq. 13935–7.
28. 'M.L.'.
29. *L.E.E.*, 5 April 1894.
30. *Ibid.*, 23 April 1894.

31 *Ibid.*, 25 April 1894.
32 Sherard, *White Slaves*, p. 3.
33 *L.E.E.*, 5 May 1894.
34 *L.W.E.*, 9 May 1894.
35 'M.L.'.
36 *Ibid.*
37 *Y.P.*, 24 January 1899.
38 Sherard, *White Slaves*, pp. 3–5. Sherard's price findings and other details are in accord with those orally conveyed to the writer by 'M.L.'. For Sherard's defence of the accuracy of his findings, see *Y.F.T.*, 11 June 1897.
39 *Leeds Mercury Supplement*, 16 February 1901.
40 *Y.F.T.*, 13 March 1903.
41 For leather prices, see B. R. Mitchell and P. Deane, *Abstract of British Historical Statistics*, Cambridge, 1962, pp. 473–5.
42 For the general price level to 1912, see W. W. Rostow, *British Economy of the Nineteenth Century*, Oxford, 1949, p. 8.
43 P. Head, 'Boots and shoes', in D. H. Aldcroft (ed.), *The Development of British Industry and Foreign Competition, 1875–1914*, London, 1968, pp. 177–8.
44 *A.F.*, 18 September 1903.
45 *The Jewish Journal*, 22 May 1905.
46 *A.F.*, 20 July 1906.
47 *J.C.*, 7 September 1906.
48 *Y.E.N.*, 8 August 1907.
49 S. and B. Webb, *Industrial Democracy*, London, 1902, p. 396.
50 Marx, *Capital*, p. 514.
51 *Ibid.*, p. 516.
52 *The Standard*, 16 January 1905.
53 Fox, *History*, pp. 231–7.
54 *Ibid.*, p. 239.
55 *Ibid.*, pp. 66–72.
56 *NUBSO Report*, May 1892, p. 13; Fox, *History*, p. 99.
57 E. P. Thompson and E. Yeo, *the Unknown Mayhew*, London, 1971, pp. 259, 267–8, 272–4.
58 *Report of the Twenty-seventh Trades Union Congress, 1894*, pp. 59–60.
59 *Report of the Twenty-eighth Trades Union Congress, 1895*, pp. 45–6.
60 *Labour Commission, 1893*, P.P. 1893–4, XXXIV, C 6894-ix, q. 33196.
61 *A.F.*, 22 November 1895.
62 *Ibid.*, 17 April 1903.
63 Trades Council Minutes, 8 February 1893.
64 *Aliens Commission*, q. 14998.
65 *Y.F.T.*, 21 April 1893. The document is in P.R.O., B 2840A/79, H.O., 45/10063, 1893.
66 B. C. Roberts, *The Trades Union Congress, 1868–1921*, London, 1958, pp. 183–4.
67 *L.E.E.*, 19 March 1884; *The Report of the Operative Riveters and Finishers*, July, 1878, p. 5.

The alien slipper industry 153

68 For registration, see *Report of the Registrar of Friendly Societies, 1884*, P.P. 1885, LXXII, 322-ii, pt C, p. 16.
69 *NUBSO Report*, January 1886, p. 11.
70 *Ibid.*, November, 1886, p. 9.
71 H. A. Clegg, A. Fox, and A. F. Thompson, *A History of British Trade Unions since 1889*, Oxford, 1964, p. 199.
72 *NUBSO Report*, May 1888, pp. 22–3.
73 *A.F.*, 27 January 1888.
74 *Ibid.*, 6 March 1888.
75 *Ibid.*, 30 April 1888.
76 *Ibid.*, 18 May 1888.
77 *Ibid.*, 4 April 1890.
78 The largest number of Jewish members of the Leeds branch of NUBSO was forty-eight, recorded in 1896. See *NUBSO Annual Report*, 1896, pp. 80–5.
79 *A.F.*, 27 June 1890.
80 *Y.F.T.*, 14 March 1890; *NUBSO Report*, April 1890, p. 12.
81 Fox, *History*, 136–8.
82 *Ibid.*, pp. 63, 88, 91–2.
83 *Y.F.T.*, 14 March 1890.
84 *Report on Strikes, 1891*, P.P. 1893, LXXXIII, C 6890, appendix v.
85 *Y.F.T.*, 9 May 1890.
86 *A.F.*, 27 June 1890; *Y.F.T.*, 20 June 1890, reports that the strike was for a uniform 4s 3d per dozen.
87 *Report on Strikes, 1890*, P.P. 1891, LXXVIII, C 6476, p. 178.
88 *Y.F.T.*, 25 July 1890.
89 *A.F.*, 19 September 1890.
90 *Ibid.*, 17 October 1890.
91 *Ibid.*, 24 October 1890.
92 *Aliens Commission*, qq. 15110–15.
93 *A.F.*, 24 October 1890.
94 *Y.F.T.*, 25 September 1891; *A.F.*, 11 December 1891.
95 *Y.F.T.*, 30 October 1891, 8 January 1892.
96 *NUBSO Report*, February 1892, p. 31.
97 *Report of the Leicester Conference of the Federation of Boot and Shoe Manufacturers of Great Britain and the National Union of Boot and Shoe Operatives*, August 1892, p. 15.
98 *A.F.*, 17 March 1893.
99 *L.W.E.*, 27 January 1894; *L.E.E.*, 23 April 1894.
100 Trades Council Minutes, 4 April 1894.
101 *Ibid.*, 27 April 1894.
102 *Y.P.*, 9 May 1894.
103 Trades Council Minutes, 9 May 1894.
104 *L.W.E.*, 12 May 1894.
105 *Y.F.T.*, 11 May 1894.
106 *Ibid.*, 18 May 1894.
107 The issues of the strike are well treated in *L.E.E.*, 11–17 May 1894.
108 *Ibid*, 18 May 1894.

109 Y.F.T., 18 May 1894.
110 L.E.E., 18 May 1894.
111 Ibid., 22 May 1894.
112 Ibid., 24 May 1894.
113 Ibid., 28 May 1894.
114 Y.F.T., 6 July 1894.
115 Report on Trade Unions, 1899, P.P. 1900, LXXXIII, Cd 422, pp. 64–7.
116 Report on Strikes, 1894, P.P. 1895, XCII, C 7901, p. 79.
117 Trades Council Report quoted in Y.F.T., 10 March 1895.
118 L.E.E., 22 May 1894.
119 D.Y.E., 1 January 1897.
120 Ibid., 6 November 1896, 15 January 1897.
121 Y.F.T., 3 September 1897.
122 Ibid., 12 February 1897.
123 D.Y.E., 15 January 1897.
124 NUBSO Report, October 1896, p. 11.
125 Ibid., November, 1896, p. 13.
126 Ibid., April, 1896, p. 12.
127 Ibid., March, 1897, p. 14.
128 Y.F.T., 15 July 1898.
129 Ibid., 22 July 1898.
130 Report on Trade Unions, 1899, pp. 74–7.
131 Trades Council Minutes, 4 August 1899.
132 Y.F.T., 3 November 1899.
133 Trades Council Minutes, 25 October 1899.
134 NUBSO Report, November 1899, p. 2.
135 Trades Council Minutes, 29 November 1899, 12 March 1900.
136 J.C., 1 June 1900.
137 For the appeals, meetings and union support, see Leeds Daily News, 24 April, 30 April 1900; Y.F.T., 27 April, 4 May, 18 May 1900; NUBSO Report, May 1900, p. 13; J.C., 1 June 1900.
138 NUBSO Report, June 1900, p. 11.
139 Y.F.T., 28 September 1900.
140 Ibid., 10 May 1901.
141 NUBSO Annual Report, 1901, pp. 72–9.
142 A.F., 18 September 1903.
143 NUBSO Report, August 1900, p. 15.
144 Ibid., February 1904, p. 17.
145 Strictly, the organ of the East London branch of the Social Democratic Federation.
146 Neue Tsait, 23 December 1904.
147 Ibid., 3 March 1905.
148 A.F., 20 July 1906.
149 Fox, History, p. 306.
150 A.F., 16 November 1906.
151 J.C., 9 November 1906.
152 A.F., 16 November 1906.
153 Ibid., 7 December 1906.

154 *Leeds Mercury*, 30 November 1896.
155 *Y.E.N.*, 6 December 1906.
156 *Yiddishe Wochentliche Tzurnal*, 12 December 1906.
157 *A.F.*, 11 January, 1 February 1907.
158 *Yiddishe Wochentliche Tzurnal*, 26 December 1906.
159 *J.C.*, 25 January, 8 February 1907.
160 *Ibid.*, 5 April, 12 April 1907.
161 *A.F.*, 12 April 1907.

Chapter 6
CONCLUSIONS

In the previous chapters attention has necessarily been focused chiefly upon the class struggle of immigrant Jewry in Leeds on the major industrial scenes. To a high degree this was due to the extent to which it was found necessary to criticise and revise established views on so many fundamental matters relating to alien industry and industrial conditions – the background to the class struggle. The many dissatisfactions which rendered this approach necessary have, it is hoped, been sufficiently clarified and treated in their appropriate places in the text.

The rich vein represented by the class struggle within immigrant Jewry is, however, by no means exhausted by exposition of the special conflicts occurring in the major industries alone. The class struggle, perceived in its totality, is a function of the total opportunities for exploitation. Classically these are very numerous in an immigrant society subject to the composite pressures of poverty, a hostile host society, and the impact of a cheap and mobile labour supply. Many quite significant, if often subsidiary, conflicts were generated in the processes of settlement, the formation of class relationships and in the vigorous and pro-active responses of the oppressed. The minor alien trades of Leeds, in fact, exhibit analogous conditions of exploitation and conflict to those obtaining in the more important occupations. The following report from *Arbeiter Freund* in 1897 illustrates the point with reference to the Jewish bakery trade:

As if it were not sufficient that the sweaters suck out our blood throughout the year in weekly work, the Jewish sweaters of Leeds now seek to extract the last drops of blood from the workers who work on the *matzos*. The workers who work on *matzos* are of various trades: footwear, tailoring and cabinetmakers, etc. Most of them are elderly people who are a burden on their young children, who wander around now without employment and who cannot even support themselves. The situation of these workers is horrible. They begin work at 6.30 in the morning and lay it down at ten at night. Those who stand at the machine are in danger every minute. The dough passes through a rotating machine where it is cut into flat pieces. The work of the men is to lift these pieces of dough from the machine. If a man turns away for a moment, a piece may get stuck in the machine and jam it so as to stop it working. He must, therefore, be very skilled and hurry and grab with the result that he may easily find himself minus a finger. The largest wages for this hard and dangerous work are 21s 0d a week and the remainder get from 6s 0d to 10s 0d.[1]

The *matzo* cake being required for the Passover festival, the trade was, in common with so many alien occupations, highly seasonal. Stocks unsold from the previous year had to be cleared in order to maintain prices, and the bakery master would halt current production and lay off his men. Beneath these imperatives, plus the fact that *matzo* prices were a matter of great concern to the community as a whole, the trade was, in its due proportion, as troubled by dissension and strike as any other Leeds alien trade. Like the slippermakers, the bakers formed a highly exploitable labour force which produced a series of *ad hoc* unions with some quaint forms of industrial action. In 1903, for example, one of their strikes took the form of an invasion of the synagogue to prevent the religious master bakers from reading the Sabbath portion of the Law.[2] By 1907 their condition was such that a coalition of social democrats, anarchists and the Leeds Tailors' union, many of whose members made the dreaded annual descent into the ranks of the bakers, had formed to organise a regular bakers' union and to carry out strikes against extreme wage cuts. As their secretary put it in his report to *Arbeiter Freund*:

Such treatment by master bakers was formerly a frequent occurrence. The workers, not being organised, had to bow to the arbitrariness of their hawk-like and bloodthirsty bosses. Now, however, the bakers are organised and their organisation, the Leeds Jewish Bakers' Union, has decided that it will not permit such disgraceful sweating of its members.[3]

Analogous conditions among the Jewish brushmakers are discernible from the reports which began to emerge in the 1900s:

A strike has broken out among our brushmakers and it has been going on for a week. The workers, despite not having a union and thus very little material support, are holding very strongly to their demands – which is rare indeed among Jewish workers in England today. The master against whom they are striking is a Jew and a leading light among the zionists but, at the same time, he is one of the most brutal sweaters alive. The conditions under which these workers worked were the most intolerable that one could meet. He demanded of them that they clean out the closets, he tore down the prices and he established a very long working day. In addition the workers had to drag, without pay, large cases of completed work to his home streets away. Besides this, he used to insult the workers in the foulest way and the wages were the worst that could be imagined.

The brushmakers had no union of their own and, though they won their strike with the support of the socialists and the tailors after a three-month battle, their approach to the English Brushmakers' Union indicates that native labour hostility was by no means confined to the tensions produced in the clothing trades. In this regard, the reported conversation between two Jewish delegates and the secretary of the English union is highly instructive:

'Tell me, [said the secretary] what will the result be for us if you win this strike without our help?'
'What will happen to you?' asked one of the delegates, mystified. 'If you help us to win this strike the sole reward is that you have fulfilled the duty of trade unionism, which is one of the first conditions of trade unions.'
The secretary replied with a smirk, looking at the strikers as if they were Indians. 'Eh, you're a clever fellow,' he said. 'If you win this strike you will only take the work away from us, but we can get more work because your work would come over to us if you lost.'[4]

A third subsidiary occupation, cabinetmaking, was of sufficient importance to warrant scrutiny under the proceedings of the Aliens Commission of 1903. This trade conveys evidence of the breadth of the struggle within alien society and is a further case of alien/host hostility beyond the clothing trades, since it encompassed a direct clash with English labour in the same trade. In 1899 there were 150 alien workers in the Leeds trade, and four years later, of the thirty-nine firms in Leeds, seven were Jewish.[5] This group had control of the whole of the cheap wholesale end, and over 50 per cent of their workers were aliens.[6] This branch, based on the machine and the subdivisional system, was in headlong confrontation with the apprentice-based craft system of the Alliance Cabinet Makers, whose leader, James O'Grady, was to inject the anti-alien malevolence he learned in Leeds into the Commons upon his election as a Labour member in 1906.[7] Jewish craftsmen who were members of the Alliance union clashed with Jewish subdivisional workers in riots during strikes in 1907 provoked by the English union's policy of seeking compensation for the undercutting of their wages by the Jewish branch.[8] As the number of rapidly trained aliens in the trade rose, wages in the Jewish branch declined to $2\frac{1}{2}d$ an hour, work became more irregular, and unemployment of three months' duration was common. At least one Jewish craftsman member of the Alliance union, affected by the cheaper branch of the trade, led the life of the tramping artisan in the slack times, sleeping in casual wards and picking oakum for his keep.[9]

Objective study of the alien industries of Leeds, along with their external relationships, has led to the conclusion in earlier chapters that many of the standard optimistic interpretations of this topic are badly misplaced. Upon a further economic relationship, that between Jewish landlord and tenant, silence has reigned, though both theory and history strongly suggest that the home of the worker was an equally fruitful field for exploitation as the workplace. J. White, the only scholar to have treated the Jewish rackrenting landlord as a symbol of the class struggle, has demonstrated how, in the East End, that personage was a leading source of communal conflict and a chief protagonist of the struggle.[10] The same problem presents itself in the Leeds case during precisely the same period and, perhaps, in an aggravated form owing to the relative self-containment of the Leeds ghetto economy. In the provincial place the distractions were fewer than in the capital, and the range of economic choice in general was narrower. In no city, said the *Standard* in 1903, after over twenty years of settlement were the aliens 'so pertinacious in their caste proclivities and so difficult to approach' as in Leeds.[11] The Jewish worker was invariably the employee of a Jewish master, whilst the ghetto landlord was also almost invariably Jewish. Thus strict parameters were established within which, as if by conscious social engineering, a microcosm of outer capitalist society was bred, with its endogenous system of hostile classes precariously superimposed upon a religious and ethnic base. That little effort has been made in recent writings to impose intellectual order – let alone dialectical discipline – on the interpretation of social aspects of Jewish immigrant experience, follows immediately from the parallel treatment of alien industry – the well-spring of social conditions and relations – in a socially abstract methodology which requires the concept of an idealised 'specially Jewish' worker, and the transformation of the deeply stratified social-economic order of the ghetto into a homogeneous population of 'temporary' proletarians. Such procedure serves merely as a cloak for awkward facts and the more distasteful aspects of Jewish class conflict.

In extending the vista of the class struggle beyond industry, no more fruitful ground may be found than that upon which the Jewish landlord functioned. In no sector was the tropism of the Jewish workshop master to the status of capitalist more extreme than in the housing of the Leeds

Jewish worker. With the tendency to the concentration of capital into few hands, landlordism waxed precisely along the classical lines enunciated by Marx in a passage which encapsulates supremely the major variables of ghetto slumdom:

Every unprejudiced observer sees that the greater the centralisation of the means of production, the greater is the corresponding heaping together of the labourers within a given space; that therefore the swifter capitalistic accumulation, the more miserable are the dwellings of the working people ... Everyone knows that the dearness of dwellings is in inverse ratio to their excellence, and that the mines of misery are exploited by house speculators with more profit or less cost than the mines of Potosi. The antagonistic character of capitalist accumulation, and therefore of capitalistic relations of property generally, is here so evident that even the official English reports on this subject teem with heterodox onslaughts on 'property and its rights'.[12]

More than any other issue, rackrenting had the power to impel the most diverse political groups into unanimous abhorrence of the Jewish slum landlord. The intimate link between the struggles on the industrial and property fronts was strengthened by the fact that investment in slum property was usually an act of business diversification on the part of the workshop master. In a reminiscence penned in 1925 by an anglicised Leeds Jew, E. E. Burgess, this is made clear. Though the masters, observed the writer, 'had their noses to the grindstone, their thoughts were concerned with the conversion of street corner cottages, or of hitting upon a block of property which the corporation might shortly ask leave to purchase'.[13] An inelastic demand caused by the incessant concentration into a single district, plus the fact that the landlord and the employer might be one and the same individual, provided the landlord with powerful sway. The wholesale displacement of the native population, despite the objective undesirability of the properties in question, aroused much local fury, augmenting the local disrepute of the immigration movement; whilst the uniquely high rents for the town imposed on the immigrants became a major scandal. Sam Fredman, the tailors' union leader, summed up the rackrenting situation and expressed the clear embarrassment occasioned the progressive workers of the Jewish community when he wrote in the English labour paper *The Trade Unionist* in 1899 that, in a few years, rents in the Jewish quarter had been doubled. The landlords, he stated, were 'taking advantage of their co-religionists who were compelled to live in the Leylands'. The landlords formed a class which was 'a disgrace to the community'.[14] The brutal indifference of the master class to either ethnic ties or co-religious sentiment, already noted in alien industry, is equally apparent in the exploitation of this most fruitful source of capital accumulation.

Apart altogether from insensitivity to the native reaction to his activities, the landlord in pursuit of the surplus values inherent in slum property was ruthless in the exercise of his powers of eviction. As Burgess put it in his reminiscences, 'Jew evicted Jew and scenes like petty Irish evictions were enacted.'[15] How useful a source of primitive accumulation the slum hovels of the ghetto proved to be becomes clear from the Quarry Hill Demolition Scheme proceedings of 1900–04. Of the 1,000 slum dwellings dealt with in this belated activity by the Leeds corporation, 508 were in Jewish ownership, for which the landlords received collectively the immense sum of £87,214 under compulsory purchase.[16] The conclusion may be drawn that a swift revolution had occurred in the ghetto between 1880 and 1904. Not only had the district been colonised by the aliens, but a significant degree of ownership had passed to a new capitalist class, the members of which can have possessed little capital upon original departure from the eastern homelands. The alien master had clearly urged on his workmen to excellent effect, investing the surpluses of sweating in the lucrative decay of the Leylands and, in the process, exhibiting to a remarkable degree the capitalist tendency to separate productive from rentier capital. The colonisation of complete districts with concomitant displacement of native populations has formed the subject of criticism and hostility on many occasions. In the Leeds Jewish case arising after 1880, the problem added directly to the burdens borne by the alien worker – not merely in the high cost of living imposed by Jewish landlordism but in the detailed local hostility of the displaced. Apart from the work of White on the East End, no attention has been paid to the problem of Jewish slum landlordism: its economic and social effects within the community, and its role as an aspect of alien entrepreneurship. From a Marxist standpoint, however, landlordism strongly illuminates the class dispositions of the community. Primitive accumulation in the workshop produced, by a clear dialectical progression, a group increasingly differentiated from the Jewish worker and with a definite capitalist consciousness. In the intimacy of a tight-knit economy such as that of the Leylands, the classless 'family' society observed by bourgeois scholars in Jewish immigrant communities did not appear.

In the interests of perception of the complex evolution of an authentic alien working-class consciousness in a community such as that of Leeds, and in its total historical connection, some attention to the ideological structure developing after 1880 is required. Under the naive scheme propounded by Professor Gartner and his followers, the Jewish worker segment consisted of two simple categories: a mass of orthodox religious workers and a hostile peripheral group of propagandising revolutionaries for ever tempting the religious mass to 'immolate' themselves by responding to socialist propaganda. The properties of such a model derive precisely from the Jewish bourgeois dream of a world of universal Jewish proprietorship which inhabits the literature of the immigration movement in Britain. They are the means of freezing in motion the energetic development of a proletarian consciousness by way of conflict within the working class pending the dawn of that wonderful day when every Jewish worker has been transformed into a master. This, however, is merely a specially Jewish form of the so-called 'metaphysic of isolated properties' in the social sciences, which proceeds by way of the imposition of some idealised feature of an earlier epoch upon a different form of society.[17] Such, for example, is the liberal vision of a society of small producers within a system of universal free trade and fair competition. When the worker is without property, however, there arise inevitably the exploiting master and, along with him, class antagonisms.

It has been demonstrated in earlier chapters that, at the least, a profound radicalism was immanent within the ranks of the Leeds Jewish workers and that it pervaded their leading institutions. Prominent revolutionaries of the community, so far from constituting a pariah class, were constantly prime movers in their progressive development. It has also been pointed out that the Gartner approach is invalidated by its metaphysical concept of human relations and experience, which rules out the hastening of a Jewish working-class consciousness through the bitter experience and disappointments of 'free' capitalism and the impact of a new, radical type from eastern Europe in the 1900s. Such sparse material as exists suggests that the substantial progress of the Leeds Jewish workers towards a strong working-class instinct and specific working-class action was, so far from a pre-ordained idealistic scheme, realistically the outcome of struggle within the worker ranks as well as that with the Jewish masters and the English trade unionists.

In that struggle the conflict between the Jewish orthodox tradition and the imperatives of the economic situation of the alien worker are clear enough. The loathing of the progressives for the local clergy, ever in the anti-socialist position, is immediately apparent in the pages of the left-wing press:

> Once upon a time the task of a rabbi was to make peace, to busy himself with visiting the sick, to provide succour to the wayfarer, piety and guardianship of widows and orphans: and, for this, he got wages of five florins a week, meat for the Sabbath and plenty of curses from the big men of the town. In this situation stood the rabbi on the same basis as all the poor, and he was familiar with the flavour of hunger and poverty. Now, however, is the order of the world quite altered, and whilst the worker, this poverty-stricken creature, has never had the chance to forget hunger and need, the rabbi, on the other hand, is no longer a dried-up, hunched, consumptive little Jew; but, rather, a fat man with thick, red cheeks, a swollen girth, a fat, rosy, overflowing-his-collar neck, a long, long, gross and large belly making the feet appear like little fat hooves which can barely move themselves ... And this rabbi no longer draws for his necessities wax candles; he sits peacefully in his chair and draws from the poor worn-out worker his last little blood and marrow; and, whilst the worker grows paler, thinner and weaker, the rabbi grows rosier, fatter and thicker.[18]

Direct command by the rabbi of anti-socialist forces is equally clear, as is the fact that they consisted of Jewish workers. As a Leeds master informed *Arbeiter Freund* in 1903:

> You ought to be in Leeds and you would see how much the workers love Rabbi Daiches such that when he instructed them to go and attack the socialists, they went in their hundreds and launched such an attack that we [the masters] were forced to call in one of the 'watchmen of the masters' in the shape of the police to prevent them injuring their own good friends who call themselves socialists.[19]

In 1904 a socialist meeting was proceeding quietly at the Leylands Board School. Unfortunately the occasion was the Sabbath. Suddenly a tumult arose:

> A gang of fanatical Jews had broken into the hall and were trying to grab the collection money. The gang were armed with sticks, knives and meat cleavers with which they attempted to attack our comrades. For us the affair is not ended. Apart from the arrest of Comrades Kurz, Sharefsky and Velinsky we will devote all our strength to defending ourselves against the brutal intolerance of these fanatical bandits.[20]

This event was followed by an inter-racial meeting of protest in the North Street Park

> to express public disgust at the ignorant and brutal intolerance of the orthodox Jewry of Leeds. The meeting was attended by countless people and English and Jewish anarchists, socialists and freethinkers energetically defended the right

of free speech, and branded the cowardly attack of the black, dark gang who had sought to emulate the bandits of London.[21]

Arrayed on the side of the reaction were, inevitably, the masters, shopkeepers and butchers, to whom the open-air propaganda of the left was distasteful, and the meetings in the North Street Park were often held with difficulty. At Louis Ellstein reported to *Arbeiter Freund*:

This summer we have held many large and successful meetings beneath the open skies. The like of this has never before been presented by Jews, either in number or content, with meetings attended by shopkeepers, masters, butchers and people of their kind who would never attend at a hall. Our meetings were naturally not to the taste of our Jewish 'upper class'. They ran to the Town Hall and we were under observation by a detective officer, and they also complained to the Park Keeper, but none of this helped them. They began to raise alarms and attempted to break up our meetings by every filthy trick, but they had to stay at home when they saw that nothing would help them. Nevertheless, they cried: 'It is a shame that Jews should say that all governments live on taxes for which the workers must labour; or that, in peacetime, governments tear off the skin of the workers whilst, in wartime, they take his whole body to feed their cannon.' How can they stand by and listen when the anarchists say that religion stands in the way of progress as, in the name of God, they spilled blood and burned Bruno, Galileo and Socrates; and that, in the time of the Inquisition, many were roasted and burned in the name of God?[22]

There was no greater unanimity concerning socialism inside the unions despite the impetus accorded these organisations by socialist workers. In 1898, for example, a Leeds tailor complained in the *Yiddisher Ekspres* that the tailors' union had spent £12 to bring an anarchist speaker from London during a time of unemployment.[23] Sam Freedman, however, asserted the right of the union to maintain a free platform. He would leave the verdict on the action to the 2,000 people who had been 'enraptured by his two-hour speech'. At the same time, he was only too aware, he stated, that 'as usual for certain people', the orator spoke 'a little too sharply'.[24]

In the absence of systematic documentation of such internal tensions, it is impossible to assess how far, by 1914, the Jewish working mass of Leeds had heeded the injunction of the social democrat Eliahu ben Dovid, who, writing in *Neue Tsait* in 1904, stated that the Jewish workers must organise themselves in a special party, separated from and opposed to all other parties of the Jewish people, and that they must join with the proletariat of all the world for the liberation of the proletariat everywhere.[25] Certainly, towards the end of the period, there are signs that the influence, authority and success of the tailors' union, the emergence of a Leeds-born generation of young Jewish workers into the workshops, and the lengthening experience of the class struggle, had exerted considerable influence in the matter of concentrating the consciousness of the individual worker upon his economic and class condition. Hence, by 1914, the impression is one of greater ideological harmony within the working class and there is an end of reports of attacks by the religious workers on the socialists and anarchists. *Arbeiter Freund* itself, in reviewing the notable victory of the tailors in the great lockout of 1911, was significantly able to rejoice in the 'instinctive union of the orthodox and the freethinkers' which had brought it about, and to exhort all Jewish unions in Britain to adopt the Leeds methods of organisation.[26]

Owing to the nature of their idealised models of alien economy, and especially in the Leeds case, Jewish commentators have seen no reason to make a serious effort to relate the economic situation of the alien to the course of development of British capitalism in general. It has been one of the special tasks of the foregoing chapters on industry to assess the stresses peculiar to the individual industries in which aliens were occupied, with a view to elucidating the problems thereby transmitted from the native to the alien branches of each industry. It has been shown, for example, that the Leeds clothing industry, so far from possessing a stability based on its huge scale, was for that very reason subject to severe crises during the immigration period. This finding led immediately to the conclusion that the relative stability of alien tailoring in Leeds, the basis of so many models, was extremely doubtful.

From the macroeconomic standpoint, the Jewish immigration to Britain coincided precisely with the onset of the crisis of profitability within British capitalism which has continued to the present time. Glyn and Sutcliffe, in tracing the movement down to the 1970s, indicate that, whereas in 1879 Britain produced one-third of the world's industrial goods, by 1913 she produced only 14 per cent. Industrial productivity grew at 2·06 per cent per annum between 1871 and 1895, but by only 0·3 per cent per annum in the period 1895–1913. During the same periods the worker's share of the output fell by 0·15 per cent and 0·32 per cent respectively.[27]

In Marxist terms, the increasing difficulty in realising the former rates of profit after 1870 was symptomatic of an advanced accumulation and concentration of capital in the maturing economy, and a concomitant rise in the organic composition of capital (increasing capital-intensity). Under these conditions, as Zeitlin has it in his work on Marxist economics, 'a battle of capitals' ensues, each capitalist employing price competition and attempting to cheapen his goods. Each capitalist attempts to obtain a larger share of the available mass of surplus value (unearned income) by intensifying the exploitation of labour and cutting his costs of production.[28] Whilst due regard must be paid to the *historical* situation of each industry in which aliens were engaged at the material time, it remains abundantly clear that the accepted economic 'analysis' that 'alien industries were in a state of transition between the workshop and the factory' fails to provide a satisfactory explanation of the fundaments of the alien economic problem. Within the native Leeds wholesale clothing industry, which constituted the main support of the Leeds community before 1914, there are the most patent manifestations of the stresses predicted by Marxist theory of capitalist development in the form of the relentless augmentation of the scale of production, in the inordinate cheapening of products, in the restless search for new products, and in the widespread employment of outside ancillary labour in the shape of the alien. Such considerations, it is suggested, do more than appeals to the state of technology to illuminate the authentic economic situation of the immigrant worker caught up in sweeping industrial developments. They go further than this, however, since the economic stresses transmitted under these conditions by native industry to the alien community point to the ultimate source and govern the intensity of the intra-communal class struggle.

Dialectic method requires the scrutiny of each historic moment in its uniqueness and in unbroken historical relationship with the preceding epoch. This, bourgeois Jewish literature on immigration and immigrant economic and social history has grossly failed to do. It is precisely the absence of analysis of this quality of transition which has impelled scholars to an arid and unhistorical utopianism and away from the bitter realities of the class struggle as the social motive power of Jewish immigrant society in the period 1880–1914.

NOTES

1 *A.F.*, 29 January 1897.
2 *Ibid.*, 3 April 1903.
3 *Ibid.*, 8 November 1907.
4 *Ibid.*, 26 January, 2 February, 30 March 1906.
5 *J.C.*, 22 September 1899; *Aliens Commission*, q. 14644.
6 *Y.F.T.*, 13 March 1903; *Aliens Commission*, qq. 14662–4, 14686–9.
7 Clegg, Fox and Thompson, *Trade Unions*, pp. 178, 396. O'Grady moved

for the prohibition of all immigration during trade disputes. Successful in the Commons, this amendment to the Aliens Act of 1905 was defeated only in the Lords.

8   *Y.F.T.*, 8 December 1899; *Leeds Daily News*, 10 January, 12 April 1900. These accounts indicate that Jewish craftsmen in the English union were prosecuted in considerable numbers for violent acts against blacklegs whilst acting as pickets.
9   Letter from Mr P. Marks of Leeds to the writer, 10 July 1967.
10 J. White, 'Jewish landlords, Jewish tenants: an aspect of class struggle within the Jewish East End, 1881–1914', in A. Newman (ed.), *The Jewish East End, 1840–1939*, London, 1982.
11 *The Standard*, 15 January 1903.
12 Marx, *Capital*, p. 722.
13 *Y.E.N.*, 7 February 1925.
14 Freedman, 'Jewish workers', p. 523. For a 'middle class' Yiddish press condemnation of the Leeds Jewish landlord, see *D.Y.E.*, 3 June 1898.
15 *Y.E.N.*, 7 February 1925.
16 Minutes of the Sanitary Committee, 3 October 1900–22, December 1904, *passim*.
17 On the methodological problems raised by this tendency in the social sciences, see M. Shirokov, *A Textbook of Marxist Philosophy*, London, 1936, pp. 211–221.
18 *A.F.*, 11 January 1907.
19 *Ibid.*, 22 May 1903.
20 *Ibid.*, 30 September 1904.
21 *Ibid.*, 14 October 1904.
22 *Ibid.*, 11 October 1895.
23 *D.Y.E.*, 14 January 1898.
24 *Ibid.*, 21 January 1898.
25 *Neue Tsait*, 22 April 1904.
26 *A.F.*, 5 January 1912.
27 A. Glyn and B. Sutcliffe, *British Capitalism, Workers and the Profits Squeeze*, London, 1972, pp. 15–49.
28 I. M. Zeitlin, *Capitalism and Imperialism*, Chicago, 1972, pp. 1–7.

APPENDIX I
The sales and profits record of four Leeds wholesale clothing manufacturers during the immigration period

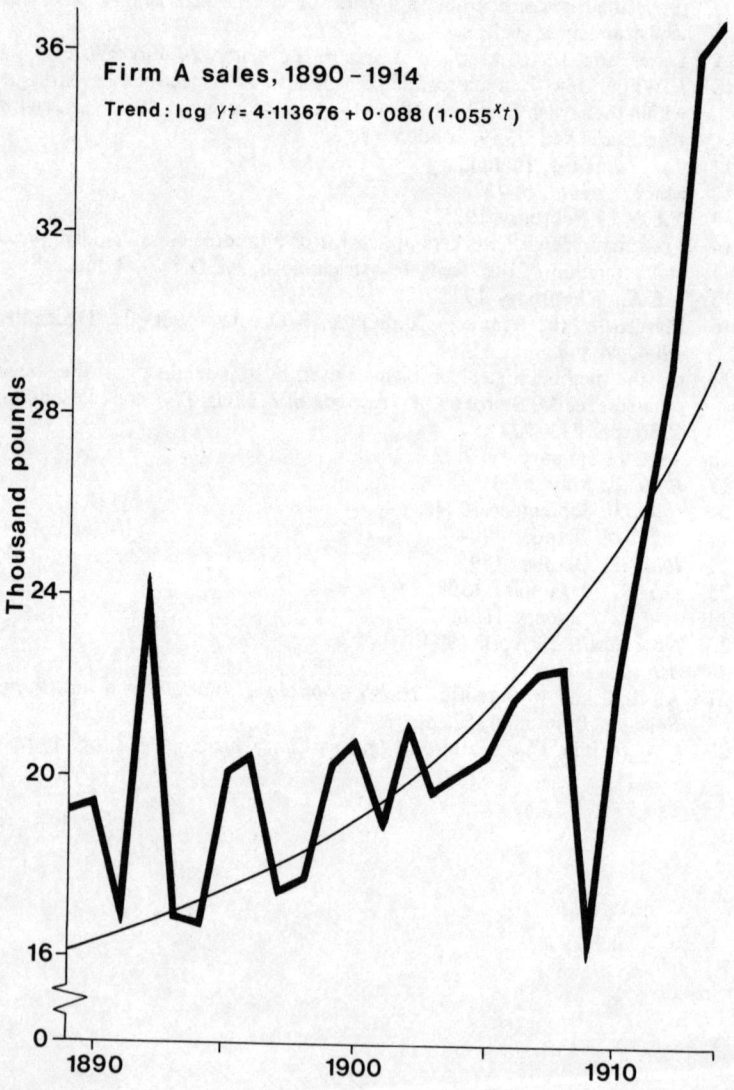

Firm A sales, 1890-1914
Trend: $\log Y_t = 4.113676 + 0.088 (1.055^X t)$

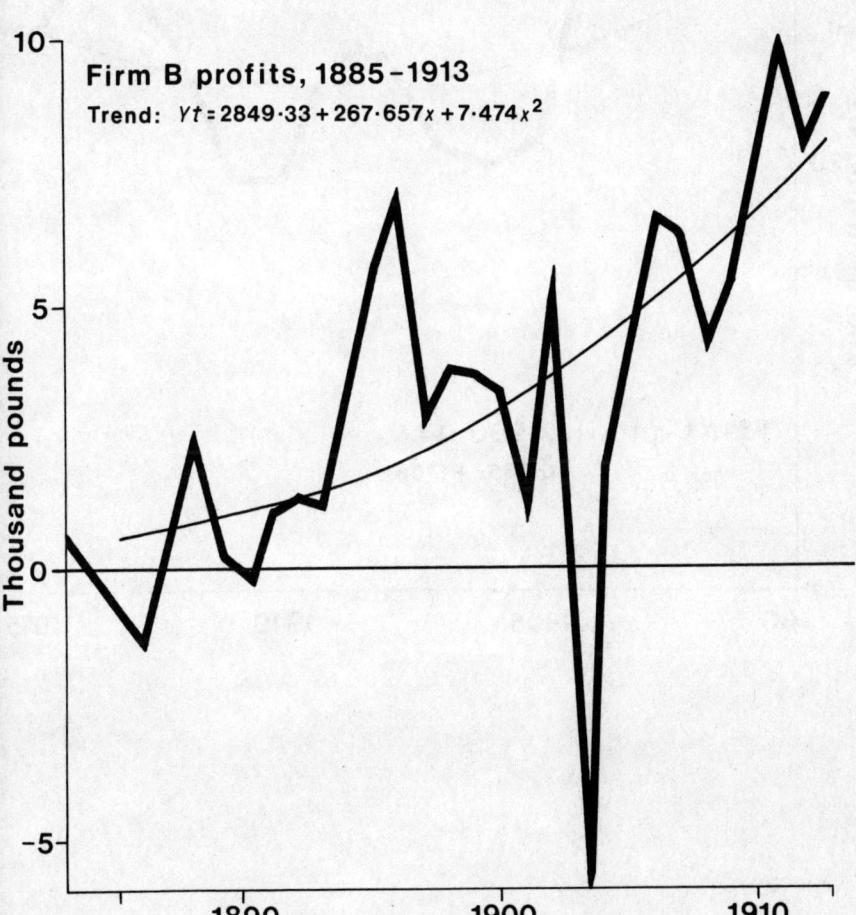

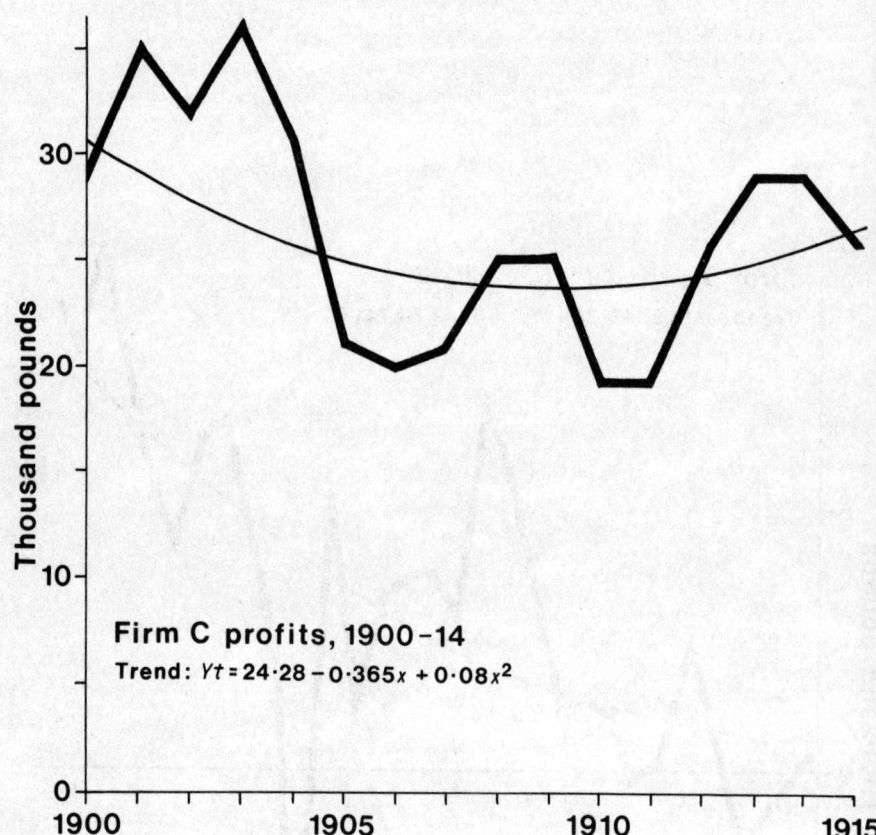

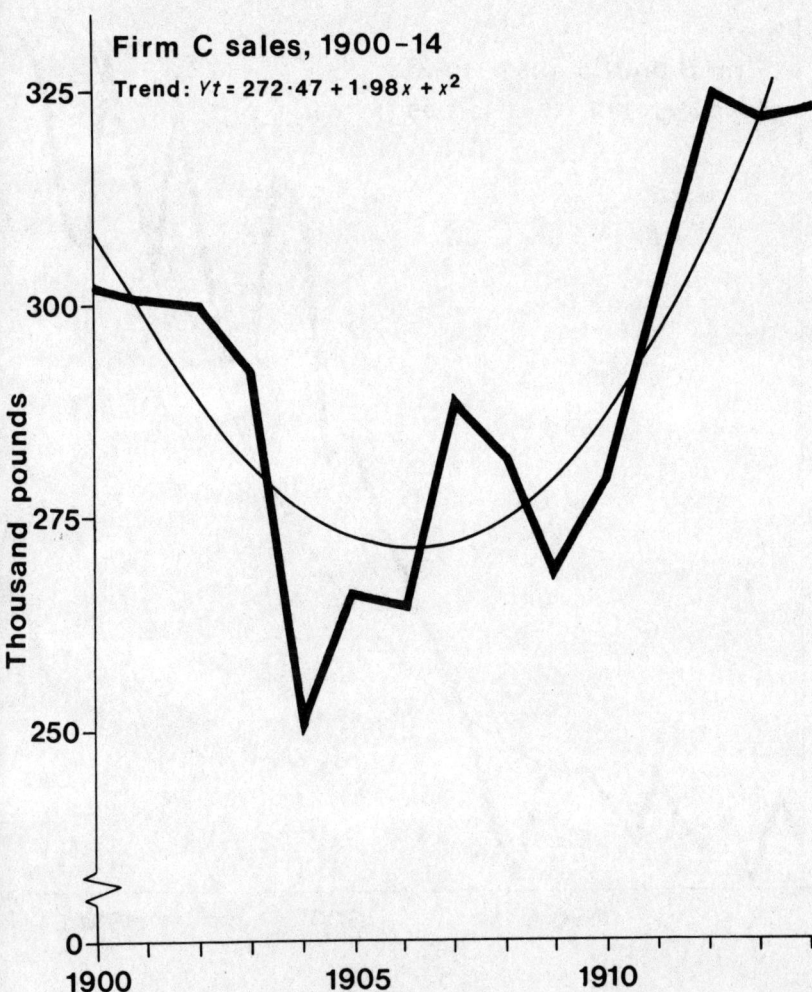

Firm C sales, 1900–14
Trend: $Yt = 272.47 + 1.98x + x^2$

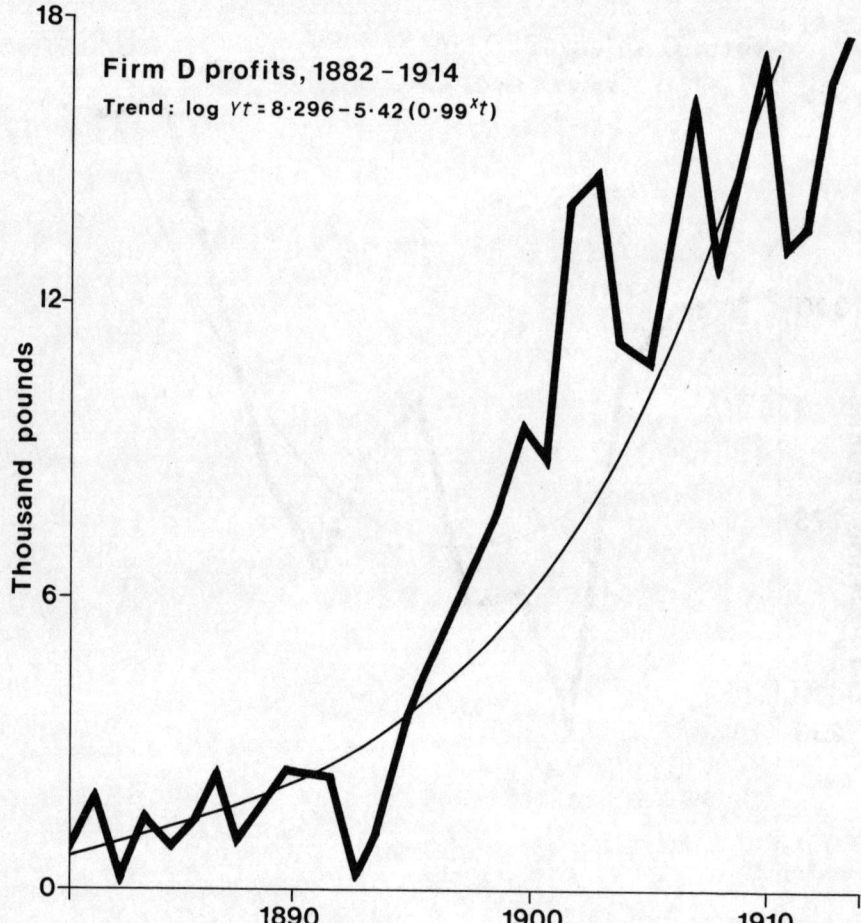

Firm D profits, 1882–1914
Trend: log $Y_t = 8.296 - 5.42(0.99^x t)$

Appendix I

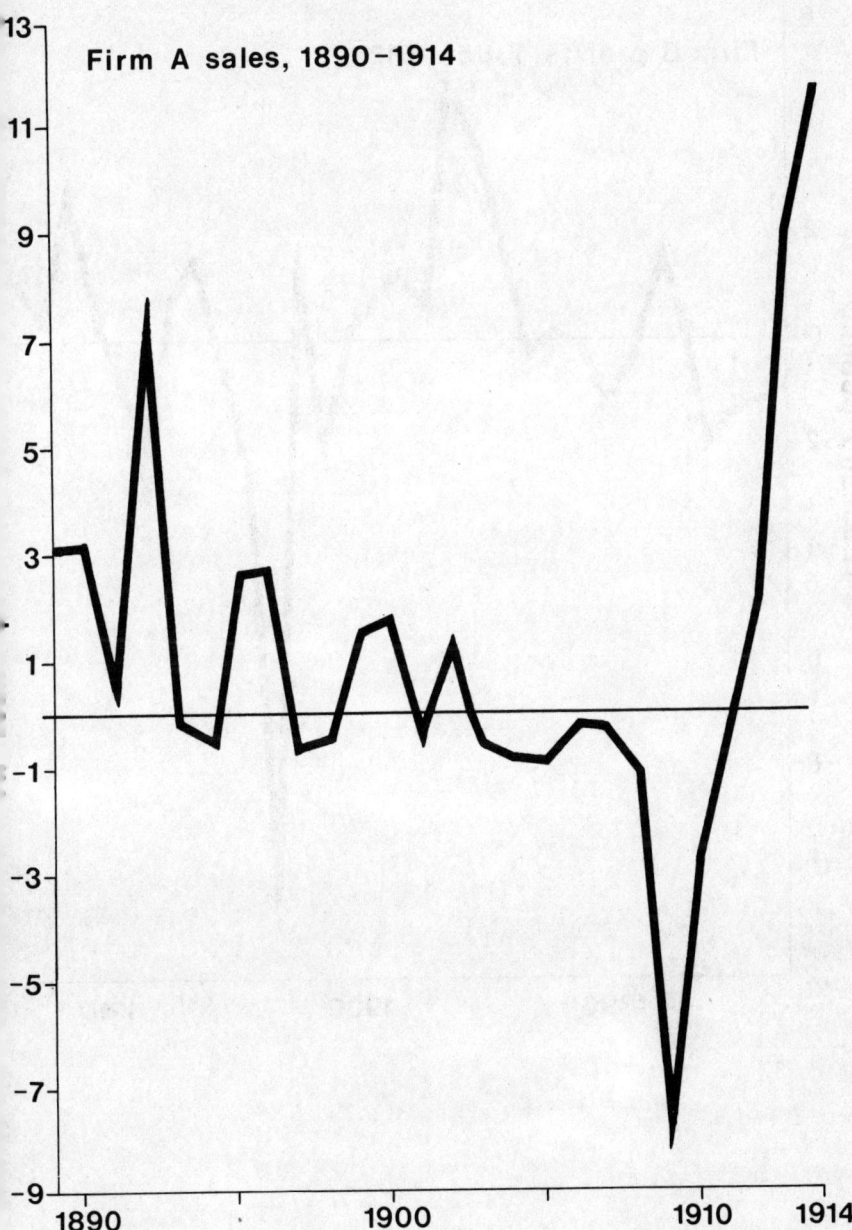

Firm A sales, 1890–1914

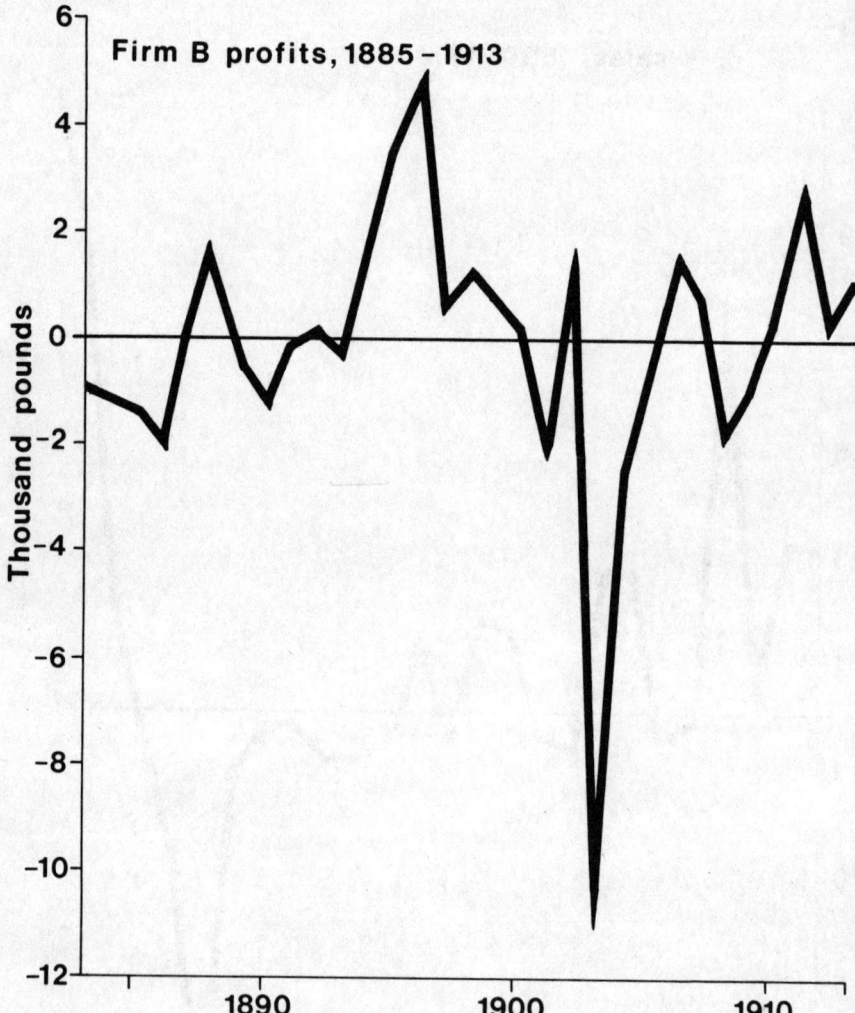

Appendix I

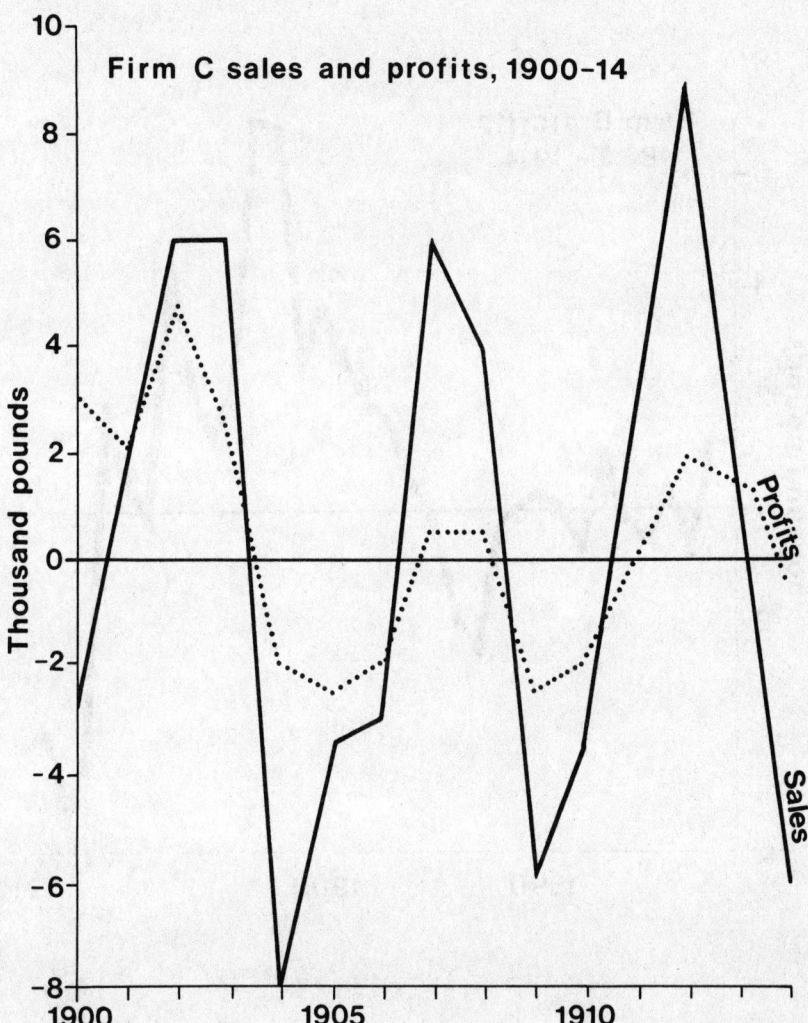

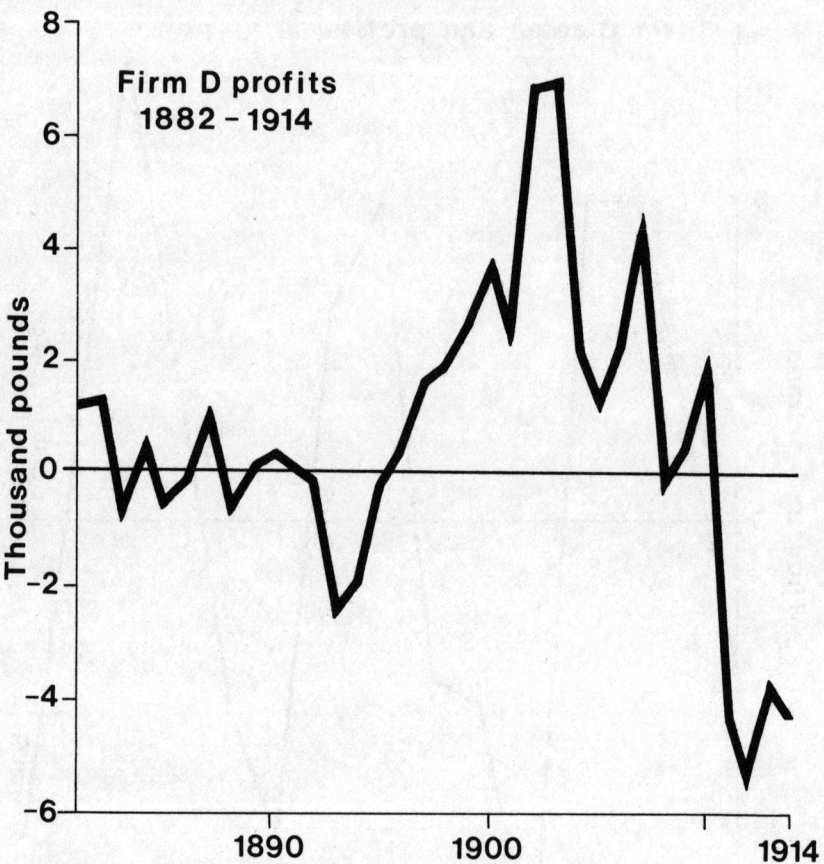

APPENDIX II
Statistical analysis of spatial conditions in Leeds Jewish tailoring workshops in 1888

The 1888 survey was divided into groups of workshops: small and large. The small were classified as those employing under twenty workers. This group had mean space per worker of 430 cubic feet, with standard deviation of 187 cubic feet. The corresponding figures for the group of large workshops were 413 and 154 cubic feet respectively.

For the respective means, we write m_1 and m_2. The null hypothesis, H_0, is that $m_1 = m_2$ and the difference is due to chance. The alternative hypothesis, H_1, is that $m_1 \neq m_2$, and the difference is statistically significant.

The mean and standard deviation of the difference in the means is given by

$$\sqrt{s_1^2/n_1 + s_2^2/n_2} = \sqrt{187^2/25 + 154^2/28} = 47 \cdot 39$$

The standardised variable, z, is therefore

$$z = (430 - 413)/47 \cdot 39 = 0 \cdot 36$$

A two-tailed test for significance at the 0·05 level requires that z lies outside the range $-1 \cdot 96$ to $1 \cdot 96$. Hence we conclude that there is no significant difference between the two categories of workshop, small and large, in the 1888 survey on the score of space per worker.

The calculation of rank correlation by Spearman's method covers the ordered data of fifty-three Jewish workshops in the 1888 survey by Leeds Town Council inspectors.

Spearman's coefficient of rank correlation, r, is given by

$$r = 1 - \frac{6 \Sigma D^2}{n(n^2 - 1)}$$

Substituting in directly the values obtained from the data:

$$r = 1 - \frac{6(24619)}{53(53^2 - 1)}$$

$$r = 0 \cdot 01$$

APPENDIX III

The address of John Lincoln Mahon to the Leeds Jewish tailors (*Der Arbeiter Freund*, 13 January 1888)

Leeds, 3 January 1888.

Dear Editor,

Last Sunday in our Tailors' and Pressers' Society, we had the pleasure of hearing the famous socialist speaker, Mr Mahon, who spoke on Socialism and trades unionism. As so many of our workers were certainly unable to understand his speech, I think it will not the superfluous to explain it briefly in your worthy paper so that our workers will be able to understand it.

Firstly, Mr Mahon demonstrated that the worker's position in general is very tragic, and that his earnings never exceeded just sufficient for a small living. That means that the worker earns just enough to enable him to retain his labour strength for his master to exploit further, and that the worker never once succeeds, especially in recent years, in gaining relief from his heavy labours or in freeing himself from his slave status.

The worker, he said, is nowadays treated far worse than a horse, for, when the capitalist's horse is ill, he does everything to cure it and sees that it gets better food etc., but, when one of his workers gets sick, even if he has given up his best years and strength to the capitalist, he drives him straight out, and, although the poor worker needs more care than a healthy man, he finds himself in such a position that he has to die of hunger and need.

For centuries the poor workers were sunk in their deep ignorance and superstition, and, because of this, they thought that God had ordained that they should be the slaves of their bloodsuckers, and that it could not, therefore, be altered. For that reason, they never made the least effort to improve their tragic condition. But, when consciousness began to develop amongst the workers, they began to struggle against their bloodsuckers, and, as soon as they recognised that a single individual could do nothing, they began to unite in societies and trade unions. The cost in workers' blood was great before they obtained in 'free England' the legal right to build trade unions. But this was only a limited step forward in the great work, for societies can only slightly ease, but not completely transform, the tragic condition of the workers. As the workers may see for themselves, the foundation of their poverty is the master; and the interests of the master are not only opposed to those of the worker, but also to the interests of the other masters. When a master seeks to obtain work from a factory, he offers to do it more cheaply than the master to whom it is already being given, and, for that reason, he reduces the wages of his workers. Therefore, Socialism, which is no more than a higher stage of trades unionism, desires that the workers, instead of pursuing a permanent struggle against the masters which they almost always lose, shall throw off the master-yoke once and for all.

And in order that they would understand well who they were and what they have to do, he recommended them to read *Arbeiter Freund*, which was the true defender of the interests of all workers.

He closed his speech with the hope that the Jewish workers, who suffered no less than any other workers beneath the capitalist yoke, would surely not remain at a distance, and that they would rapidly organise and unify themselves in order to bring about the general liberation all the quicker.

Other Leeds socialist speakers and a lady were present, but, owing to the late hour, they were unable to speak. The president of the society, Mr Frank, thanked Mr Mahon deeply in the name of all the members and expressed the hope that he would visit other meetings in the future from time to time and awaken the sleeping spirit of our workers to the general struggle against the exploiting class.

D.B.

INDEX

Abrahams, Moses, communal minister, 2
Alien population of Leeds, 2
Alien unions, neglect of, 59–60
Amalgamated Society of Tailors, 105–6, 113
Anarchists, in Leeds alien society, 81, 96–7, 134, 144, 157
Anti-religious forces, 162–4
Antisemitism in tailoring, 70
Anti-socialism, 163–4
Arbeiter Freund, Der (*The Worker's Friend* – anarchist-communist journal in Yiddish), 8, 69–70, 72–3, 75, 78–9, 81–3, 94–5, 115, 125, 147, 149–50

Bain, J. S., on size of firms, 11
Balsam, Harris, Jewish tailors' leader, 84
Baron, S. W., Jewish historian, 3
Bribery, in Leeds tailoring trade, 16
Burgess, E. E., Jewish journalist, 62, 160
Burnett, Robert, Labour Correspondent of the Board of Trade, 18
Bythell, D., on alien unionism, 60

Cameron, Dr Spottiswoode, Leeds Medical Officer of Health, 49
Caplan, Jacob, Leeds Jewish anarchist leader, 81, 96, 99, 102, 104–6, 108, 133, 136, 138, 145
'Cohenovitz' (pseud.), Yiddish journalist, 50–1, 95–6
Collet, Clara E., industrial investigator, 19, 43
Commonweal, The, organ of the Socialist League, 82, 103
Communal institutions in Leeds, x
Concentration and workshop efficiency, 11
Connellan, Owen, Leeds Trades Council secretary, 140
Coyle, John, Leeds footwear union leader, 127–8, 133, 140–1
Cunninghame Graham, R. B., socialist politician, 103

Dawson, E. T., Leeds Factory Inspector, 49
Dubnow, S., Jewish historian, 7
Dyche, John, Leeds Jewish labour leader, 6, 71, 75, 77, 96, 98, 103, 105, 109

Economies of scale, 11
Ellstein, Louis, anarchist labour leader, 92–3, 96, 108–10, 164
Ellstein, Saul, social democratic leader, 97, 142

Factory legislation, in alien workshops, 43–4
Fagenbaum, Benjamin, Jewish orator and author, 100
Finn, Joseph, Jewish labour leader, 19, 40–2, 63–4, 69
Fisher, John Greevz, 74
Foster-Fraser, John, antisemitic journalist, 131
Frank, Lewis, Leeds Jewish tailors' leader, 70, 98

Freak, Charles, NUBSO president, 132, 135
Freedman, Sam, Leeds Jewish Tailors' Union secretary (1895–1906), 68, 79, 99, 107, 109, 112–13

Gainer, B., historian, on social outlook of aliens, 6; on state of alien trades, 9; on alien workshop scale, 10; on long-term trends in alien trades, 21; on Leeds working conditions, 37; on socialism and the aliens, 93
Garrard, J. A., historian, on fewness of Leeds alien workshops, 1; on alien entrepreneurship, 5; on state of alien trades, 9; on long-term trends in alien trades, 20–1; on Leeds working conditions, 36; on division of labour in Leeds, 39; on alien unionisation problems, 61
Gartner, L. P., historian, on social outlook of aliens, 6; on state of alien trades, 9; on alien workshop scale, 10; on stability of Leeds alien trades, 21; on Leeds working conditions, 36; on alien unionisation problems, 61; on socialism and the aliens, 68, 93–4
Gasworkers' and General Labourers' Union, 99–106
German competition, in clothing trade, 23
Glyn, R., and Sutcliffe, B., on declining rate of profit, 165
Goldie, Dr John, Leeds Medical Officer of Health, 47, 49
Grossbart, Benjamin, Leeds Jewish slipper workers' leader, 145–6

Hillman, Arthur, Leeds Jewish anarchist journalist, 96
Hobson, J. A., economist, 4–5
Holmes, C., historian, on antisemitism, 6
Hunt, E. H., on alien capitalism, 6; on state of alien trades, 9; on alien workshop scale, 10; on Leeds working conditions, 36; on division of labour, 39

Immigrant trade unions, neglect of, ix
Inskip, W., NUBSO secretary, 132, 139
Irish National League, 77

Jewish clergy, 162–3
Jewish population pressure, xi
Jewish worker, neglect of, ix
Joseph, Davis, Leeds master tailor, 17, 43
Judge, John, NUBSO official, 73

Kemelhor, Morris, Leeds Jewish tailors' leader, 71–2, 74, 77–8, 80, 83, 85
Korn, Jacob, Leeds Jewish tailors' leader, 74–5, 77, 84
Krausz, E., Jewish author, on Leeds class system, viii
Kropotkin, Prince Peter, 98–9

Lancet, The, 17
Leeds alien tailoring industry, perfect competition, similarity with, 7; role in clothing industry, 14–16; workshop scale, 17–20; Town Council survey of, 18; changing role, 21–2; increasing skills in, 22; seasonality of trade in, 22–3; reduced demand for services, 26–8; bedroom system in, 29–30; growth of small workshops in, 29–30; relations with native firms, 38; division of labour in, 39; malpractices in, 40–3; length of working week in, 45; sanitary conditions in, 46–55; similarity with East End, 92; female competition, 92–3, 114; political influences in, 94–8
Leeds Jewish bakery trade, 156–7
Leeds Jewish brushmaking trade, 157–8
Leeds Jewish cabinetmakers, 158–9

Leeds Jewish settlement in the 1870s, x
Leeds Jewish slipper trade, communal significance of, 121; scale of, 121–2; technological basis of, 122; size of labour force, 124; Rossendale Valley competition, 125; hostility of native interests, 125–7, 134–5; wages and conditions in, 126–9, 137, 139, 142, 144–5; source of anti-alien feeling, 130–1, 139–40
Leeds Jewish slipper unions, revolutionary leadership, 134; the union of 1888, 136; amalgamation with Leeds Gasworkers, 136–9; external relations, 137–9; break with the Gasworkers, 138–9; organisational problems, 138, 141; revival of 1893, 139; supported by Leeds Trades Council, 140; membership, 141, 150; co-operative workshop, 141–2; union of 1898, 142–3; union of 1904, 145 et seq.; final clash with NUBSO, 147 et seq.
Leeds Jewish tailoring masters, antisemitic policy, 75; use of boycott, 80–1
Leeds Jewish Tailors' Trade Society, 61
Leeds Jewish Tailors' Union, views on the bedroom system, 51; origins of, 61; organisational problems, 61–2, 107–9; co-operative system, 64–5, 82; strike of 1885, 65–7; membership, 70, 90, 107; general strike of 1888, 74–81; post-1888 policies, 86; trade problems, 91–3; socialist influences in, 93; amalgamation with Leeds Gasworkers, 99 et seq.; anti-piecework campaign, 102, 110; break with Gasworkers, 103–6; reorganisation of 1893, 106; relations with English labour, 111–13
Leeds Socialist League, 70–1, 74, 77, 82, 103, 136
Leeds Town Council, 18, 47, 49–50
Leeds Trades Council, 65, 70, 73–4, 79, 82, 105–6, 109, 125, 133–4, 139–41, 143
Leeds wholesale clothing industry, expansion in the 1870s, ix–x; scale of, 13; technological organisation of, 14; retention of work indoors, 15–16; secular trends in, 20, 24–5; revolution in demand, 20–1; increased productivity in, 23–4; seasonality of trade, 24; relations with domestic system, 25; sales experience, Appendix I; price reductions, 40; length of working week in, 45–6
Lenin, V. I., on growth of Russian clothing industry, 3–4; on capitalist domestic industry, 14–15
Lerner, Mrs S. W., on Talmudic background of alien masters, 2; on alien entrepreneurship, 5; on division of labour, 39; on alien unionism, 60, 99
Leylands, Jewish quarter of Leeds, x, 160–1
Lipman, V. D., Jewish author, on alien social outlook, 1; on alien class attitudes, 5; neglect of alien unions, 60
London Jewish clothing industry, 11
Lubelski, David, Leeds Jewish master tailor, 74–8
Lyons, Lewis, London Jewish labour leader, 3, 78–80, 91

Maguire, Tom, Leeds socialist leader, 15, 71, 74–7, 82, 84, 99–100, 103, 105–6, 136
Mahon, John Lincoln, 71–2, address to the Leeds Jewish tailors, Appendix III; 78, 103, 105, 109
Marston, William, A. S. of T. secretary, 51
Marx, K., on demand for labour, 22–3; on the apparel industry, 25–6; on division of labour,

39–40; on effects of mechanisation on domestic industry, 122–3, 129–30; on slum rackrenting, 160
Matlovsky, Jack, Leeds slipper union leader, 136
Mendelsohn, Bernard, Leeds slipper union leader, 140
Mendelsohn, E., Jewish historian, 3
Men's Wear, trade journal, 15, 26
Meyer, Morris, editor of *Neue Tsait*, 146, 149
Myers, Isaac, Leeds Jewish tailors' leader, 65

National Union of Boot and Shoe Operatives (NUBSO), 131 *et seq.*
Neustatter, H., statistician, 5, 60

O'Grady, James, Alliance Cabinetmakers' leader, 158

Paylor, Tom, Leeds socialist leader, 71, 74–7, 79, 82–3, 99–100, 103, 136
Proletarianisation of Russian Jews, 7

Quarry Hill, Leeds, Demolition Scheme, 161

Rackrenting by alien landlords, 159–61
Raskin, H. M., Jewish inspector of alien workshops, 50
Rickards, J., Leeds Factory Inspector, 17, 20
Rollin, Aaron, Jewish historian, 80
Rosenbaum, S., Jewish statistician, 1–2
Rosenberg, Lewis, Leeds Jewish tailors' leader, 84
Rowlands, J., Labour politician, 65–6
Rudman, Morris, Leeds Jewish slipper workers' leader, 136–7
Russian Jews, changes in economic and social status, 7

Sacher, H., Jewish author, on Jewish proletariat, 7
Schleich, Abraham, Leeds Jewish slipper workers' leader, 143

Sclare, Moses, Leeds Jewish Tailors' Union secretary, 1906–, 30, 68, 107, 115
Seasonality of clothing trade, 24
Shaw, Arthur, Leeds Trades Council president, 110–11, 140
Sherard, R. H., author, 43, 127–8
Social democrats, 97–8, 157
Socialism in Leeds Jewish unions, 68, 73
Stewart, L., and Hunter, M., 98
Sweeney, James, Leeds labour leader, on unskilled nature of immigrants, 4; on methods of Jewish masters, 43; as leader of 1885 tailors' strike, 65; as Jewish link with Leeds Trades Council, 70; role in tailors' general strike, 74–8; views on general strike, 81; as leader of 'scab' committee, 84; role in Leeds gasworkers' strike, 99; lecturer to the Jewish tailors, 109; protest against alien slipper trade, 125–6; attitude to alien slipper unions, 136, 139

Taylor, Isaac, Leeds Jewish tailors' leader, 85, 96–7, 108, 114
Technology, new, in clothing industry, 14
Thomas, Joan, 98
Thorne, will, 113
Trades Union Congress, 132

Ward, Alderman J., chairman of Leeds Sanitary Committee, 48
Webb, Beatrice (Potter), 2, 5
Webb, Sidney, 23
Weltanschauung, aliens of, 7–8
White, J., author, on Jewish landlordism, 159
Wholesale clothing industry, demand changes in, 21; cyclical nature of, 24

Yorkshire Post, The, 4, 37
Yorkshireman, The, 47, 66–7

Zeitlin, I. M., economist, 166